Complacency and Collusion

Complacency and Collusion

A Critical Introduction to Business and Financial Journalism

Keith J. Butterick

First published 2015 by Pluto Press
345 Archway Road, London N6 5AA

www.plutobooks.com

Copyright © Keith J. Butterick 2015

The right of the Keith J. Butterick to be identified as the author of this work has been asserted by him in accordance with the Copyright, Designs and Patents Act 1988.

British Library Cataloguing in Publication Data
A catalogue record for this book is available from the British Library

ISBN 978 0 7453 3204 8 Hardback
ISBN 978 0 7453 3203 1 Paperback
ISBN 978 1 8496 4836 3 PDF eBook
ISBN 978 1 8496 4838 7 Kindle eBook
ISBN 978 1 8496 4837 0 EPUB eBook

Typeset by Swales & Willis
Text design by Melanie Patrick

Contents

Introduction	vii
1 The origins of business reporting and early crises	1
2 *The Economist*, *The Times* and railway mania	18
3 New Journalism, the *Daily Mail* and Charles Duguid	32
4 Harry Marks, *Financial News* and the *Financial Times*	43
5 The crash of 1929 and Keynes	60
6 The emergence of modern financial journalism	71
7 The 2008 financial crisis	83
8 The structure of modern financial and business journalism	101
9 Ideology, business discourse, news values	120
10 Financial communication and financial PR	137
11 Financial journalism: its role in the creation of economic paradigms	156
12 The future of financial and business journalism	172
Notes	182
Bibliography	189
Index	200

Introduction

Almost daily it seems the headlines of the newspapers and broadcast news feature another scandal or story about a business. Too often it's about corporate wrong-doing and not about a good-news story, such as a successful company or an innovation. If bad news sells newspapers, then there has certainly been enough for a lifetime from the banks.

The prominence of business stories is why we need financial and business journalism, but for all its current high profile we do not know enough about its origins, its function, or what the modern-day financial journalist does. This book puts that right, because it is the first book to provide a detailed analysis of financial and business journalism.

Inevitably, the financial crisis of 2008, given its size, provides a recurring lens through which we can analyse the role of financial and business journalism and, crucially, look at its role in those events.

In November 2008, during the royal opening ceremony of a new academic building at the London School of Economics (LSE), Professor Luis Garicano, director of research at the LSE's management department, was explaining to the Queen how the then unfolding economic crisis had started. Having listened to his explanation, Her Majesty asked the question that puzzled not just her, but millions of her subjects: 'If these things were so large, how come everyone missed them?' Professor Garicano replied that 'At every stage, someone was relying on somebody else and everyone thought they were doing the right thing' – a situation which the Queen described as 'awful' (Greenhill, 2008).

'How come everyone missed them?' is a question millions of people throughout the world have asked since the start of the financial crisis in 2008. In the UK every taxpayer has paid directly for the crisis by contributing financially to the bail-out of the banking industry.[1] In the longer term, the recession that developed after 2008 has been paid for by the poorest and the working-class through lost jobs and lower wages and living standards. They have paid a cost for a crisis that was not of their making.

There are other unanswered questions, such as why those who caused the crisis have not been brought to account for their actions. If the crisis was caused by greed and the type of activity that many would describe as criminal, how is it that so few have escaped prosecution?[2]

Perhaps the most crucial question is how a crisis that was so clearly a failure of free-market capitalism and an unregulated banking system led in the UK to a Coalition government that then intensified the same economic policies that had been a major factor in contributing to the problem.

It was not only the economics profession that stood accused of failing society by missing the warning signs and not alerting everyone to what was happening. Questions have also been directed at financial and business journalists as to why they did not or could not identify the impending crisis. A Reuters Institute report (Picard *et al.*, 2014: 28), for example, said, 'Business news failed to predict the [2008] crisis, possibly being "guilty" of seeking opportunities to report on business news in a positive light because no significant source was raising questions about developments in the sector.' Business and finance journalists are supposed to be close to events, watching and occasionally boasting of their special and unique relationship with the financial and business world. Many newspapers also have specialist banking correspondents who have personal access to the leading figures in the industry. So if their relationship was as close as they claimed, why could they not see the story that was developing in front of them?

There is another angle to this question: did the fact that they were so close to their sources prevent them from identifying the story? What we see when we explore the nature of the relationship is a systemic failure which goes right to the heart of business and financial journalism.

If most of the financial and business press missed the emerging 2008 crisis, does this raise questions about its function? Or was the 2008 crisis so unique that, along with the politicians and economists, it is not surprising that many business and financial journalists failed to identify it?

Our historical research demonstrates that this failure was not an isolated event but systemic. Earlier crises have also been missed, and it is likely that future ones will be too, unless there is a re-evaluation of the role and purpose of the financial media.

'While the root causes of the [2008] crisis lie in the behaviour of and regulation of banks and other investors, many have asked what the role of financial reporting may have played in the crisis and whether the crisis would have been so sudden and deep if a different approach to the practice of financial journalism had been taken' (Tambini, 2008: 5). At the heart of this failure is the relationship that the financial media has with public companies.

The 2008 crisis unleashed a torrent of soul-searching and self-criticism from practising financial journalists keen to try to understand how, as a former *Wall Street Journal* writer put it, 'Could 9,000 Business Reporters Blow It' (Starkman, 2009: 15). How, he asks, could an 'army of professional business reporters – an estimated 9,000 or so nationwide [in the USA] in print alone – for all practical purposes miss the biggest story on the beat'. In the UK, leading practitioners of financial journalism were hauled in front of the House of Commons Treasury Select Committee in February 2009, not only to explain why they had failed to identify the crisis, but to answer accusations that they had made the situation worse by the way events had been reported as it developed.

A welcome, if unintended, consequence of the 2008 financial crisis is that, possibly for the first time, business and finance journalism has been considered seriously, and that its practitioners have been encouraged to look at their practice. Whether they have drawn the appropriate conclusions from their analysis is, however, another question. Most practitioner responses, perhaps predictably, have focused on the problems and difficulties faced by the newspaper industry and journalism as a whole. Important examples of such 'pre-2008' analysis include Anya Schiffrin's *Bad News* (2011), which consists largely of contributions from the USA. In the UK the journal *Ethical Space* (Mair and Keeble, 2009) produced a special edition 'Playing Footsie with the FTSE? The Great Crash of 2008 and the Crisis in Journalism'.

According to Schiffrin, the 'failure' of business and financial journalists to identify the crisis was caused by the same problems and difficulties affecting all sections of the print media. Crucially, therefore, this means that the failure to spot the impending crisis was not primarily the fault of either the journalists or the genre of financial and business journalism. Common industry factors include cut-backs in the number of journalists and increased work loads caused by the need to produce more copy in order to supply online versions of the newspaper. The consequence of this is that journalists have less time to spend on detailed investigative reporting. 'The disintegration of the financial media's own financial underpinnings could not have come at a worse time. Low morale, lost expertise, and constant cutbacks, especially in investigative reporting – these are not conditions that produce an appetite for confrontation and muckraking'[3] (Schiffrin, 2011: 4). Furthermore, under-resourced financial and business journalists faced, in financial public relations (PR), one of the PR industry's most powerful and influential sectors. And, in the uneven battle between PR and journalism, it was PR that came out on top.

Complacency and Collusion: A Critical Introduction to Business and Financial Journalism looks at the history and development of financial and business journalism, key figures and key incidents and its current functions.

However, understanding its role, purpose and functions means setting it in context, which can be done only by a detailed exploration on the nature of the public company. The history of financial and business journalism is linked to a particular form of business organisation: first the joint stock company and then its successor, the public company. Any book looking at modern financial journalism has to take account of its relationship with financial PR and the communication obligations of the modern public company.

Financial and business journalism, despite the high-profile that business news occupies, remains under-studied and under-researched. This book is an introduction to it and, while aimed at journalism/media/PR students, it is also intended for the general reader interested in the media. It aims to fill what I believe is a glaring gap in the journalism studies market. This book builds on the efforts of a number of individuals who have explored different aspects of financial and business journalism. Wayne Parson, in his excellent book *Power of the Financial Press*, explores how financial journalism has transmitted economic ideologies. Aeron Davies, who has been important in exploring the role and influence of corporate PR in a number of papers, and has exposed the growing influence of financial PR on business and the link with the corporate elite. Gillian Doyle has raised perceptive questions about the nature of financial journalism following the collapse of Enron. More recently, Damien Tambini has produced a first-rate analysis of some of the ethical considerations.

Dilwyn Porter is one of the few historians to have explored some of the historical roots and seminal figures in business history, and his research has opened up new insights into some of the main historical characters and episodes of financial and business journalism. I hope that my exploration of these themes will encourage others to explore financial and business journalism. As this is an introduction and deals only with the printed media, I recognise that some subjects may not be covered in as much depth as possible.

Financial and business journalism has the following functions. Firstly, it is the sphere through which the corporate world prefers to interact with society. Businesses are happier to be scrutinised and analysed in these pages of the press, rather than elsewhere. It is an area in which businesses can receive legitimation and validation because corporate interests are more able to control the news agenda, especially through their PR activities.

Secondly, it has been and continues to be the vehicle through which economic ideas and philosophies are discussed and promulgated. From the eighteenth century, when Adam Smith's economic philosophy became the established economic paradigm, to the emergence of neoliberalism in the 1970s, economic writers have played an important role in disseminating arguments and helping to establish an economic philosophy's intellectual credibility. Keynes, for example, quite deliberately used the media and not academia to try to influence policy. In the 1970s, Samuel Brittan of the *Financial Times* and Peter Jay of *The Times* were influential apostles of neoliberalism. The economic columnists, like their counterparts in the news and editorial sections, play an important role in voicing and reinforcing readers' opinions.

Chapters 1 to 6 trace the origins of financial journalism from the first recorded versions down to the current day. Chapters 7 to 12 look at modern financial journalism and are based on research undertaken at the University of Huddersfield Centre for Communication and Consultation Research. Looking at the history of financial and business chronologically reveals – perhaps not surprisingly – that financial crises keep reoccurring and our lack of collective memory means that we keep on walking into them. One of the functions of financial journalism should be to act as the guardian of that memory.

The origins of this book lie in my working background, which is in financial and business journalism. I have edited a business magazine and worked in newspapers as a financial and business journalist. I have also worked in financial PR and experienced at first hand the many ways that PR practitioners attempt to influence the media. I believe this cross-disciplinary background provides me with the ideal skills to look at this.

In the final chapter of the book, I attempt to answer the question 'What is financial and business journalism?' The 2008 crisis was the largest failure of free-market economics since 1929. That should have led to a reassessment of our profession's relationship with business. This chapter also attempts to answer the question 'What is the role of financial and business journalism?' Is it to 'fight for business' and articulate its interests and encourage politicians to implement policies that are in business's interests? Or is it to adopt a more critical and sceptical tone? It seems that too many of our current business and financial journalists believe that it is the former, and have in the process become the willing or unwilling apostles of neoliberal, low-tax, less-government interference, loose labour laws policies and the transfer of wealth from the poor to the rich. To suggest that financial and business journalism should have a more critical function is not anti-business, but can play an important role in building a new relationship with society. I hope that this book will help to stimulate the debate about what that role should be.

I'd like to thank Sadaf Shabbir and Nannette Brimble for their work on the research and my colleagues in the Media and Journalism Department at Huddersfield University for their support and encouragement.

I would also like to thank Anne Beech of Pluto Press for her advice, support, encouragement and belief that there was a worthwhile project.

Finally, thanks to my wife and family for the many absent hours that they endured during the researching and writing of this book.

1

The origins of business reporting and early crises

The exchange of financial and business information between companies oils the wheels of trade, and the history and development of business and financial journalism in both the UK and the US is inextricably linked with the provision of information on and about companies. The forerunner of the modern public company was the joint stock company,[1] and, just as the modern investor needs information about a company, so did the earliest investors in joint stock companies.

While in England companies that offered shares to investors date back to at least the thirteenth century (Micklethwait and Wooldridge, 2005), the joint stock company really began to take off in the seventeenth century, stimulated by the wealth of gold and silver from South America and the economic potential of trade with colonies in North America. This encouraged traders to look at other continents for similar opportunities. The companies created to open up trade in new areas were risky enterprises with no guarantee of success – or even of a return on the money invested. The common feature of all the companies was that they needed large amounts of capital to finance buying ships and paying the sailors (Scott, 1951). Such finance could be raised only through a joint stock company because it spread the risk among a large number of investors. Joint stock companies were granted a charter by the crown which gave them exclusive rights to trade in a specific part of the world. 'Chartered companies represented a combined effort by governments and merchants to grab the riches of the new worlds' (Micklethwait and Wooldridge, 2005: 25).

Chartered joint stock companies were used to open trade with Virginia (1606), Bermuda (1611), Guyana (1619), New England (1620) and Nova Scotia (1621). One of the most famous and long-lasting of these trading companies was the Hudson Bay Company, formed in 1668 to develop trade with Canada. In contrast, one of the least successful was the Muscovy Company or to give its full name, 'The mysterie and companie of the Merchants Adventurers for the discoverie of regions; dominions; island and places unknown'. It was created by the explorer Henry Cabot in 1555 to trade with Russia but, despite a promising start, it was not successful and, around 1630, disappeared from view without giving its investors any return on their investments.

The buying and selling of shares in joint stock companies was strictly controlled: if, for example, further capital was needed by a company after the initial issue of shares, it had to be provided by existing shareholders. Investors who wanted to sell their shares could do so only through private negotiations.

The investors of the seventeenth century share a common problem with twenty-first-century investors: information asymmetry – that is, the unequal flow of information between the company and the potential investor. Information asymmetry was the term used by the Kay Review (2012) into UK equity markets established by the government in 2011. Led by the economist Professor John Kay, its purpose was to review how the equity market was working in the UK and, especially, whether companies were too focused on short-term outcomes. If they were, the Review would recommend actions to address the problem. The Kay Report was published in 2012 and welcomed by the government on its publication; however, so far, none of its recommendations have been implemented.

Information asymmetry suggests that the information balance always seems to lie with the company, and the investor can struggle to find adequate information to inform their investment decision. The history of financial and business journalism demonstrates that companies cannot always be relied upon to produce the objective, accurate information that investors need. One of the most important functions of business and financial journalism has been – and continues to be – to balance this information asymmetry and provide the critical information and analysis that can help investors to make informed investment decisions.

Early beginnings

The first recognisable business newspaper was born out of the trading activity centred on Antwerp in the eighteenth century, which at the time was part of the Spanish Empire and the leading financial and trading centre in Europe. Antwerp was a major port, and hundreds of ships passed in and out of it every day, sailing to and from the Spanish possessions in the Americas. Many trading ventures that needed finance found support through the merchants and traders at the Antwerp Stock Exchange.[2]

Trading houses[3] produced handwritten sheets that contained information on tides, what ships were sailing in and out of port and what their cargoes consisted of; these were distributed to their customers to help their investment decisions. These handwritten publications (McCusker, 1991) emerged in Antwerp in 1540. The first printed 'newspaper' was a development of this, and was produced by the Antwerp trading house Van der Molen (McCusker, 1991). The information it contains is still the same, giving customers advice about visiting ships and what goods are being unloaded in the port[4] (Roush, 2006). We know that other licensed brokers of the Antwerp Stock Exchange (McCusker, 1991) published two different kinds of business newspaper; one was known as the commodity price current account and the other as the exchange current account. Significantly, these publications were intended not just for domestic consumption but also for distribution outside Antwerp to other cities in order to try to stimulate trade for local businesses and attract investors and customers to the city.

Another client newsletter, produced by the powerful German banking family the Fuggers[5] in 1586 (Roush, 2006), shares more of the features of the modern financial and business newspaper. The core information on the tides and currents was similar to that of the Antwerp newsletter, but what made it a 'newspaper' was that the factual material was complemented by news and information on the political and economic events of the day. There was news on, for example, the activities and intrigues of Europe's ruling dynasties; such information was important for traders and merchants, as wars and dynastic changes impacted on commercial activity and the fortunes of their clients. The collection and dissemination of information to produce the newsletter was a sophisticated operation, indicating just how important it was to both the clients and the Fuggers. The main providers of news were the Fugger bank agents who were based throughout Europe; there was also trading news from America.

In the last decade of the seventeenth century, London replaced Antwerp as the financial capital not only of Europe but of the world. And in London, as in Antwerp, a network developed to disseminate trading information. However, in the early eighteenth century this was not initially based around a stock exchange building but around a unique public sphere, the London coffee house.

London at the beginning of the eighteenth century had over 2,000 coffee houses,[6] many of which became associated with a particular clientele or profession; authors, for example, frequented Will's in Covent Garden, while scientists preferred the Grecian in Devereux Court. Life insurers used Tom's in Exchange Alley. Politicians had their own coffee houses: the Whigs used St James, whilst Tories frequented the Cocoa Tree. The legal profession gathered at Nandos in Fleet Street and even the clergy had their favourite spot, Child's, near St Paul's. Traders from different parts of the world also had their own meeting places such as the Jamaica, Jerusalem and Pennsylvania in Exchange Alley (Dale, 2004).

Two coffee houses, Jonathan's and Lloyds, were to have a long-term impact not only on London's financial history but also on financial and business journalism. Edward Lloyd opened his first coffee house in 1687 near the docks, and, with its mercantile and shipping connections, Lloyds soon became the headquarters for a profession that became known as marine 'underwriters'[7] (Dale, 2004). In 1691 Lloyd moved his establishment to Lombard Street in order to be nearer to the General Post Office, then an important source of shipping information (Kynaston, 1995).

One of the main attractions for the customers of the coffee houses was that they had access to the expensive newspapers of the day. Some coffee house owners, however, found that either the newspapers did not provide information that was relevant to their customers or, if they did, it was often unreliable. This led a few of the more enterprising newspapers to start publishing their own newsletters to meet their customers' requirements. Another factor that led the coffee house owners to set up their own publications was a 'war' that broke out between the 'coffee-men' (the owners of the coffee houses) and newspaper proprietors. The coffee men said that the newspaper subscriptions were too high and that newspaper journalists harassed coffee shop customers. Journalists were accused of attempting to eavesdrop on private conversations in order to gather information. For their part, the newspaper owners argued that as the availability of newspapers was the main attraction of the coffee houses for their customers, then the coffee-men should pay higher subscriptions (Dale, 2004).

Edward Lloyd produced his *Lloyds List* to provide reliable news and information on shipping matters for the ship owners and merchants who used his coffee house. So valuable and accurate was it that after his death in 1713 publication was taken over by the association of underwriters that took its name from his coffee house. Both Lloyds and *Lloyds List* still exist. Lloyds is the home for UK insurance underwriters; *Lloyds List* is owned by the Informa Group and still covers insurance-related matters. In common with many modern publications, in October 2013 it announced that it was ending the print edition and would in future be available only online.

Jonathan's coffee house was established by Jonathan Miles in Exchange Alley in 1680 (Kynaston, 1995) and attracted customers who were involved in or associated with the buying and selling of company shares. The information that Jonathan's offered to customers was its main attraction because it was so regular and up to date. While it had some information similar to the first Antwerp trading newsletter it also had wider editorial coverage on lost cargoes, problems caused by diseased crews and delays in sailing caused by repairs to a ship. In fact, the news was on anything that could impact on a trading mission. Jonathan went to great and sometimes unusual lengths to gather the information and deliver it faster than his rivals. He had an army of boys who waited around London's docks for ships to arrive to pick up any relevant news. These young, early investigative journalists also badgered the servants of merchants for scraps of useful information (Dale, 2004). Their collective findings were displayed on boards inside the coffee house, entry to which cost a penny (Dale 2004, Roush 2006).

One of Jonathan's regular customers, a Huguenot named John Castaing, was a broker at the Royal Exchange and he spotted a gap in the information market and produced his own publication to meet it. His newsletter contained the now basic trading news of ships and tides, but what Castaing added was up-to-date information on company share prices, bullion prices and also changes to the currency exchange rates. His newspaper, *Course of the Exchange*, first appeared in 1698 as *John Castaing, Broker at his office of Jonathan's Coffee-House* and was delivered every Tuesday and Friday in the City of London for an 'all-in' subscription of 3s per quarter (Dale, 2004: 17). While some publications such as *Whiston's Merchants Weekly Remembrancer, of the Present – Money Prices of Their Goods Ashoar in London* had covered share prices since 1681, the information in them was often inaccurate. What made the *Course of the Exchange* different was the reliability of its information. It was so reliable, in fact, that the listing eventually became the accepted standard and benchmark for other traders and city coffee houses (McCusker, 1991). As with *Lloyds List*, there is a direct link to one of the modern Stock Exchange's most important current publications; Castaing's list evolved into the current official price list of the London Stock Exchange. When Jonathan's burnt down in 1748, a replacement building was funded by a number of brokers and, as the new site was close to London's livestock market (the 'Stocks Market'), the two were combined to become the 'London Stock Market'.

The South Sea Bubble

In the early years of the eighteenth century, 'London was a town for making money and journalism and coffee thrived on the passion for profit. Thus it was that coffee houses emerged to provide a means by which personal exchange and information, gossip and rumour could take place more easily' (Parsons, 1989: 13). This was the background to one of the notorious incidents in financial history – the South Sea Bubble. The South Sea Bubble is significant in the history of financial and business journalism because for the first time we see a combination of circumstances that continue to recur at different historical periods. The Kay Review (Kay, 2012) highlights the South Sea Bubble as the first, and ideal, example of information asymmetry, where potential investors in a company lack independent advice on whether it is a worthwhile investment proposition. The combination of naïve investors with rising share prices and a financial media which not only misses the danger signals but actually exacerbates the problem by the way it reports on events can be a toxic one. Understanding that incidents such as the South Sea Bubble and the financial crisis of 2008 are linked should also enable us to have a better understanding of why they occur and how we might identify similar ones in the future.

Up until the end of the seventeenth century, trading in joint stock company shares was limited in both scope and volume. After 1695 this changed dramatically, for two main reasons; firstly, following the revocation of the Edict of Nantes, thousands of Huguenots[8] were expelled from France and arrived in London with cash to invest after selling off their assets. This flood of new money coincided with the second factor, a period of peace and domestic prosperity which encouraged investors and companies to look for trading and business opportunities.

While joint stock companies were still restricted by Royal Charter, there were no such limitations on share trading by unincorporated companies, which could offer their shares to investors. It is estimated that by 1695 there were at least 140 companies with a total combined capital of £4.25m (Scott, 1951). Many of these companies were a risky proposition for potential investors, who had little information by which to judge the company, other than through what it provided. While success is not and cannot be guaranteed on any investment, what reduces the risk for an investor in any period, as we shall consistently see, is accurate information about the company and its prospects and about those behind it.

In the 1690s, among the companies looking to raise funds from investors were some that must have taxed the imaginations of those responsible for producing information about them. How, for example, could a potential investor assess the risk associated with an enterprise that wanted to take advantage of new diving equipment to find and raise treasure from shipwrecks? Another wanted finance to manufacture goods in England such as wallpaper, fine linen, plate glass and tapestries, that were currently being imported from France (Dale, 2004).

While financial and business journalism would eventually evolve to offer the type of objective information that can help potential investors make their investment decisions, in the late eighteenth century this role was in its infancy. Newspapers, though, did have an important function for new businesses: they were eagerly used by company promoters to advertise a company's prospectus, which gave potential investors information about the company and its prospects.

The advertising generated from new company flotations was to provide newspapers with a valuable source of income down to the twentieth century. For journalism, though, this was sometimes to be a double-edged sword, with the power of advertisers often being used to compromise editorial integrity.

The improved conditions for business at the end of seventeenth century and the opening up of new investment opportunities came just as newspapers were beginning to emerge as a serious voice in and for the community. When newspaper censorship ended in 1695, newspaper production in London and the rest of the country soared (Temple, 2008). In 1702 the first regular daily newspaper, the *Daily Courant*, appeared, priced 1 penny, and, while aimed primarily at foreigners, it also contained the all-important shipping news.

Freed from the restraints of censorship, many of the new publications either adopted a critical line on the government or advocated outright radical political change. Worried about the potential impact that a free press might have, in 1712 the government introduced the Stamp Act to control it. Basically, this was an attempt to limit newspaper ownership to the wealthy, the rationale being that they would be less likely to be critical of the government and the established order. The duty of 10*d* per whole newspaper sheet, a halfpenny for a half sheet and 1*s* for every advert was harsh and expensive, hitting both editorial and advertising content (Downie, 1979). In an attempt to disguise the duty's real purpose and give the impression that the government was not against newspapers, the tax was also imposed on other printed documents such as pamphlets and legal documents. This iniquitous piece of legislation lasted over 140 years, ending only in 1855 (Conboy, 2004). For the government of 1712, the Act did have the desired effect of severely restricting the growth of newspapers and magazines. However, despite the Act, in the early eighteenth century London still had at least 18 newspapers – a mixture of dailies and weeklies with an estimated weekly combined circulation of around 44,000.

The London papers and coffee houses were the information distribution network at the heart of the South Sea Bubble. The network functioned through a combination of rumour spread through the coffee shops and the newspapers which carried advertisements about potential investments. One of the reasons why the South Sea Bubble is significant is that for the first time we can see, firstly, how an information distribution network shapes and then influences the decisions of investors and, secondly, how this network itself could be abused and manipulated.

The South Sea Bubble took place over the summer of 1720. In many ways it is an almost meaningless incident, as it involved only one company, which survived the crisis and carried on trading. And while for those who lost money it was undeniably traumatic, with a number of deaths associated with it, it was not, however, a crisis that had any wider economic impact, unlike many later financial bubbles. It did not, for example, plunge either the national or international economy into recession.

The South Sea Bubble originated in the attempt by the government of the day to privatise £10m of the country's £50m national debt by persuading government bond holders to swap them for shares in a joint stock company – the South Sea Company. Hoping that the South Seas would offer the same rewards as India and Canada had in 1711, the government created the South Sea Company (joint stock company) to develop trade with South America. Setting up the company was also an attempt by the Whig government to build a commercial counterbalance to the Bank of England, which had been created by an earlier Tory government. The bond holders who held the £10m of national debt were required to transfer their bonds into shares worth the same amount in the South Sea Company. To encourage the company to take on the debt, the government paid it an interest of 6% per annum on the debt. And, to finance the interest payments, the government introduced taxes on a range of products, including wines and vinegar (Dale, 2004).

This apparently ingenious scheme was, however, fundamentally flawed. South America[9] was no unknown territory as North America or India had been in the 1600s. By 1711 it was a relatively mature trading market and the main sources of wealth – gold and silver – had already been identified and exploited. Trade to and from South America was still dominated and controlled by Spain and any success that the South Sea Company might have would be dependent on the co-operation of the Spanish government, which was hardly likely to encourage a rival such as Britain. To add to the problems, it took five years for the company to start trading, which ended almost as soon as it started when war between Britain and Spain broke out in 1718 (Dale, 2004).

Despite the lack of trading activity by the South Sea Company, there was, however, an active market in the buying and selling of its shares. In the absence of any actual trading results by which to judge the company's performance, what drove investor activity was its perceived potential. This was unscrupulously and aggressively promoted by a publicity and lobbying campaign carried out by those involved in trading the shares – the company directors and the share promoters. A key role was played in the company's share promotion by a new intermediary that emerged between the buyers and sellers of company shares: the 'stock-jobber'. The stock-jobber became a reviled figure: many of them amassed fortunes from their activities and were viewed with both disdain and envy by the landed classes (Dale, 2004), even though they became a useful source of wealthy individuals to whom impoverished aristocrats could marry their daughters. It would not be the last time that 'the City' would produce a hate figure. There was a widespread contemporary perception that stock-jobbing and rumour mongering were synonymous, as it was in the interest of the stock-jobber to push the share price of a company whose shares they were dealing in as high as possible.

The information distribution network of coffee houses and uncritical newspapers proved to be an ideal combination for spreading unsubstantiated rumours. By 1720 newspapers such as *Weekly Journal*, *London Journal*, *Daily Courant*, *Evening Post*, the *Postman* and *Postboy* were beginning to offer a form of news and editorial commentary on financial matters. However, the main sources of information about companies that were looking for investors were the advertisements that the companies paid for (Temple, 2008). The South Sea Company used advertisements to communicate information about new share issues, its favourite publications for this purpose being the *London Gazette*, *Daily Courant*, *Daily Post* and *Evening Post* (Murphy, 2009).

In January 1729 the company submitted a new proposal to the government that it would take on the entire national debt on a similar basis as the earlier scheme; government bond holders would swap their bonds for shares in the South Sea Company. However, this time, its great rival, the Bank of England, alarmed at the power this would give the South Sea Company, put forward an alternative proposal. The government then had a choice between the speculative trading operation of the South Sea Company and the Bank of England, which, although private, was a conventional bank. As Members of Parliament would decide in a vote on which scheme would be chosen, the supporters of both companies lobbied other MPs intensively. The scale of this activity was later exposed by a parliamentary inquiry into the activities of the South Sea Company and its directors. It was lobbying activity on an industrial scale, putting modern efforts to shame, with MPs and members of the House of Lords on both companies' payrolls (Balen, 2009).

During the debate in the House of Commons Robert Walpole, the leader of the opposition and future prime minister, attacked the basis of the proposal in words that have a modern resonance: 'The scheme by diverting the genius of the nation from trade and industry; it held out a dangerous lure for decoying the unwary to their ruin by a false prospect of gain and to part with the gradual profits of their labour for imaginary wealth.' Success for investors, he said, depended on the rise of the South Sea Stock: 'The great principle of the project was an evil of the first magnitude; it was to raise artificially the value of the stock, by exciting and keeping up a general infatuation and by promising dividends out of funds which would not be adequate to the purpose' (McKay, 1852: 50).

Walpole, however, was not quite the sainted visionary he might appear from such words, as he too had bought South Sea Company shares. However, he was lucky enough to sell them at a profit before the share price collapsed. He became the political beneficiary of the bubble: after the government fell, he came to power and went on to become the UK's longest-serving prime minister. On 2 February 1720, the South Sea Company scheme was passed, first in the House of Commons by 172 votes to 55 and then by another large majority in the House of Lords. Clearly, the South Sea Company's lobbying had been more effective than that of the Bank of England.

The passing of the Bill prompted another rise in the share price: on 1 February it was £130 per share and only a day later rose to £300. The directors and Chairman Sir John Blunt used the coffee houses and newspapers to spread rumours to raise the share price (Murphy, 2009). They claimed that a free trade agreement between England and Spain was imminent, and that Mexico would trade all the gold in its mines for English cotton and woollen goods. They also promised that for every £100 invested in South Sea Company shares, investors would receive hundreds of pounds of dividends a year. Feeding on such rumours, the share price continued to rise, reaching a high of £400 before settling at £330 (Dale, 2004).

The problem for the company directors was that they had to keep pushing the share price up to attract more investors to buy the shares so that the company could pay dividends to the existing shareholders. Every time the share price fell, the company intervened to try to push it back up again. For example, the day after the Bill received the royal assent in April, the share price fell from £310 to £290. In response, the

South Sea Company spread more rumours that it was being allowed to build and charter as many ships as it wanted to trade in South America and that the king of Spain was waiving a 25% tax so as to encourage its trading activities.

On 12 April 1720 a further one million shares were offered to the public at £300 per share, which could be paid in £60 instalments. This instalment plan opened up share buying to a new market and this became the first share issue where working people such as maids and porters bought shares in a company (Dale, 2004). These were naïve, inexperienced investors and their enthusiasm only added to the share-buying frenzy, which also helped to keep the share price rising[10] (Paul, 2011). The South Sea Company also lent money cheaply to potential investors so that they could buy shares. Following the success of the one million share offer, another one million new shares were offered at £400 per share, which also sold out in a few hours.

That millions of pounds were being spent on the shares of a company that had not even traded did not go unnoticed by other businessmen – and crooks – who believed that in such a febrile atmosphere an inexperienced investing public would buy anything. In the summer of 1720, in a testament to the creativity and invention of company promoters who saw the chance to fleece a gullible public, a number of wild and implausible schemes were promoted. For example, investors could buy shares in a company that wanted to purchase Irish bogs (McKay 1852); another company proposed manufacturing an invention known as Puckle's Machine Gun 'Which was to discharge round and square cannon balls and bullets' (round for Christians and square for Turks). Other schemes included making salt water fresh, constructing a wheel of perpetual motion and importing large jackasses from Spain to improve the stock of English mules (McKay, 1852).

Perhaps the most infamous scheme was one whose prospectus invited the public through a newspaper advertisement to invest in 'A company for carrying on an undertaking of Great Advantage, but no-one to know what it is …'. The prospectus said the company needed half a million pounds but did not say what it was to be used for. The shares were priced at £100 each with a deposit of £2 per share. As an additional inducement subscribers who paid the deposit were promised an annual dividend of £100 for every share held. The enterprising company promoter opened an office in Cornhill at 9.00 a.m. and closed at 3.00 p.m. the same day.

During the opening hours the London information distribution network did its work and he sold one thousand shares, raising £2,000. Happy with his efforts, he closed the office, disappeared off to the Continent and was never heard of again (McKay, 1852). Between 1719 and 1720 an estimated 190 companies raised a total of £121m (Scott, 1951).

With the South Sea Company share price soaring, it was little wonder that crooks were tempted; within just three months the company's share price rose from £128 to £300, then £500. The government, worried that investment in both legitimate companies and fraudulent scams would divert finance away from the South Sea Company, decided to act to stop other companies and scams by passing the Bubble Act. This made non-chartered companies illegal, and from 1720 only companies incorporated by Royal Charter were allowed to sell their shares.

The South Sea Company share price reached its highest point at the end of May and the beginning of June 1720, rising from £550 to £890: at such high prices, investors began selling their shares in order to make a profit on their investments. This, however, turned into panic selling in July when Sir John Blunt, the Chairman of the South Sea Company, and other directors sold their shares. Investors often regard share sales by company directors as a lack of confidence in their own businesses, which in the case of the South Sea Company, it most certainly was.

The sale or purchase of shares by the directors of a public company is still regarded as a sensitive issue that can affect a company's share price. The question to which other shareholders want to know the answer is, whether the directors are selling or buying shares based on their knowledge of what is happening in the company or will happen in the future. As actions that can impact on the company share price, share sales and purchases by directors have to be notified to the Stock Exchange and the information shared with everyone. So important is this for many investors that newspapers carry regular updates on the various share dealings of directors.

If the sales by the South Sea Company directors represented the actions of directors desperate to get out of a business before it collapsed, there are also reverse situations where directors buy shares in a company to demonstrate their confidence in it. An example of this occurred in 2008 when, in a collective show of belief in the company, the directors of the troubled bank HBOS bought an additional 1.4 million HBOS shares. Mark Kleinman (2008), writing in the *Daily Telegraph*, commented:

'HBOS led a rally in the banking sector this morning after its shares soared as much as 17%, helped by the news that its chief executive Andy Hornby had spent hundreds of thousands of pounds on shares in the high street lender in the days surrounding last week's share price plunge.' Hornby bought 92,812 shares. Colin Matthew, Bank of Scotland treasurer and HBOS chief executive of strategy and international, bought 58,543 shares and head of insurance and investment Jo Dawson picked up 57,115 shares. HBOS's finance director, Mike Ellis, bought more than 10,000 shares. 'The purchases were a way of demonstrating confidence in the bank,' said a source.

As the share price of the South Sea Company started to fall, the directors once again attempted to use the tactics that so far had served them well and embarked on another round of rumour mongering. They even called a public meeting to try to address the worries and concerns of investors. It was all, however, to no avail as, during September, the share price continued to fall (Dale, 2004). An orgy of selling in South Sea Company shares began in October 1720, and, as panic spread among shareholders, the share price collapsed to £150. Thousands of people who had bought shares at the higher prices were ruined. The impact was indiscriminate; porters and ladies maids, along with bishops and poets, were all equally affected. There were daily reports in the press of suicides by investors who had lost their money – the Post-Master General poisoned himself and Stanhope, the Chief Minister, was said to have died from the strain induced by the crisis (McKay, 1852).

Walpole, who had already sold his shares, rescued the company, with the Bank of England taking part of the South Sea Company capital and reconstructing the national debt. The South Sea Company survived and remained a trading company with a licence to operate in the South Seas. Even though it was never as successful as the East India Company, it did subsequently pay dividends and provide a return to its shareholders (Paul, 2011).

The most lasting effect of the crisis was the Bubble Act, which restricted the creation of joint stock companies for nearly a century. Joint stock companies could be created only by a private Act of Parliament and incorporated firms could not transfer shares or have more than six partners. For many people this was no bad thing. The activities of the South Sea Company and other companies created at the time had confirmed their fears that the joint stock company was a dubious form of enterprise which made it hard to distinguish between good and bad businesses. There was widespread criticism of this form of company structure where management and ownership were separated. Adam Smith, looking to learn the lessons of the South Sea Bubble and other problems created by joint stock companies, warned in the *Wealth of Nations* that 'The directors of such companies however, being the managers rather of other people's money rather than their own, it cannot be expected that they should watch over it with the same anxious vigilance with which the partners in a private company would watch over their own ... negligence and profusion, therefore, must always prevail, more or less in the management of the affairs of such a company ... They have, accordingly, very seldom succeeded without an exclusive privilege and frequently have succeeded with one' (Smith, 1776: 606–607).

Smith's preferred company structure was the partnership where the managers were also the owners of the firm and therefore directly responsible for any debts and liabilities incurred by the business. In a partnership, an individual commits their own resources and capital to the venture and this gives the business more credibility in the eyes of many. In a joint stock company, because the company managers did not have personal responsibility for any company debts, this could result in their running-up huge debts for which they had no personal liability.

The 1820s boom and crash

With few domestic public companies to invest in because of the restrictions imposed by the Bubble Act, British investors in the 1820s turned overseas, and especially to South America, for investments. Although, a hundred years earlier, investors had lost money on the false promises offered by South Sea trade, this appears to have been forgotten by the investors of the 1820s. As with the South Sea Company, the investment opportunities on offer to investors seemed guaranteed to make money and proved irresistible to many. Henry English, a contemporary stockbroker, strongly disapproved of both the companies and their promoters. Many projects, he wrote, ranged from 'the fantastic to the downright fraudulent' (Dawson, 1990).

The 1820s equivalent of 'The Company to Produce Everything' of the South Sea Bubble era were the bonds issued by an imaginary South American republic called Poyais,[11] the creation of a Scottish fraudster

George McGregor, a former officer in the Duke of Wellington's Peninsula Army who went to fight along with other British army veterans in South America. McGregor offered potential investors a number of alternative ways of investing. The wealthy investor, for example, could buy 2,000 bonds at £100 per bond, while the less wealthy could buy land at 3s 3d per acre (later 4s), about a day's wages in 1822. The offers worked and the necessary finance was raised to enable prospective settlers to go to Poyais, an area in modern-day Honduras. The venture failed because of the hostile nature of the jungle and the devastating impact of tropical diseases on the settlers. McGregor's success in raising substantial funds, however, also encouraged other 'mini-Poyais' schemes (Dawson, 1990).

The collapse of the Spanish Empire saw the emergence of new and independent countries such as Venezuela, Bolivia, Chile and Mexico in South America. These countries needed huge amounts of capital to invest in their infrastructure and to help grow and develop industries such as mining that were vital to their futures. Between 1822 and 1825, seven Latin American nations issued over £20m in bonds (Dawson, 1990). However, the companies set up to develop mining schemes proved disastrous for investors, with virtually every one of them losing money. In these investments we see the same situation repeated as occurred during the South Sea Bubble: legitimate companies competing for funds alongside fraudulent ones. 'Among the companies which sprang up daily, was one to make gold; and success was declared to be undoubted. The shares were all greedily taken; and it was then advertised that, as the expense of producing one ounce of gold would cost double the value of the produce, the company would be dissolved, and the deposits kept to pay expenses' (Robb, 2002: 15).

In April 1825 there was a major economic crisis. Although it is not clear what specific incident caused it, the main difference between this and the South Sea Bubble crisis was that it affected both the UK and the international economy. The initial spark was a share price collapse in various South American mining companies, which in turn triggered a series of commercial failures, including a number of regional banks in the UK that had lent money to individuals so that they could invest in the failed South American companies. This led to the recession of 1826 in the UK, which was so severe that the Bank of England was forced to restrict the flow of credit so as to avert a possible balance of payments crisis. In practice, this turned out to be one of worst financial crises of the nineteenth century.

Although British investors had limited investment opportunities, this was to change dramatically as the government handed responsibility for building the UK's canals and railways over to private companies. Government in the 1820s and 1830s believed in *laissez-faire* economic philosophy – that the state should have no role in the management of the economy – and applied this to developing the country's railways and canals. Building both networks demanded huge amounts of capital and, as the state was not going to provide the finance, the only vehicle capable of raising it from private sources was the much-maligned joint stock company. By the 1820s the restrictions on joint stock companies imposed by the Bubble Act were beginning to hinder the growth of the national economy. The scale of the problem is illustrated in the way that Parliament struggled to cope with the number of Bills from companies that had applied, wanting corporate status to be granted. In April 1825 there were 250 bills before the Commons from different groups wanting to set up companies to invest in the UK's railways and canals. In the face of such pressure, in June 1825, the Bubble Act was repealed (Robb, 2002). It was not, however, replaced by any new legal structure, which meant that unchartered companies were now governed by commercial law. Provided that the purpose of the company was legitimate, anyone could now legally form a company. No one could see how fortuitous this was in terms of timing, as this new, unrestricted company structure, with no limit placed on the number of potential shareholders, would be the main vehicle for the financing of one of the most important periods in UK industrial history. However, as history again and again demonstrates, unregulated corporate structures create problems that are not just commercial: they impact on the rest of society.

2

The Economist, The Times and railway mania

By 1800 newspapers had established themselves as the most important element of the public sphere (Conboy, 2011), with four daily newspapers published in London: the *Morning Post*, the *Morning Chronicle*, the *Morning Herald*, and *The Times*. Newspapers at this time were often associated with a cause or class; the *Morning Post*, for example, was the preferred reading of the aristocracy, with a circulation of around 3,000 copies in 1847 (Brown 1992). The *Morning Chronicle* (started in 1765) was originally a Whig paper, but was purchased by a consortium of Peelites in 1848. The *Standard* started in 1827 as an evening paper holding conservative views and specifically opposing Catholic emancipation.

The Times, established in 1785 as the *Daily Universal Register*, was the UK's first national daily newspaper and raced ahead of its rivals under the energetic ownership of John Walter (1776–1847). Its success in the early part of the nineteenth century was down to it being the first paper to recognise the importance of news as an essential element of a newspaper. Walter was prepared to commit both personnel and resources to gathering not just domestic but also foreign news (Temple, 2008). He also invested heavily in the latest printing technology, enabling the paper to go to press later and contain more up-to-date news than its rivals. The Koenig steam press introduced by *The Times* in November 1814 produced 1,000 sheets per hour, while in 1827, with the installation of the Applegarth press, production was raised to 4,000 impressions per hour (Black 1992).

This policy was both editorially and commercially successful, as circulation rose from 5,000 copies in 1815 to 10,000 by 1834; then to 18,500 in 1840, 23,000 in 1844, passing 30,000 in 1848 (Temple, 2008).[1] The newspaper's editorial success was demonstrated by an increasing political influence.

On his death, editor Thomas Barnes was succeeded by 23-year-old John Delane, whose appointment marks a new era of expansion for the newspaper. Under his editorship, while *The Times* was loosely identified with liberalism, his main concern was to maintain its independence from political parties and factions, recognising that its strength lay in its being critical of whichever government was in power. Any support for the government of the day was lent rather than given, and could at any time be replaced by criticism or outright opposition (Hamilton, 2004).

Modern company news and editorial effectively began in the 1820s. Its limited scope reflected not only the available information from business sources at the time but also the prevailing social attitudes of the landed aristocracy, who held employment in business, commerce or trade of any kind in low regard. The emerging business class was still waiting to find a channel that would articulate its views and interests.

The first modern 'City' reporting started in 1820 in the *Observer*, when the owner, William Innell Clement, introduced a City column because he needed to increase the amount of news in the paper in order to produce what he called a 'seventh-day' (i.e. a Sunday) newspaper. He also introduced a City column in the *Morning Chronicle*, which he took over in 1821; encouraged by the economic boom of the 1820s, other newspapers followed and developed their own City columns.

The introduction of financial news was also part of the emerging professionalism of newspapers, where the use of trained reporters was becoming more common. From the 1830s specialist commentators started covering political events and, following the lead of *The Times*, other newspapers began to appoint foreign correspondents. Another significant move was the emergence of dedicated journalists covering City and finance stories.

Although the first company news reporting appeared in the *Observer*, the honour of the title 'father' of financial journalism belongs to Thomas Massa Alsager, who was appointed financial editor of *The Times* in 1817. This, however, was only one of his functions at the paper. A brilliant linguist, he was also responsible for organising the collection of foreign and domestic news which was so important to the newspaper's success.

Newspapers in the early part of the nineteenth century had a simple structure. *The Times* only had three sections: first, the Leader, which was more extensive than its modern-day counterpart, the editorial; second, a news section covering both domestic and foreign news and readers' letters. The growing importance of business coverage is illustrated by the fact that the business column or the 'City article' was the third section. The importance *The Times* attached to business reporting is illustrated by a pledge it made in 1785, that it would give due attention to the 'interests of the trade, which are so greatly promoted by advertisements' and facilitate 'commercial intercourse between different parts of the community'.

It is significant that three of the most successful business editors of the nineteenth century also had successful careers in business and commerce. Alsager, James Wilson and Walter Bagehot (editors of *The Economist*, see below) utilised their experience and understanding of business in their writing and commentary. Alsager's business experience was probably crucial in enabling him to take the defining role in covering business and financial issues and, especially, taking a critical stance over the issue of railway mania (see below).

Thomas Massa Alsager began working as an apprentice setter in the family business. A self-educated man, he was a first-rate scholar and linguist and could also perform competently on all instruments of the orchestra (Porter, 2004b).

Alsager entered journalism in 1819, aged 38, and only because he was friends with the new editor, Thomas Barnes. Using his business experience to report on market or City activity, Alsager's money article was published daily from 1825. Although other newspapers developed their own financial columns, *The Times* was regarded as the most authoritative, due to Alsager's business knowledge, experience and contacts.

Harry Marks (see Chapter 4) said that Alsager was regarded as 'the chief authority on these (financial) matters, and became the favourite medium for circulating official and semi-official communicators'. Marks's views on Alsager are interesting, and Alsager is an early example of how some financial journalists became trusted conduits for business and establishment sources to disseminate news and information. Alsager certainly had excellent business and social connections: he was close to such key figures as the Rothschild banking family, sharing their conservative views on issues such as the currency, foreign investment and joint stock banking. Because his financial articles were popular with both readers and business this helped to attract advertising to the paper. Alsager was so important to *The Times* that he was made a partner in the business in 1827 and, with joint manager William Delane, the paper prospered and grew. By the 1840s *The Times* was the paper read, and in some cases feared, by the establishment, with the apparent power to shape and influence government opinion (Conboy, 2004).

The Economist

The newspaper that became the outspoken champion of Adam Smith's free market philosophy and articulated the views of the industrialists and manufacturers who were transforming the UK's industrial and physical landscape was *The Economist*. It was founded by manufacturer James Wilson in 1843 to articulate the views of people like him and fight for their interests. The cause that prompted its foundation was one that came to epitomise the battle between landowners and industrialists: the repeal of the Corn Laws. Once established, *The Economist* was to become, and remain, the most influential voice of *laissez-faire* economic philosophy and free market economics.

The Economist called itself a 'newspaper' rather than a journal, such as the influential *Edinburgh Review*, because it carried news about current events rather than just feature articles and economic debates. *The Economist: A Political, Commercial and Free Trade Journal* was formed in the heat of a fierce political debate that dominated the politics of the period, with governments rising and falling over where they stood on the issue of free trade or protectionism. These issues all fused together in the arguments over the Corn Laws (Gambles, 1999).

The first Corn Law was introduced in 1804 by a Parliament dominated by landowners who were attempting to protect their profits by imposing a duty on imported corn. The Napoleonic Wars, however, restricted corn imports from Europe, and while wheat farming in Britain increased, so did bread prices. When the war ended in 1815, farmers and landowners feared that the price of wheat would fall quickly; so, under their pressure to keep prices artificially high, Parliament introduced new Corn Laws in 1815 (Gambles, 1999).

A number of political and economic issues crystallise around the debate over the Corn Laws and the way British society was changing during this period. Their introduction demonstrated the strength of agricultural interests in politics and the way that landowners, and especially aristocratic landowners, dominated the political landscape.

The laws were deeply unpopular with the rapidly growing urban working class and also the emerging industrial bourgeoisie and factory owners. One reason was that they were a stark reminder to the working class, for all their increasing prosperity, that political power still lay with the landowners. The argument about the repeal of the Corn Laws became one between the largely disenfranchised urban classes and the landed aristocracy. Manufacturers were opposed to the Corn Laws not only on ideological grounds, but also for practical reasons, as high bread prices led to increased demands for higher wages. Countering this, landowners argued that if the price of bread fell, manufacturers would attempt to drive wages down. The debate also encompassed arguments over free trade versus protectionism and which served the interests of the UK economy better (Howe, 1997).

In October 1837 the Anti-Corn Law Association was formed in London; Richard Cobden, a Manchester industrialist joined in 1838 and established a new centralised Anti-Corn Law League. The economic depression of 1840–42 increased membership, and in 1843 *The Economist* was set up, with help from the Anti-Corn Law League, under the editorship of its founder, James Wilson from Hawick, who was similar to many early financial journalists in combining business and journalism. Wilson started as an apprentice in a hat factory which his father eventually bought for him and his brother. They ran the business successfully until the 1837 economic crash, in which he lost most of his wealth (Pickering and Tyrrel, 2000).

Wilson in fact is one of the most interesting businessmen of the period, the setting up of *The Economist* being only one of his accomplishments. In 1847 he became the Liberal MP for Westbury, Wiltshire and, on account of his economic experience, Prime Minister Lord John Russell appointed him Secretary of the Board of Control, a department responsible for Indian affairs. In 1853 he founded the Chartered Bank of India, Australia and China, which eventually merged with the Standard Bank to become the Standard Chartered Bank. He also held a number of senior financial and economic posts in different government administrations, including Financial Secretary to the Treasury and Paymaster General. He resigned in 1859 to sit as a member of the Council of India to re-order the country's financial structure following the revolt of 1857. He died of dysentery only a year later, aged 55.

While the Corn Laws had no significant impact on Wilson personally, he was a believer in free markets and objected to the Corn Laws on principle. He first wrote and published a pamphlet, *Influences of the Corn Laws as Affecting All Classes of the Community* (1839). Free trade, Wilson believed, benefited everyone. In his prospectus for *The Economist* he wrote: 'If we look abroad, we see within the range of our commercial intercourse whole islands and continents, on which the light of civilisation has scarce yet dawned; and we seriously believe that free trade, free intercourse, will do more than any other visible agent to extend civilisation and morality throughout the world – yes, to extinguish slavery itself' (www.economist.com).

Wilson's outlook, whilst moral, was not moralistic, believing 'that reason is given to us to sit in judgment over the dictates of our feelings'. Reason convinced him in particular that Adam Smith was right, that, through the invisible hand, the market benefited profit-seeking individuals (of whom he was one) and society alike. As he was a manufacturer, he wanted especially to influence 'men of business' through *The Economist*.

Wilson remained the paper's publisher and also writer of most of its content for seventeen years. Walter Bagehot, Wilson's son-in-law, took over as the paper's editor from 1861 until 1877. Before taking over at *The Economist* he wrote for a variety of publications and set up the *National Review* in 1855. Like Wilson and Alsager, Bagehot also combined business and journalism, running the London office of the family banking business, Stuckey & Co., while also editing *The Economist*. Bagehot's popularity as a writer was based on his direct, almost colloquial style. He tried 'to be conversational, to put things in the most direct and picturesque manner, as people would talk to each other in common speech, to remember and use expressive colloquialisms' (www.economist.com).

Bagehot understood how to write for his audience and had the ability to take complicated economic ideas and put them into understandable language. What he was doing for his readers was putting capitalism into words (Parsons, 1989). Under his editorship *The Economist* expanded its coverage of both domestic and international politics. Bagehot was a banker and his book *Lombard Street* (1873) is still regarded as one of the most important books on banking, revisiting what he described as the principles of banking following the collapse of Overend Gurney in 1866. Overend Gurney had been known as the 'bankers' bank' that could not collapse. When it did, it had a profound impact on confidence in the banking system, and *Lombard Street* is Bagehot's restatement of what banking principles should be. However, he is probably best remembered for his work on constitutional matters. *The English Constitution* (1867) offers a definitive account of the relationship between Parliament and the monarchy; the monarch, he argued, was head of the 'dignified' parts of the constitution, those that 'excite and preserve the reverence of the population'; the prime minister was head of the 'efficient' parts, 'those by which it, in fact, works and rules'. A political Liberal, he twice stood unsuccessfully for Parliament.

Bagehot believed that 'The object of the *Economist* is to throw white light on the subjects within its range', and under his editorship the paper's influence grew. One British foreign secretary, Lord Granville, said that whenever he felt uncertain, he liked to wait to see what the next issue of the *Economist* had to say. Wilson and Bagehot were not, however, simply observers on economics and business but participants; their writings were informed and guided by their practical experience of the business world. They also knew their audience and understood how to write for business owners and entrepreneurs and rationalise their collective experience. These practical business readers wanted facts rather than abstract theories, because facts were indisputable and could change opinions. Wilson insisted that all the arguments and propositions put forward in *The Economist* should be subjected to the test of facts.

The Economist became more than just a newspaper, providing the Victorian business community with a coherent set of ideas, information and news. The economic theories of Adam Smith, for example, offered a justification and rationale for what practical men were doing. Wilson and Bagehot's journalism helped to shape the views of Victorian businessmen. Politically, this helped to bring about the triumph of manufacture over agriculture, the collapse of the rotten boroughs and the victory of free trade over protectionism.

Railway mania

In 1830 the Liverpool and Manchester Railway opened the first steam passenger-railway service, demonstrating that rail transport could be commercially viable. Its success was the catalyst for the beginning of large-scale railway construction in Britain, which then spread throughout the world. The so-called 'Railway Mania' in the UK was also a significant event for the emerging financial and business press. Its most important impact was to demonstrate, probably for the first time, that a newspaper could take an editorial position opposing commercial interests and be editorially and financially successful. This was a victory for editorial credibility. The episode also demonstrates the impact that advertising in newspapers could have for advertisers, as huge amounts of finance were raised because of the railway advertising.

The scale of the undertaking by the private railway companies to build a network was immense. 'In 1845 Parliament sanctioned 2,816 miles of new railway line. An additional 4,540 miles were sanctioned in 1846. At its peak in 1845–46, railway expenditure absorbed almost 7% of national income' (Robb, 2002: 13). The whole country appeared to be affected by a railway investment fever. A writer of the time, Thomas Tooke, observed, 'In every street of every town persons were to be found who were holders of railway shares. Elderly men and women of small fortunes, tradesmen of every order, pensioners, public functionaries, professional men, merchants, country gentlemen – the mania had affected them all' (Robb, 2002: 31).

In accordance with *laissez-faire* philosophy there was no rational planning of railway routes by the national or local authorities; the decision about where to go was made by regional railway companies, with several often competing to open similar routes between different towns. In such situations what determined which company won the route was who reached agreement first with all the landowners involved (Robb, 2002).

In the beginning, the railway companies were all regionally based, and to fund their ambitious investment plans both to lay down the track and operate a railway service they turned to local sources to raise the necessary finance. While the regional county banks that could issue their own notes provided debt finance for working capital, the investment funds had to be drawn from other sources. It was local investors who could see the benefits and attractions of a local railway company who became the investors in the railway joint stock companies. The investment opportunities that the railway companies promised appeared too good to be true, as they made extravagant claims about the returns investors could expect.

The various rail schemes attracted new and inexperienced investors, including some of the most famous names of the day: Charles Darwin,

Charles Babbage, John Stuart Mill, the Brontë sisters, William Makepeace Thackeray, for example. Politicians who invested included Disraeli, Gladstone, Palmerston and Robert Peel (Odlyzko, 2010).

All the Brontë sisters were enthusiastic investors in railway shares; Charlotte Brontë, in her diary, provides an interesting insight into how the sisters researched their investment decisions, demonstrating the importance of local newspapers:

> Emily has made herself mistress of the necessary degree of knowledge for conducting the matter, by dint of carefully reading every paragraph and every advertisement in the newspapers that related to the rail-roads. (Quoted in Odlyzko, 2010: 4)

In the Haworth parsonage such information could only have come from their preferred local newspaper, the *Leeds Mercury*, owned by Edward Baines. Emily Brontë's share-buying research illustrates the key role played by local newspapers in helping regional railway companies to raise their funds, and would be typical of most middle-class families.

Although by the 1840s British newspapers had increased the volume of their business editorial coverage, most information about companies still came from the display advertising that companies took out in the newspapers. Advertising columns at the time were used for a variety of purposes and played a wider role than modern newspaper advertising. The minutiae of local life were often expressed in these advertisements, which frequently occupied the whole front page of each issue. Companies looking to raise funds would advertise lengthy company prospectuses providing details of the proposed venture and information on why the funds were needed, how they were going to be used and what returns or dividends the potential investor could expect. There would also be adverts for notice of company meetings such as the Annual General Meeting, and the resulting minutes would also be advertised. Information for investors and potential investors would also be generated by the many and varied invitations to contractors to bid for large and small building projects. In a paper such as the *Leeds Mercury*, readers like the Brontë sisters would probably find more information about the railways in the advertisements than the editorial.

Railway mania and the opposition of The Times and The Economist

Railway mania was an important event for *The Times*, *The Economist* and business and financial journalism generally because it demonstrates how editorial coverage can influence opinion and also bring commercial benefits. After its principled stance, the circulation of *The Times* grew several times larger than that of all the other dailies combined (Odlyzko, 2010).

In a leader of 1 July 1845 *The Times* came out in opposition to the way the railway network was growing: 'Whence is to come all the money for the projected railways? Is a question which at the present day we often hear repeated ... The pace of railway speculation has fairly outrun the power and control of the legislature ...'.

Another leading article stated: '[T]he mania for railway speculation has reached that height at which all follies, however absurd in themselves, cease to be ludicrous, and become, by reason of their universality, fit subjects for the politician to consider as well as the moralist' (Odlyzko, 2010: 88). The position taken, and the writing, was all the work of Alsager.

The Times was joined in its opposition to railway mania by *The Economist* and these two became the most significant and influential of the anti-railway newspapers. Neither was opposed to railway development per se – they both recognised and accepted that railways would bring economic and social benefits; nor did they deny that the new railway companies would eventually produce a profit and a return for their investors. *The Times* in fact declared itself to be an 'enthusiastic' railway supporter, regarding them as vital to the transport infrastructure (Odlyzko, 2010). The concern of both papers, however, was that there was too much railway development taking place and that the amount of investment going into developing the railway network would have an adverse effect on other areas of the economy.[2] A further concern was that the speed of the investment in the railways was too fast and could destabilise the rest of the economy. In October 1845, for example, the *Economist* argued that the nation did not have enough capital to pay for all the proposed railway construction, a line repeated in *The Times* in November, which estimated that the cost of an additional 620 new railway schemes was £563m, or more than two-thirds of the total national debt. Such finance, it said, could not be raised without 'the most ruinous, universal, and desperate confusion' (Robb, 2002: 47). *The Times* criticised not only the financial impact but also the activities of the share promoters and the way they raised the money through spreading dubious claims.

Another concern of both *The Times* and *The Economist* was that the railway network could eventually, through mergers and acquisitions, end up as a private monopoly,

> The question then is, are we in thirty years' time to have a vast *imperium in imperio* – a railroad union with a capital of a thousand millions, and an income of fifty millions, besides a proportionate expenditure, – in *private hands*; or are we to have this wealth and power in the hands of the state? Is there no inconvenience, no danger in the existence of so vast an independent body? The patronage of the state will be a trifle in comparison. (Odlyzko, 2010: 88)

Despite the derogatory comment about the state, this was a significant statement for a conservative paper to be making that believed in property rights and private enterprise. If the railway network was to be a monopoly then, surely it would be better in public rather than private hands. 'Its advocacy of government ownership or at least closer government oversight of railways indicates an unusual situation. This paper felt that the potential size, power, ubiquity, and indispensability of the growing new transportation infrastructure called for departure from ordinary principles, including risking all the inefficiencies and corruption that government operations were associated with in most minds at that time' (Odlyzko, 2010: 88).

In another line of attack *The Economist* argued that many of the many proposed lines were already redundant: 'We see nine or ten proposals for nearly the same line, all at a premium, when it is well known that only one can succeed, and the rest must, in all probability, be minus their expenses.' The unrestrained speculation of 'railway mania' was, *The Economist* said, 'a tale of national delusion' (Robb, 2002: 47).

The opposition of *The Times* rattled the railway companies, which hit back by threatening to withdraw their lucrative advertising from the paper. This was a defining moment. Would the newspaper maintain its position and editorial integrity, or succumb to the pressures from the advertisers for the sake of commercial expediency? Sacrificing the former for the latter would be a severe blow to the credibility of the paper. Significantly, both the editor, Thomas Barnes, and owner, John Walter II, supported Alsager and his firm, uncompromising line. The position taken by *The Times* enhanced not only its reputation but also that of financial and business journalism; and, confirming that readers respect editorial independence, its circulation actually grew as a result of its opposition to railway mania. The role *The Times* played in helping to prick the railway bubble was recognised by other publications. In October 1845, for example, the *Law Times* wrote, 'It is to the energetic efforts of *The Times* to expose the folly of the railway mania that the country is mainly indebted for the check which it has received and which though attended with present inconvenience, will prevent more extended mischief' (Robb, 2002: 84).

From this professional high point, however, Thomas Alsager was to suffer a rapid and tragic fall. A rival newspaper accused him of hypocrisy, claiming that at the same time as *The Times* was criticising railway mania it had been promoting the direct London and Exeter line in which Alsager held shares (Porter, 2004b). While this damaged his reputation, however, this was not the cause of his downfall. In October 1846 Alsager left *The Times* under a cloud, following a row with the owner, John Walter II, over the way he had apparently misrepresented the financial position of the printing department. This controversial end to his connection with the paper he had served for almost thirty years was a huge blow to Alsager. The depression that had afflicted him following the death of his wife a year earlier intensified, and on the first anniversary of her funeral, 6 November 1846, he attempted suicide, cutting his throat and slashing his left wrist. He eventually died on 15 November 1846 (Porter, 2004b).

Although the speculative mania around railway shares began to abate in 1846 as the demand for new capital subsided, the financial problems of many railway companies were only beginning. Their biggest financial losses came between 1846 and 1849, when construction started on the approved schemes.

For those companies that managed to build a network, as soon as they started operating it became clear that many schemes and companies were unviable. The financial situation of many was exacerbated when, in late 1865, the Bank of England raised interest rates, with the result that funds moved from railway shares into government bonds. This prompted falls in the share price of railway companies, leaving many of them with little or no funding and their investors with no prospect of getting a return on their investment. This presented the larger railway companies such as Great Western Railway with opportunities, and many started buying failed lines to expand their network. Investors in the failing railway companies had little choice but to accept the situation and sell their shares well below the price they had paid for them, or risk losing everything.

The estimated total overall losses of the railway investors were about £80m, or almost a third of the total amount invested, and the impact was devastating, especially for all those new to investing. At the end of 1849, when railway shares were touching their lowest level, a rueful Charlotte Brontë wrote:

> My shares are in the York and North Midland Railway. The original price of shares in the company was £50. At one time they rose to £120; and for some years gave a dividend of 10% they are now down to £20 and it is doubtful whether any dividend will be paid this year ... (Quoted in Odlyzko, 2010: 4).

Charlotte Brontë, however, could at least afford to be relatively relaxed over her losses, as her novel *Jane Eyre* had been a best seller when published in 1847.

Many middle-class investors like the Brontë sisters invested not because they wanted a huge return from any rise in the value of the shares, but because the promoters promised shareholders a steady and regular income over the operational lifetime of the railways. The twelve main companies paid an average dividend of 7.6% in 1846, but by 1848 this had fallen to 5.3% and by the early 1850s it remained around 3% (Robb, 2002).

Railway mania demonstrated to company promoters that regional and national newspapers were a vital means of reaching potential investors and could influence purchasing decisions. The advertising income of the papers from new company placings and the associated follow-up announcements became over many years a valuable source of revenue. In such circumstances it would have been easy for the newspapers to be meekly compliant with the editorial demands of company advertisers and to collude with them to produce the editorial that they wanted.

However, both *The Times* and *The Economist* had demonstrated, in their editorial stance on the railways, that financial reporting could be critical, editorially independent and also commercially successful. A confident *Times* went further, becoming the first newspaper to outline an editorial policy on how it would treat company reports. In future, it announced, company reporting would be on its terms: rather than simply reproduce verbatim reports written by the company, it would publish only reports written by its own journalists.

The repeal of the Bubble Act in 1825 had left joint stock companies largely free from regulation. However, the activities of fraudulent company directors during the railway boom had once again demonstrated that joint stock companies could be a vehicle for financial abuse. Despite the opposition of supporters of *laissez-faire* in Parliament, regulation was pushed through to control their activities. Starting in 1844, a series of Companies Acts began to define the role of shareholders and the responsibilities of company directors. Under the requirements of the 1844 Act, a company could claim limited liability status, provided that it had at least twenty-five shareholders and that 75% of the company's capital was subscribed, with 15% paid.

In 1856, the Joint Stock Companies Act codified the law by imposing a two-stage process, jettisoning the requirements about the amount of capital to be subscribed and paid for. Any group of seven or more persons could now form a limited company by registering its objectives and that it was limited. A better-known Act of 1862 simply codified all these measures.

These changes led to a substantial increase in the number of companies being created. In 1853, there were 339 provisional registrations; ten years later, under the new rules, this had increased to 689 (Scott, 1951). In practice, dealing in company shares was limited to a handful of companies, as there was nothing in law to compel a registered company to offer its shares to the public. Furthermore, the number of companies in which there was an active share market was always small in proportion to the overall number of registrations.

3

New Journalism, the *Daily Mail* and Charles Duguid

In 1855 the stamp duty that had restricted newspaper ownership was repealed. The repeal marked the end of government attempts to use taxes and duties to control newspapers and opened up a new era for journalism. Before the repeal, most newspapers were created to argue for a political cause or social campaign or class interests. After 1855 a new model appeared: a low-price newspaper that attracted advertisers because of its large circulation. This was the beginning of the 'dual-product' status of newspapers: on the one hand, they are bought for their editorial content, and on the other hand, advertisers use them as a platform to reach readers.

A series of technological developments made the mass production of newspapers commercially viable. Steam-driven presses, for example, which were four times faster than the older presses, were introduced in the 1830s. The development and growth of the telegraph improved the sourcing and delivery of news; newspapers could now report on events happening on the other side of the world within hours of them happening, giving them an added credibility as a source of news. The telegraph also impacted on financial and business information, enabling reports and stories to be written about companies and stock exchanges around the world.

Improved delivery processes through postal communications and the development of the railway industry enabled up-to-date newspapers to be delivered faster and more efficiently. Large metropolitan centres made large-scale distribution of newspapers possible, and in a cost-effective manner. Increasing literacy levels among all sections of a growing population also helped to stimulate overall demand for newspapers.

Nowhere is the impact of these changes better illustrated than in the way the *Daily Telegraph* developed. The original *Daily Telegraph &*

Courier had been created by Colonel Arthur Sleigh in 1855, like many other newspapers at the time, to fight for a political cause. That of the *Daily Telegraph*'s had, however, to be one of the more obscure issues of the day: to air a personal grievance against Prince George, the Duke of Cambridge and future Commander-in-Chief of the British army. The new paper was printed by Joseph Moses Levy, owner of the *Sunday Times*. The *Telegraph*'s first edition was published on 29 June 1855. Due, perhaps not surprisingly, to the limited appeal of its cause, it was not a success. Colonel Sleigh could not pay the printing bill, so Levy took it over.

In 1855 ten newspapers were published in London. *The Times*, priced at 7*d*, although the most expensive had a circulation of 10,000. Its two main rivals, the *Daily News* and the *Morning Post*, both cost 5*d* each. Levy, however, in line with the new thinking, believed that if he produced a cheaper newspaper than the competition, he could expand the size of the overall market. On 17 September 1855, he relaunched the *Daily Telegraph* with the slogan, 'the largest, best, and cheapest newspaper in the world'.

Levy appointed his son, Edward Levy-Lawson, and Thornton Hunt as joint-editors. Soon after joining, Thornton Hunt wrote a report on the possible future of the *Daily Telegraph*: 'We should report all striking events in science, so told that the intelligent public can understand what has happened and can see its bearing on our daily life and our future. The same principle should apply to all other events – to fashion, to new inventions, to new methods of conducting business' (Burnham, 1995: 89).

After only a few months the *Daily Telegraph* was outselling *The Times*, and, by January 1856, its circulation was 27,000. The early *Daily Telegraph* supported the Liberal Party and progressive causes such as the campaign against capital punishment, reform of the House of Lords and the abolition of corporal punishment in the armed forces. It was not a paper that would necessarily appeal to its modern readers.

New Journalism

The repeal of the stamp duty freed newspapers from space restrictions, enabling new and radical design innovations to be introduced.

The old layout had originally been a response to space restrictions imposed by the stamp duty and had become the standard design in all newspapers.

The technological changes and the influence of US-designed newspapers brought a new style of journalism, the so-called 'New Journalism'. This was characterised by radical, stylistic changes and design innovations such as cross-heads in copy to break up the cramped columns of undifferentiated small type. Editorially, New Journalism had a more 'personal' tone, designed to engage the attention of the reader through shorter paragraphs and illustrations.

This type of editorial appealed to a new type of readers who were the products of industrialisation. By the late 1880s, the transformation of the UK from a rural to an industrial economy was almost complete, with new towns, and new suburbs in old towns. Industrialisation had transformed the structure of society, producing an urban, factory-based working class, a managerial class and a *petit-bourgeoisie*.

To reflect the social and political changes taking place in society, newspapers began covering a wider and more diverse range of editorial subjects. The verbatim reporting of political speeches was replaced by lighter, human-interest gossip stories and sports news. New types of display advertising were also introduced.

The Daily Mail *and Charles Duguid*

It was an ex-journalist, Alfred Harmsworth, who created in the *Daily Mail*, the newspaper that articulated the views and reflected the interests of the class created by industrialisation. Harmsworth was born in 1865, and his interest in journalism started at school, where he edited the school magazine; after school he began his journalism career working on a boys' magazine owned by the *Illustrated London News*. In 1868 he became editor of *Bicycling News*. Two years later, aged just 23 and in partnership with his 26-year-old elder brother, he set up on his own, launching *Answers to Correspondents*, a competitor to the UK's then most popular magazine, *Tit-Bits*. Within four years *Answers* was selling over a million copies a week. It was based on a deceptively simple idea: readers sent in questions which were answered by the magazine and the most interesting questions and answers were then published in the magazine (Boyce, 2011).

Harmsworth started in newspaper publishing in 1894 by buying the struggling London newspaper the *Evening News*. The new owners radically redesigned the paper, with the news presented and laid out in the sharper modern style, using eye-catching headlines and illustrations to break up the text. Advertisements were also changed to be more appealing to readers, placed in a single column on the left side of the page. In just two years Harmsworth had transformed the loss-making *Evening News*: circulation had grown to 800,000 and it was making profits of £50,000 (Boyce, 2011).

In 1896, Harmsworth launched the *Daily Mail*, a newspaper deliberately aimed at the new classes working in jobs that were the result of mass industrialisation and urbanisation. These were the people who travelled to work from their houses in the new suburbs; they were shop assistants and clerks, 'busy people' who needed interesting stories that could be consumed quickly. Harmsworth, the consummate publishing professional, invested significant financial resources to ensure that the launch was correct. By the time of the first issue of the *Daily Mail* was launched on 4 May 1896, there had been over sixty-five dummy runs, each one costing £40,000.

The eight-page newspaper cost one halfpenny, with the tagline highlighting its good value, 'A Penny Newspaper for One Halfpenny', and describing it as 'The Busy Man's Daily Journal'. The paper size, declared the first edition, 'has been selected with a view to the consideration of the travelling readers'. These were the people who got things done – they were productive, ambitious, hard-working and loyal. And when they found their collective political voice, aristocratic politicians such as the prime minister of the day, Lord Salisbury, would rue the day when he dismissed the *Daily Mail* as 'a newspaper produced by office boys for office boys' (Boyce, 2011).

The *Daily Mail* had a successful and winning formula that combined hard news along with softer news such as sport and personal items. Stylistically, the stories were shorter, with innovations such as a banner headline going across the page, making it easier to read and follow. It was also the first newspaper to include a woman's section, covering fashion and cookery. Another new feature introduced by the *Daily Mail* was the publication of serials, which were personally selected by Harmsworth. The planned print run of the first issue was 100,000 copies, but on the first day it actually sold 397,215 copies. By 1899 circulation had risen to 500,000. Net sales peaked at 989,255 in 1900 and never fell below 713,000.

Financial journalism was important to Harmsworth and it was not just as a commercial proposition to attract advertising. He believed that, for his readers, the clerks, office workers, shopkeepers and middle managers, investing in stocks and shares would not only produce a welcome financial return for them, but also enhance their social status. Owning shares would be a demonstration that they were rising up the social ladder. Harmsworth understood that his readers were aspirational and wanted to better themselves, and this was one means of doing so. However, he also recognised that he had a responsibility to such new, inexperienced investors, and encouraged a style of financial journalism that would both encourage and help them.

The importance that Harmsworth gave to financial news was such that it led on the second page. In a format that was to remain until the 1920s, the *Daily Mail*'s 'City' column was news about share price movements during the previous day's trading, while 'Chat on "Change"' was a column offering comment and background information on companies and classes of shares. In the first issue it suggested that consols[1] might fall in price because 'There is now added the fear that the Shah of Persia will prove very pliable in the hands of Russia and may lead to the Eastern question being reopened. If consols go, Home Rails will follow, that is, if the reason for going is political and financial. Regarded from the investment standpoint, the tendency of everything is upward, and the public have not yet bought as much Home Railway stock as they want. So that, barring accidents, Rails should attain a higher level' (*Daily Mail*, 4 May 1896).

In 'Advice to Investors', the new paper laid out its position:

> The wants of the small investor will receive particular notice. We will explain technicalities to those who do not understand them. We shall endeavour to interpose between the inexperienced and the loss of their money; but they must get in the way of asking our advice before they act. Investors frequently fall into trouble first and ask advice afterwards. We shall of course do the best we can for all: but if they will seek counsel before they invest it will be better for them. (*Daily Mail*, 4 May 1896)

Although changes to company law during the 1850s and 1860s had provided more security to shareholders, the way shares were offered to investors remained broadly the same in the 1880s as it had at the time of the South Sea Bubble in 1720. Investors bought shares based on information provided by the companies, with little or no external check on the veracity or accuracy of that information.

At every stage of the sale process the party involved had a vested interest in promoting the interests of the company and would attempt to push up the share price. Stockbrokers, for example, took a commission on the sale of company shares, and so their advice was compromised. Company promoters and share pushers who promoted shares to the public had little or no regulation over their activities or the claims they made. Opportunities for unscrupulous, crooked share promotions and bogus schemes were rife.

Financial journalism had developed little since its emergence in the 1820s, and while most newspapers carried a 'City' column, it was dry and usually little more than a review of company share price movements, similar, in fact, in content to the share price columns carried by modern newspapers. The journalists who wrote the market news columns followed the share price movements at the Stock Exchange, which was also where they gained their information about companies and their markets. They relied on what the financial intermediaries told them, with little or no direct contact with companies. The writing was mainly a recitation of facts, with few opinions expressed in the City columns by their writers.

Charles Duguid (1902: 39), one of the most important figures in the history of financial and business journalism, provides a picture of the way traditional newspapers reported: 'Sometimes there will be found on the same money page one of these colourless notices and, on another part of the page, a criticism of the prospectus as well. The one is the customary concession to the advertiser or to the advertising agent; the other is the expression of the opinion of the paper for the benefit of the reader. But as a general rule the money articles of the great morning papers contain the colourless prospectus notice alone.'

In the 1860s and 1870s the daily money article in *The Times* still maintained its 'unrivalled authority' (Kynaston, 1998), established at the time of railway mania. The City editor carrying the mantle of

Thomas Massa Alsager was Marmaduke Sampson, another impeccably connected journalist, and known as the man who could not be bought. A former Secretary to the Treasury Committee of the Bank of England, he had contacts at the highest level of government and reflected the views and opinions of the establishment. He was another of the 'safe conduits' used by the political and business establishment to transmit information.

Sampson, ironically, was also another *Times* City editor whose career was to end in disaster for him personally, in an incident that also compromised the position of financial journalism. It was a major scandal when it was discovered that Sampson had accepted bribes from the share promoter Albert Grant. *The Times*, in an editorial, expressed 'astonishment and indignation' at the revelations. Grant, during a criminal trial, said he had given the money to Sampson as compensation for the losses Sampson had incurred on investments Grant had recommended to him. The man who 'could not be bought' had been bought, and was forced to resign (Kynaston, 1998).

This incident, however, had wider consequences for financial journalism, seriously damaging its reputation, as, once again, a financial journalist had been unable to resist the temptations offered by a company promoter. And this at the newspaper that supposedly epitomised the highest and best standards of journalism!

The reality was that bribery of the press by commercial interests was endemic in late nineteenth-century journalism. In 1898, for example, the magazine the *Nineteenth Century* complained: 'That the City has a large number of "reptile" journals, which will praise – and for that matter also condemn – anything as long as they are paid for it, is by this time well known to anyone who is not a tyro in finance. But unfortunately investors are mostly tyros in finance' (Robb, 2002: 117).

The problem was compounded because corruption worked both ways as company promoters attempted to seduce and bribe journalists. There were examples of corrupt newspapers that blackmailed company promoters for payment to *withhold* critical stories about the company. Ernest Terah Hooley, financier, property developer and company promoter who numbered among his achievements developing Trafford Park industrial estate in Manchester into the largest industrial park in Europe, complained at his bankruptcy hearing:

I have promoted companies that I have not made a single penny out of, because the newspapers took all the profit. I have paid one alone £40,000. A single article in another cost me £10,000. As soon as it is known that a company is coming out I am besieged by them and their representatives. They come quite openly and say. 'Well what we are going to get out of this?' (Quoted in Robb, 2002: 117)

Reflecting[2] on the differences between the new and old types of journalism, he wrote that the 'Older form of financial journalism' was boring and uninteresting, 'With a dull coldness, [it] set forth mere price movements, without embellishment, hint or explanation of any kind. There was little danger that readers would be misled; neither it was to be said, was there much danger that they would be usefully informed' (Porter, 1998: 50). The new financial journalism, however, was characterised, according to Duguid, by 'crisp' and 'outspoken' commentary, 'successful tips' and 'trenchant disclosure of financial fraud' (Porter, 1998). The success of the new financial journalism had, he said, 'been evinced over and over again ... the wiles of the unscrupulous company promoter have been laid bare, and hundreds and thousands of pounds have been retained in the pocket of the thrifty investor'.

Duguid believed that the financial journalist had to make the 'dry bones of finance live' for the city clerks, country clergymen, retired colonels and small shopkeepers who now invested in stocks and shares (Porter, 1998: 54). However, while making the financial pages accessible, the real duty of the financial journalist was to offer advice to readers, and this meant building a relationship of trust with them.

The challenge for both journalist and editor in such situations was similar to the one we saw at *The Times* during the period of railway mania, and one that also exists today. How far could editorial standards be compromised when confronted with commercial temptations and pressures from advertisers?

In a testament to the influence that financial journalism had on its readers, another nineteenth-century financial journalist, Salomon Van Oss (1898), said: 'Those who have shares to unload can well afford to give needy or unscrupulous journalists an inducement; and after seeing a number of paragraphs in newspapers praising up certain shares of which he knows nothing, many an investor decides to put his money into what afterwards proves to be a foredoomed concern. Investors have such a childlike faith in anything that is printed!'

Duguid pointed out the temptations that financial and business journalists at the time were subject to: 'The City editor from the highest to the lowest is subject to the constant temptation of those financiers who would have him withhold his criticism or praise their wares ...' (Porter, 1998: 52). He went on to describe the different and often creative ways companies exerted their influence, including direct bribes paid in either cash or shares to journalists or editors.

In Hooley's 1898 bankruptcy trial, Duguid, at the time the financial editor of the *Westminster Gazette*, told the court how Hooley had tried to bribe him while he was at his previous paper, the *Pall Mall Gazette*: 'I was asked to accept £1,000 shares in a hydraulic syndicate company, which would have been immediately bought back for £5,000' (*Daily Mail*, 11 August 1898). These so-called press calls were a common bribe offered to financial journalists and eventually resulted in a Stock Exchange investigation (see Chapter 4).

Duguid and other financial and business journalists were attempting to produce a code of practice for financial writers by defining what their roles and responsibilities should be. The ideal City editor, according to Duguid, should practise a code which would mean being 'Assiduous in collecting his financial facts, level-headed in appraising them, precise in arraying them.' He should be prepared to express 'a definite opinion on his facts', which should be delivered with 'honesty and rectitude'. The emphasis in the proposed code was on the professionalism and integrity of the journalist (Porter, 1998: 54). He also suggested that the financial journalist should act in a similar fashion to a magistrate when considering evidence: disinterested and capable of arriving at an independent judgement.

Charles Duguid took over as City editor at the *Daily Mail* in August 1906, and held the position until 1920. According to his obituary in the *Daily Mail*, he was one of the first to convert the City article from a 'lifeless presentation of dreary market reports and quotations into a readable story of the day's financial news. He was alike a lucid exponent and trenchant critic of financial subjects' (*Daily Mail*, 15 December 1923). He worked as a freelance journalist, at the age of 26 became assistant editor of the *Economist*, then financial editor at the *Pall Mall Gazette*, the *Westminster Gazette* and the *Morning Post*. He also became a consulting financial editor at *The Times*. He was also the author of two of the most influential books on finance at the time, *How to read the Money Article* and *The Story of the Stock Exchange*.

Duguid at the *Daily Mail* was fortunate to have the support of the owner, Alfred Harmsworth, who intervened directly to make sure that the City column, 'Chat on "Change"' was written and produced on ethical lines. Harmsworth was concerned about the relationship between advertising and editorial and was determined to keep them separate. While it might be an exaggeration for Harmsworth's biographers to claim that before the *Daily Mail* 'the investing public had been given almost no guidance and protection' and that the paper 'changed the character and improved the quality of financial journalism' (Porter, 1998: 57), the *Mail* did unquestionably have a positive influence in raising the standards and professionalism of financial and business journalism.

However, despite the improvements brought in by the New Journalism, they did not automatically mean that all the old practices disappeared overnight. An historian of nineteenth-century financial journalism, writing in 1904, describes in detail the problems facing investors at the time:

> Investors had great difficulty in obtaining trustworthy information about the securities in which their money was embarked. The Money articles of the general newspapers were chiefly taken up with the bare records of movements in the Funds, foreign stocks, and English railway securities. About the various American railways, Erie, Wabash, Central Pacific – in which millions of English capital were invested they had no information except that which was contained in the inspired memoranda sent to them from time to time by the London agents of the American directors, which was frequently stale and sometimes misleading. Of the operations of the syndicates, formed to manipulate stocks, nothing was known outside the inner rings of the Stock Exchange speculators. Mine shareholders were at an equal disadvantage, having to wait for news from their properties until it suited the directors, in their own good time, to communicate so much of the intelligence to hand as they saw fit to publish. Many of them were even kept from week to week in ignorance of the price of their shares, for in those days the

few daily papers which condescended to quote any mining shares paid no attention to those that were not included in the Official List. They dealt with quotations generally in the same perfunctory manner, omitting to record any prices made after the official hours in the Exchange, although the changes made by late dealings were sometimes very important and gave the operator on the spot a considerable advantage over the investor at a distance. (Kynaston, 1998: 4)

Journalists such as Duguid were not critics of the system; they wanted to make it operate efficiently and effectively by removing the crooks. The quality of their writing, however, did raise the standard of financial journalism, turning it into a source of information that by and large could be trusted. The contributions of the new financial journalists normalised share ownership and made it acceptable for a whole new class. Their lasting significance was ideological; 'Late nineteenth-century financial journalists were effectively popularizing capitalism, facilitating the spread of share ownership among their readers. Along with this came an enhanced awareness of the particular responsibilities attached to financial journalism as an occupation or profession' (Parsons, 1989: 51). They were crucial in legitimising 'economic values, ideas and language' (Poovey, 2002). They normalised the market and the activities of the joint stock company, and brought them into common use through discussion and comment, and helped marker operations appear, 'a law-governed, natural, and – pre-eminently – safe sector of modern society'. Alex Preda (2009) sees the mid-nineteenth century as a turning point, arguing that the old way of seeing financial speculation as gambling gave way to a new of 'science of financial investments' which stressed rationality and downplayed human agency. This new scientific vision 'promoted the notion that financial markets are governed by principles which are not controlled by any single individual or group. Even if some persons may occasionally manipulate markets, these principles will ultimately prevail.' Market activity was made 'socially legitimate and morally acceptable', and large numbers of investors were, by these means, incorporated into the market (Preda, 2009).

4

Harry Marks, *Financial News* and the *Financial Times*

In 1883, 28-year-old Harry Marks, a journalist and former editor of an American business newspaper, arrived in London with ambitious plans to set up a similar publication to the one he had successfully edited in New York. His arrival opens one of the most controversial and fascinating periods in the history of financial and business journalism. Marks divides opinion: to some he was the epitome of the fearless, campaigning, investigative journalist, editor and publisher who fought for the interests of the small investor against powerful and vested interests. To others he was a charlatan, only interested in the pursuit of his personal financial interests. His career in journalism, according to this perspective, was designed to exploit the gullible and enrich himself. Even his departure from the USA was mired in controversy: he left accused of defrauding, and then deserting, the widow of a business associate with whom he had an affair. Later, Marks attempted to clear his name of these accusations by suing George Butterfield, an aggrieved company promoter who had published the details about his alleged New York indiscretions. Marks, however, failed to convince an Old Bailey jury, which found against him, though the judge made it clear that he regarded the verdict as perverse (Porter, 2004a). The suspicions about his conduct therefore remained.

Harry Marks was born in London in 1855. His father, David, was an eminent Hebrew scholar and chief rabbi at the West London Synagogue (Porter, 2004a). Aged 16, Harry moved to the USA, where his father had friends in New Orleans. He learned his journalism craft on various Texas newspapers which he later described as 'the roughest and most thorough literary training that America offered' (*Financial News*, 27 December 1916 quoted in Porter, 2004a). Marks moved to New York, working for the *New York World* from 1873 to 1878, and in 1880, aged 25, he became the editor of *Daily Mining News*, the world's first daily mining newspaper. A year later he started a new title, *Financial and Mining News*, which he described as 'a price list, with reports from the mines and small paragraphs' (Porter, 2004a).

During his editing tenure in New York, Marks used his contacts and the knowledge gained through his position to trade in mining and oil shares for his own personal financial gain. This was also to be a constant and controversial feature of his career in England. Marks, however, never saw these two activities as contradictory, nor did he believe that they raised any ethical problems or that his role as an editor might be compromised by his commercial activities.

Marks had clear and high ambitions for his new UK newspaper:

> I dreamed of a journal that should treat of financial subjects as the most thorough and the most enterprising newspapers deal with political and general news topics, aiming to give the earliest, completest, and surest information upon all matters of public interest, even 'premature' information when its prematurity would enhance its value to my readers. My dream contemplated a journal doing bold and seasonable service in the interests of the community. (Marks, quoted in Kynaston, 1998: 5)

However, London investors did not share Marks's vision for his new newspaper, and the financial support for it came from Colonel Edward McMurdo, an American who knew Marks from his time in the USA. McMurdo was in London in 1883 to support the share issue of a US railroad company and agreed to invest £1,000 in the new paper and guarantee all expenses in return for a share in the company.

On Wednesday 23 January 1884 the first edition of the *Financial and Mining News* appeared, describing itself as 'A Daily Journal Devoted to the Interests of Investors'. A column titled 'Our Programme' outlined its rationale; 'great stress was laid on the paper's unique supply of early and reliable news from the United States, especially in relation to its mines' (Kynaston, 1998: 7). *Financial and Mining News* adopted the American format (New Journalism), with a new, modern layout, with short editorial snippets about business personalities and opinion pieces on shares and companies. Its tone was lively and fast paced in order to hold the attention of the reader. Priced at 1*d*, it consisted of four pages, with the lead on page 1, headlined the 'Stock Market', carrying a description of the previous day's trading:

> Business as a whole was far from active in the Stock Exchange yesterday, but the features were somewhat of a more favourable character than on the previous day; though it cannot be doubted the general public evince a strong disinclination to venture into new engagements of a speculative nature, which is not surprising considering the heavy losses incurred during the past year or two. (Kynaston, 1998: 7)

This editorial format was to remain broadly the same for more than 60 years, with news from foreign exchanges and company shareholder meetings combined with more in-depth investigative features. From the first its news coverage was determinedly international; the first editorial, for example, contained news about Mexico and how the country had developed since the introduction of railways.

Page 3 of the first issue was a full page 'Guide for Investors' with information on securities quoted on the London Stock Exchange and the number of shares traded along, with details of the dividend paid by each company. Crucially, on page 4 it had the all-important advertisements for the share issues of two new waterworks companies. There were also notices from smaller companies and a report of the board meeting in New York of the Northern Pacific Railway (Kynaston, 1998).

Although similar copy could also be found in other contemporary newspapers, the first edition of *Financial and Mining News* clearly stated what would make it different from other publications. This was a serious, international business newspaper aimed at keen but not necessarily experienced investors and, crucially, this was a paper that was on the side of the small investor. Marks believed that what his readers needed was clear and independent guidance about what to invest in. The problem in Marks's case, however, was that such noble ambitions appear to have not been pursued solely for altruistic reasons – because it was worth doing – but with a commercial rationale, from which he benefited. Marks believed that if the paper was honest and critical this would attract readers, which in turn would bring in more advertisers. However, in the circumstances of the day, given the amount of corruption that existed in financial and business journalism, this was still a bold editorial position to adopt. The difficulty with it, as we shall see, was that such a principled line was not always followed, undermining the paper's credibility.

Marks believed in a style of journalism that could be challenging and controversial. An editorial in the third issue, for example, said: 'The swindling operations of a certain class of money-lenders and loan-officers seem to engage the attention of everyone except the police. If the police could spare a little time from the engrossing occupation of unearthing imaginary dynamite plots, they might do something to curtail their operations' (quoted in Kynaston, 1998: 8).

In May 1884, five months after its launch *Financial and Mining News* carried the type of editorial scoop which for Marks demonstrated the nature of the publication. The story was about a financial crisis in America caused by the collapse of the Marine National Bank and the failure of one of New York's leading brokers, Grant & Ward. Recalling the events twenty years later, Marks wrote:

> Day by day (in the newspaper) we had given warnings of an impending crash, and night by night our New York correspondent had cabled news of the increasing embarrassments of the stock-jobbing combinations which controlled the market. While the other daily papers in complete ignorance of the situation, were discoursing on the great improvement in American business, the *Financial and Mining News* alone saw and told the truth about the situation and urged investors to sell their holdings in American railways. It predicted the panic almost to a day, and when the collapse came, when Erie and Central Pacific, Lake Shores and New York Centrals were tumbling down $5 and $10 at a time, those who had followed the *Financial and Mining News* reaped large profits, the accuracy of our information was established and the reputation of the paper made. (Quoted in Kynaston, 1998: 18)

In July 1884 'Mining' was dropped from the title as it was regarded as being too restrictive and affecting the paper's credibility in the City. The paper continued to campaign against fraudulent activities during August 1884. A number of schemes and dodges carried out by some stockbrokers attacked. The year ended with the December issue featuring an article criticising company directors whose social prestige and influence on investors were matched, so the article said, only by their incompetence. This was heady stuff for the period, and was an attempt to mark the paper as being on the side of aspirant, hard-working people and against the privileged elite who ran the Stock Exchange.

As both circulation and advertising grew, *Financial News* expanded the number of its sections and introduced a letters page, 'Answers to Correspondents', which in time became one of the most popular parts of the paper. The readers' letters in a way typified its rationale. The letters tended to be from new, inexperienced investors requesting information on investments. Readers believed that the answers provided by *Financial News* could be trusted, as it appeared to offer disinterested, objective advice that could be relied upon even though it charged for an answer (Kynaston, 1998). The letters and their responses were a direct forerunner of the personal financial columns that are an essential element of the modern newspaper. The editorial line *Financial News* worked, as it became the leading financial newspaper of the day, setting a trend that others attempted to follow and imitate. 'Financial News became the flagship of the new financial journalism, accessible as well as authoritative, which characterised the money pages of most London newspapers by 1900' (Porter, 2004a).

By the first anniversary of the paper, on 23 January 1885, it had become a 'solid and authoritative organ of record and opinion' (Kynaston, 1998) with international coverage of companies in USA, Canada, Latin America, South Africa and a comment on Germany's economic growth.

Criticising companies and individuals, however, carries with it the risk of being sued, and in October 1886 Marks appeared in court in what, down the years, would be the first of many similar cases. For Marks and other serious journalists, being sued for libel can be a testament to their editorial impact; however, as ever with Harry Marks, there was a commercial angle. While being sued appeared to confirm his reputation as a fearless, campaigning newspaper editor, critics suggest that Marks deliberately created situations which forced people to sue. The evidence for this accusation is the number of similar cases where he was sued by a disgruntled company promoter or owner who claimed he had deliberately created offensive articles in order to generate publicity for the magazine. Typical of these cases were the accusations made against Marks by John Barr, of the London & Leeds Bank. He accused Marks of launching what he described as a 'vicious, libellous attack' on the collapsed bank because, so Barr claimed, the bank had refused to advertise its prospectus in the paper (Kynaston, 1998). Similar accusations were to be repeated time and again. Were these the groundless accusations of disgruntled advertisers, or was there something to them, a case of no smoke without fire?

Marks in his defence against Barr claimed that *Financial News* had refused to accept the advertisements of the London & Leeds because its investigations had proved the whole scheme to be a sham. In this case the court found in favour of Marks, deciding that the articles had been published without malice and for the public benefit, so 'Barr's Bogus Bank' lost the case. The problem for Marks was that similar accusations recurred time and again.

Critics of the time, including not surprisingly rival publications, were keen to undermine the paper's credibility and argued that the campaigns carried out by Marks and *Financial News* were illusory:

> By the exposure of a few dubious cases, the opinion is engendered in the public mind that the *Financial News* is a genuine friend of the investor, and this makes it all the easier and safer for its proprietors and editor to play other games, where the interest of the investor is the last consideration that would ever occur to them. (Robb, 2002: 117)

Despite such accusations, *Financial News* did undertake outstanding serious investigative journalism that had an impact and made a difference. The best example of this was the exposure of corruption at the London Metropolitan Board of Works (MBW). A series of articles in *Financial News*, some of which were written by Marks himself, revealed how officers of the Board were paid by developers to use land it owned. The articles resulted in a Royal Commission being appointed in 1888 to investigate the accusations, which found that they were correct. The MBW was abolished and replaced by a new and democratically elected London County Council. By any standards, this case was a triumph for campaigning journalism, which in the UK was equalled at the time only by the articles of W. T. Stead in the *Pall Mall Gazette*.[1]

While the MBW articles can be regarded as Marks's finest editorial achievements, perhaps his finest court-room hour came in November 1887. On this occasion, rather than being on the receiving end of a writ, he was the plaintiff. W. R. Grenfell was a director of the Bank of England (Kynaston, 1998) and involved in the promotion of the Harney Peak Tin Company, which was attempting to raise £2m of capital. *Financial News*, however, attacked the company so strongly that the prospectus had to be withdrawn. Marks and Grenfell then started a bitter and acrimonious exchange, with Marks eventually suing Grenfell for slander. Once in court, Grenfell capitulated and apologised to Marks, agreeing to pay 50 guineas in damages and £300 costs. This was another case where Marks was vindicated, and another demonstration that he and *Financial News* were on the side of the investor in exposing fraudulent schemes and poor investment prospects.

Financial News did, though, tread a fine line. It needed advertising revenue in order to be commercially successful but some of the methods it used to attract advertisers, at times, cross the line between ethical and unethical behaviour. In addition to prospectus advertising by companies looking to float, *Financial News* also deployed a variety of other schemes to try to attract advertisers (Kynaston, 1998). One, for example, was to make companies pay for extended reports of their company meetings. Another was to charge companies to have their share price listed; if the share price rose, a charge was made, but there was no charge if the price remained the same. While these schemes may have been worthwhile commercially, they were ethically dubious, with companies in effect paying for editorial coverage. More damaging to the newspaper's reputation, however, was that Marks appears to have compromised his editorial judgement by promoting companies in which he owned shares, hoping to benefit financially if the company share price rose as a result of what he wrote (Kynaston, 1998). Share ramping of this kind was to occur regularly in the history of financial and business journalism, one of the most notorious cases being the activities of the so-called 'City Slickers' of the *Daily Mirror* (see Chapter 6).[2]

Although *Financial News* claimed to sell more copies than any other financial newspaper, there were no independently verifiable figures available, so its actual circulation may have been only a few thousand. In 1887 *Financial News* began a Monday edition and increased its pagination to six pages in response to the first so-called 'Kaffir' boom on the Stock Exchange, where South African mining companies started using the London Stock Exchange to raise finance for their operations. It is one of these mining companies that provides evidence that Marks promoted company shares for his own benefit. He 'appears to have used [*Financial News*] to create a market for shares in the Rae (Transvaal) goldmine, unloading his holding through dummy vendors before the price collapsed' (Porter, 2004a).

However, perhaps a worse example of Marks's unethical behaviour was his acceptance of a £17,000 bribe from Ernest Terah Hooley to promote the flotation of the New Beeston Cycle Company in *Financial News*. During Hooley's bankruptcy proceedings he said that he had given the money to Marks because he was a friend. This argument, though, failed to convince contemporary critics (see Porter, 1986). Hooley also admitted paying a leader writer on *Financial News*, one H. J. Jennings. Hooley told the court, 'The articles [by Jennings] I saw in the *Financial News*, I thought the cleverest I had ever seen in my life. I found out who the writer was and gave him £500' (quoted in Kynaston, 1998: 48).

Marks's association with Hooley was more complex than this appears. He was a shareholder in at least one other company with Hooley. This company was the publisher of a newspaper called the *Sun* and in 1897 Hooley had apparently agreed to appoint Charles Duguid as its city editor on an annual salary of £1,250. Marks, however, overruled the appointment and Duguid was paid compensation of £3,000 by Hooley, which critics said was evidence of another bribe to journalists – which Duguid hotly disputed (*Daily Mail*, 11 August 1898).

The Financial Times

One of the new papers hoping to emulate the success of *Financial News* was the *London Financial Guide*, which first appeared on 9 January 1888 with the slogan on its masthead of 'Without Fear and Without Favour' (Kynaston, 1998). The new publication was the brain-child of James Sheridan and his brother, about whom little is known.

The first edition had the by now standard reports on company meetings, but with a noticeably different approach from the at times overly aggressively, critical, *Financial News*. The line taken by the *London Financial Guide* suggested that it would attempt to present a more balanced and nuanced picture of companies and their promoters. While one article in the first edition attacked the Stock Exchange's 'old-fashioned mode of secrecy and closed doors', a second argued that the company promoter was often unfairly blamed by the press when things went wrong. There was a page of foreign news and one detailing Stock Exchange prices, and a full page advertising the prospectus of the Upper Trent Navigation Company. Editorially it had a consistent line, with two main editorial targets, the Stock Exchange and *Financial News*, which was criticised in virtually every issue for getting something wrong (Kynaston, 1998). We do not know whether this line was adopted in order to attract the advertising of disgruntled companies unhappy with *Financial News* or whether there was a real dissatisfaction with the position of *Financial News*. However, while the new paper criticised *Financial News* for supposed lax editorial standards it was not averse on occasions to bending its own principles to attract advertising. On 11 January and 6 February 1888, for example, it carried adverts from two new companies offering shares to potential investors. The adverts for the Hull Brewery Company and the Manchester Brewery Company included the company prospectus on one page and 'copy' editorial matter on a separate page that appeared to be part of the paper's editorial (Kynaston, 1998).

The new paper failed to meet its target of publishing three times a week, and in only its second month it announced on 10 February that from 13 February 1888 a new newspaper would appear from Monday to Saturday, to be known as the *Financial Times*. Leopold Graham, its first editor, does not appear to have had a promising background for a newspaper editor. According to one contemporary profile, 'He had no notion of writing and was poorly educated, but he had a smattering of common French phrases and a real understanding of company promoting and speculative City business' (Kynaston, 1998: 9). Was he, then, appointed less for his journalism abilities than because he knew how to produce a product appealing to companies and company promoters? Was this an indication that the approach of the new newspaper would be to attempt to be more commercial than its predecessor?

The *Financial Times* declared itself to be 'The friend of the honest financier, the bona fide investor, the respectable broker, the genuine director, the legitimate speculator.' Its enemies were 'the closed Stock Exchange, the unprincipled promoter, the company wrecker, the "guinea pig", "the bull", "the bear", "the gambling operator"'[3] (Kynaston, 1998: 17).

The first issue was an 'impressive' effort and superior to the paper it replaced. The middle two pages contained up-to-date market information along with market and company meeting reports. There were also legal updates relevant to finance and more general financial news. It also contained the all-important new company adverts such as the prospectus for the European & American Machine Made Bottler Company.

If it was to be a commercial success, then it had to dislodge *Financial News* from its position as market leader. To do this it criticised its editorial standards. One editorial, for example, attacked *Financial News* for its hypocrisy for on the one hand criticising so-called 'bucket shops',[4] yet on the other hand carrying adverts from them. The *Financial Times*, the paper grandly declared, would never be guilty of such double standards: 'Our advice to all our readers is to leave this class of business alone: but if they *will* try their luck, then let them be careful to deal only with houses of known respectability, whose code of honour – at any rate in this matter – is not that of the *Financial News*' (quoted in Kynaston, 1998: 18).

Despite the moral stance of its editorial line, the new paper quickly ran into financial problems and was taken over by its printers, MacRae, Curtice and Co., who appointed their own directors. Ironically, given its editorial position against the 'unprincipled promoter' and the 'company wrecker', the new chairman of the company brought in by the printers was Horatio Bottomley, who already had a reputation as an unscrupulous if very successful company promoter.

The *Financial Times* described Bottomley in 1897 as 'a man of millions' (Morris, 2004) who was appointed because of his publishing experience and his apparent ability to make money. However, his involvement in the newspaper lasted only a few months. One contemporary commentator said he left because the size of the *Financial Times* business was not big enough for Bottomley, who wanted a larger canvas for his ambitions. In 1889 he floated the Hansard Publishing Union, known on the Stock Exchange as 'Bottomley's swindle'. Within two years he was bankrupt and charged with conspiracy to defraud investors. Undaunted, he went on to run a series of fraudulent ventures, and in the First World War produced the infamous mass-circulation paper *John Bull*, described as a 'cheap organ of hate'. In 1922 he was finally convicted of fraud and sent to prison (Kynaston, 1998; Morris, 2004).

The financial uncertainty and editorial instability at the *Financial Times* was resolved at the end of 1893 with the appointment of Douglas

Gordon MacRae as managing director, 'Probably the most important figure in its early history' (Kynaston, 1998). Born in Fyvie, Aberdeenshire in 1861, MacRae was a printer by trade and part of the team that had taken the paper over. In addition to being the largest shareholder, he also controlled the editorial line. The better controls and financial management introduced by MacRae enabled the paper to develop editorially.

The *Financial Times* and *Financial News* competed fiercely against each other, often taking opposing sides on issues simply because the other was in favour. During 1888, 'As hard as the *Financial Times* slung mud at the *Financial News*, the *Financial News* slung it back' (Kynaston, 1998: 25). Their warring reached a peak in a dispute over Colonel J. T. North, known as the 'Nitrate King' because of his various nitrate companies in South America. *Financial News* opposed him, with a headline warning of 'The Coming Crash in Nitrate Rails'. The article went on to say, 'Colonel North is a Pactolus[5] among promoters. Whatever he touches turns, if not to gold, at least to premiums. In the end there is often a considerable difference between gold and premiums, but at the outset they may be easily mistaken for each other' (quoted in Kynaston, 1998: 25).

The *Financial Times*, however, supported the Colonel and in 1889 devoted pages to his impending trip to Chile and his investiture with the freedom of the City of Leeds. The dispute over whether Colonel North was a charlatan or an original and successful entrepreneur, however, marked the end of direct hostilities between the two papers. Management at both papers recognised that such open and direct warfare was harming the two titles. In future, while they continued to compete vigorously against one another, it was never with the same degree of animosity.

In 1893 the *Financial Times* adopted the distinctive light salmon-coloured paper to distinguish it from *Financial News*. *Financial News* was always larger in size than the *Financial Times*, though whether it had, as it claimed, 'a circulation greater than that of all the other Financial Journals in England combined', is doubtful, as it never attempted to verify circulation claims. The *Financial Times*, on the other, had its circulation verified by a firm of accountants, demonstrating that sales increased in 1891 by 73% from the previous year (Kynaston, 1998).

In November 1890 the *Financial Times* was nearly brought down by the Baring crisis, an incident with echoes of the financial crisis of 2008, in which an overconfident bank made a deal too far that impacted on the rest of the financial system. While the resulting economic crisis had a severe effect on all financial newspapers, the *Financial Times* was especially badly hit and the paper had to be subsidised with profits from other publications such as *Drapers Record* that were owned by the printers.

At the end of the nineteenth century South America once again was the cause of another financial crisis that impacted on the UK's banking system. On this occasion it was the highly respected merchant bank Barings, which nearly collapsed because of an investment that went wrong in Argentina. The Barings director responsible for the investment was the arrogant Lord Revelstoke, who had achieved notoriety on the flotation of the brewer Guinness in 1886. The Guinness share issue of £4.5m was heavily oversubscribed and the issue price of £10 per share rose to £16 10*s* when the market opened. Barings controlled the distribution of the shares and made certain that their friends and family benefited from it; one-third of the shares went to the Barings' circle; another £800,000 was taken by the bank, Barings' partners, their friends and City contacts. The profit made was said to be over £500,000. 'Even among insiders who had benefited from the operation, there was a feeling that it had gone too far' (Fay, 1997).

In 1890 Revelstoke agreed to underwrite a £2m share issue by the Buenos Aires Water Supply and Drainage Company, but the shares proved virtually impossible to sell. As Barings had most of its capital tied up in a variety of investments in South America, the failure to sell the shares raised serious questions about its capability, and confidence in the bank fell. The main problem was that it did not have enough finance to meet the obligations and commitments it had already made. With more debts than assets there was a real danger that Barings would go bankrupt. This was a major problem for both the City and the government, in much the same way as the problems at RBS and HBOS were in 2008. If Barings was allowed to go bust, this would impact on other financial institutions and affect the UK economy. The bank was, in the modern terminology, too big to fail, so Barings, like RBS and HBOS more than a century later, was bailed out in November 1890 with the finance provided by a consortium of banks and the government and organised by the governor of the Bank of England, William Lidderdale.

In another forerunner of 2008, the near-collapse of Barings eroded confidence between the financial institutions, which stopped lending to each other as the all-important ingredient, trust, disappeared. This grew into an international problem because the investment boom of the late 1880s was based on excessive expectations about the economic prospects of countries such as the US, Argentina and Australia. Huge sums were invested in land, railways and urban construction companies on the basis of very limited knowledge. With such high expectations they could not possibly produce the required profits (Cain and Newton, 2011). The near-collapse of Barings, one of the most prestigious investment banking houses in the world, was a profound shock to the international investment community and hit confidence in the international financial system. The outcome was that international lending to countries by the banks was severely restricted for the next decade.

In the wake of the Barings crisis, British Gross Domestic Product (GDP), as expressed in terms of 1900 prices, fell by about 1% per annum between 1891 and 1894 and the subsequent economic crisis also led to a crisis for the financial newspapers as new share issues and financial advertising all but dried up.

The differing approaches of the two newspapers to specific issues reflected the readerships they had developed. The *Financial Times* tended to be less aggressive and populist in many of its positions, recording what was happening rather than commenting just for the sake of it. It saw its main readership as the financial community of the City and openly aimed at becoming the 'stockbroker's Bible' or 'parish magazine of the City' (Kynaston, 1998: 28).

Financial News, however, as we have seen, saw itself from the very beginning as the 'outsider', outspoken and critical about what it considered fraudulent company schemes and those who promoted them. Its readers tended to be the ordinary investors who loyally trusted what the paper said. Taking such a stance, the paper believed, would attract readers who trusted its position and the advice it offered. Such tactics, whilst commercially successful, also drew criticism because there was a clash between its public position as the fearless pursuer of truth, on the one hand, and the reality of some of its dubious commercial activities, on the other.

The libel case of 1886 was followed between 1888 and 1890 by three similar cases where Marks and *Financial News* were sued for libel. In one of them an insight was provided into how widespread corruption was in financial and business journalism at the time. At the public examination of the winding up of the London & Globe Finance Corporation the chairman Whitaker Wright made the following assertion:

> It is well known in the City that all the financial daily press and those who publish the reports of transactions on the Stock Exchange and call attention to them, put in the official lists and the transactions of the tape and everything of that kind, will not do it, will not assist companies in any shape or form unless they have consideration in some form or other. (Quoted in Kynaston, 1998: 53)

Wright also detailed other examples of how newspapers abused their position, claiming that some companies sold their shares at an artificially low price to newspapers. They were then, by pre-arrangement, bought back by the company at a higher price. So serious were the allegations about these so-called press calls that a Stock Exchange committee was forced to investigate them. The inquiry found that brokers acting on behalf of Wright had 'sweetened' ten financial journalists, including Marks and three other journalists from *Financial News*. For all its attack on *Financial News*, the *Financial Times* proved not to be immune to temptation either, with one of its journalists accepting an offer including, 'last but not least the great MacRae himself who had picked up 6,500 shares at a bargain price'. Wright, tried for fraud in 1903, was sentenced to seven years in prison but killed himself with a tablet of cyanide when the trial finished (Kynaston, 1998: 37).

The end of the nineteenth century was generally a good period for the Stock Exchange and also therefore for the financial media, and the papers were able to increase their pagination. In the week beginning 10 May 1897, for example, *Financial News* totalled fifty-eight pages and *Financial Times* fifty-four. Their rising revenues encouraged two other new financial dailies to start, but their subsequent fates demonstrate the hold that *Financial News* and *Financial Times* by now had on the specialist financial market. *Financial Truth* (1889–1904), while described as a thin paper, was surprisingly long lived. *Financial*

Post (1895–98), although more solid and reputable in feel, could not attract the necessary advertising. The commercial success of *Financial News* encouraged competitors to try their hand and a number of new titles emerged during the 1880s, hoping to emulate its success. In among the legitimate publishing attempts, some papers were established to deliberately defraud company promoters (Porter, 1998). In February 1888 one of the new magazines, *The Statist*, dismissed these 'so-called financial journals':

> In the course of a few weeks many of them disappear, and another swarm takes their place. The promoter of financial newspapers seems to be not only ubiquitous but inexhaustible. He will do anything to catch the wayward taste of the public – from cheating his printer to libelling his mother-in-law. If Throgmorton Street will not have him under one spicey title he will try it with a spicier one still ... The one end and aim of this vagabond industry is to be seen about the street, so that he may be able to bully advertising agents and tradespeople into giving him a few advertisements. (Quoted in Kynaston, 1998: 14)

Such dominance effectively ended attempts to launch specialist financial newspapers until technological developments reduced production and costs, making it easier for new publications to enter the market (Kynaston, 1998).

By the late 1880s Harry Marks was in sole control of a prosperous and thriving company and enjoying the lifestyle of a successful publisher. A profile in *Vanity Fair* magazine provides the following description of him: 'He lives in anything but Grub Street style at Loudoun Hall in St. John's Wood. He is fond of horses, and owns a promising colt, which lately began to carry his colours at Newmarket. He has a fine picture gallery, wears tight boots, suffers from the gout, and is fond of music. He cannot sing, although he sometimes tries to do so' (quoted in Kynaston, 1998: 67). Marks was politically ambitious, standing as a 'progressive conservative', and was elected first in 1888 as a councillor in Marylebone and then as Conservative MP for St George's-in-the-East, becoming a prominent supporter of the Salisbury government.

The twentieth century

Financial News and the *Financial Times* suffered at the start of the twentieth century. The Boer War depressed business on the Stock Exchange, with a consequent fall in the papers' advertising revenues. However, a longer-term and more dangerous threat to all financial papers came, ironically, as a result of the activities of both newspapers working to expose corporate abuse. As an MP Marks was involved in the committee stage of the Companies Act 1900, which is best remembered for the introduction of the compulsory audit of company accounts. One section of the Act, however, also affected company prospectuses and the way shares were allocated and underwritten. While *Financial News* welcomed the legislation, the *Financial Times* attacked it, describing the Bill as 'that excessively feeble embodiment of the joint wisdom of our legislators …' and likely to 'hamper the movements of the honest promoter, while carefully setting up danger signals to warn the rascal where his hazard lies'. The eventual outcome was that promoters stopped issuing prospectuses and the newspaper advertising also dried up (Kynaston, 1998: 51). 'According to one account, the only reason why Parliament in 1900 declined to make the issuing of a prospectus or its equivalent compulsory was because that provision was proposed by Marks, who for some mysterious reason was suspected thereby of lining his own pocket' (Kynaston, 1998: 9). The advertising revenue of *Financial News* slumped alarmingly.

In 1904, on the twentieth anniversary of the establishment of *Financial News*, Duguid reckoned that only four of the main morning and evening papers still subscribed to what he called the 'older form of financial journalism', in the sense of merely providing 'the bare record' and 'seldom indulging in any outspoken comment or venturing any opinion'. 'In the course of two decades he [Marks] had initiated and then sustained nothing less than a revolution' (Kynaston, 1998: 53). Others, however, were more critical. 'Mercenary publishers such as Harry Marks exploited their positions of trust for illicit profit' (Robb, 2002: 116).

As Marks concentrated on his political career his influence at *Financial News* declined. This brought a noticeable change in style with higher 'ethical standards' and a greater 'professionalism' among the journalist staff. The Edwardian *Financial Times*, meanwhile, had by now achieved its goal of being *the* paper of the Stock Exchange and was regarded as the 'stockbrokers' Bible'. The Chairman of the *Financial Times* said in 1906 that it 'accurately reflects the conditions of business in the City' and that 'when there is activity', of which in 1906 there had been little, 'and new companies [are] being formed, we get the prospectuses' (quoted in Kynaston, 1998: 51).

While it still investigated wrong-doing by companies, the *Financial Times* was becoming more cautious, adopting a 'fairly neutral tone to new issues, and summarising the main aspects of the particular prospectus' (Kynaston, 1998: 67). There was also an attempt to lessen the dependence on flotations as a source of advertising revenue.

The reaction of the *Financial News* and the *Financial Times* to Lloyd George's so-called People's Budget of 1909 demonstrated that for all their differences they were both largely uncritical supporters of capitalism and the establishment. The *Financial Times* said: 'It is obvious that the Budget has been introduced without that previous careful study of the probable incidence and effects of new taxation which such legislation imperatively demands in the interests of the community' (quoted in Kynaston, 1998: 71); while the *Financial News* observed in its more direct style: 'We find in Mr Lloyd George's first Budget a patent and deliberate determination to use the machinery of finance to establish schemes which, for want of a more specific term, may be called Socialistic' (Kynaston, 1998: 71). It also commented on 'the nervousness which has pervaded alike the financial world and the investing classes' as a result of the budget. Marks stood down as an MP in 1900 but was re-elected in 1906 in Thanet. He finally resigned as the editor of *Financial News* in 1909, bringing to an end a colourful and controversial, fascinating career in journalism.

5

The crash of 1929 and Keynes

By the twentieth century, Britain was a fully fledged industrial economy. The scale and speed at which the economic structure and the physical landscape of the country had changed was dramatic, with the changes taking place in under fifty years. The Great Exhibition of 1851 was a showcase for Britain's industrial dominance, produced by the first phase Industrial Revolution. The economic advantage was based on key industries' being located close to power sources such as water and coal. However, by the end of the nineteenth century and the beginning of the twentieth, Britain's once-dominant economic advantage was beginning to wane. The USA and Germany especially were starting to benefit from later industrialisation and from newer, faster, more productive technologies.

There is a debate about whether the 'City' (the collective term for the UK's financial world) could and should have done more in the late nineteenth century to help Britain's manufacturers re-equip in order to compete with these new industrial power-houses. Critics of the City contrast its attitude towards investment in industry with that of the German regional banks, who invested in companies by taking shares in the businesses. By investing in companies in this way they became long-term investors. In contrast, the City was (and continues to be) purely focused on making short-term returns to satisfy the demands of investors.

The City's lack of interest in investing in UK industry is illustrated by the fact that in 1882 out of a total of nearly £5,800m of quoted securities only £64m was invested in British industry (Scott, 1951). When asked to finance a coal products company in 1911, Lord Revelstoke of the merchant bank Barings (see Chapter 3) famously remarked that 'I confess that I personally have a horror of all industrial companies and that I should not think of placing my hard-earned gains in such a venture' (quoted in Hutton, 1995: 123). UK domestic companies accounted for only a small proportion of the London Stock Exchange, with shareholders preferring to chase investments abroad rather than help domestic industries. In 1913 for example, home companies accounted for only 17% of all securities traded in London, while 83% went on foreign issues, ranging from Indian and American railway bonds to foreign government bonds.

However, it must be remembered that at this time the majority of investors were retail/individual investors and not institutional investors. While there has been much analysis and debate about the role of the City, less attention has been given to the role played by the financial press in encouraging investors to pursue short-term profits. Investing in shares had become, in the late Victorian period, a mark of improving social mobility. Papers such as *Financial News* and the *Financial Times* depended for their existence on company announcements and new flotations. The financial press of the day expressed the interests of the investors, who wanted companies to produce profits that could be distributed to shareholders rather than re-invested for the benefit of the company. When the *Daily Mail* was launched and *Financial News* and the *Financial Times* were opening, neither the newspapers nor their readers were demanding long-term investment at the expense of the dividends they earned. The newspapers were therefore eager participants in the short-term investment culture that existed at the time.

The Victorian love affair with the buying and selling of stocks and shares was commented on by the notorious company promoter Albert Grant, who made a fortune through selling shares in both good and bad companies to investors. Reviewing the year 1871 he said,

> That was a year and an era when everyone was seeking what he could make on the Stock Exchange. There is a peculiar fascination to some people in making money on the Stock Exchange. I know hundreds who would rather make £50 from the Stock Exchange than £250 by the exercise of their profession; there is a nameless fascination and in the year 1871 the favourite form of making money on the Stock Exchange was by applying for shares, selling them at whatever premium they were at, and that the money was considered honourably made. They seemed to think that premiums grew like mushrooms in the night, in a public way and that in Capel Court,

inside the Stock Exchange they grew like cherries and only had to be plucked off the tree. (Quoted in Kynaston, 1994: 266)

Grant represented the darker side of the stock market – the type of company promoter from whom *Financial News*, the *Financial Times*, the *Daily Mail* and Charles Duguid, for example, wanted to protect their readers. As a company promoter active in the 1870s, Grant floated nineteen new domestic and, significantly, foreign companies, many of which proved to be fraudulent. He was also MP for Kidderminster and was described as having a 'masterful' use of the press (Kynaston, 1994).

By 1914, investing in public companies had become a less risky proposition due to the tighter regulation introduced in the 1900 Companies Act, which gave more security to investors. Interestingly, in this period one way that the City could refute accusations that it was not interested in investing in UK businesses was by pointing to the wide range of businesses that turned to the Stock Exchange to finance their growth. These were often family-owned businesses, and also companies looking to develop new technologies.

Between 1919 and 1920, after the war-time controls on company formation were relaxed, a mini-boom in company formation took place, with approximately £400m of new company issues. It was to the City that these companies turned for long-term finance. Many of the companies going public were private businesses, particularly in the textile and coal mining industries (Scott, 1951). This buoyant situation, however, was ended by the depression of 1921–22, with a gradual recovery between 1927 and 1929. During this period, with society undergoing major structural and cultural changes, new companies and products begin to emerge that aimed at satisfying personal consumer needs. Car companies such as Morris floated in 1926, alongside new businesses supplying radios and gramophones such as Thorn, and Pye in 1931 (Scott, 1951).

In the 1930s, companies based on new technologies such as radio-based electricity, chemicals and motor introduced mass-production methods to meet consumer demand. These processes in turn created a professional managerial class, and publications emerged to cater for their needs and interests. Business magazines such as *Business Week*, *Fortune* and *Barrons*, for example, rapidly became mandatory reading for aspirant and ambitious managers in the USA who were interested in economics and company affairs (Parsons, 1989).

Professional managers working in national and international markets wanted objective information on how government activities and policies would impact on their careers and businesses. In the UK after the Second World War, this managerial class would eventually become the primary readership of newspapers such as the *Financial Times* and *The Economist*. This demand for a different editorial policy also led to an increasing professionalisation among financial journalists, leading to the end of the dubious share promotion schemes and puffery that had become so endemic in financial media before the First World War and in the 1920s.

The 1920s were difficult times in which to try to float a company, and many that were floated were short lived. By the end of May 1931, of 248 companies formed in the UK in the 1920s, 70 had gone and the shares of another 136 had no value. Despite the tighter regulations, new company flotations brought with them the by now all-too-familiar unscrupulous company promoters. All that the 'share pushers' or 'bucket shops' needed to con the investor was a good address near the Stock Exchange and an imposing title, acquired either by taking over an existing firm or inventing one. One of the main reasons why both the fraudulent company and crooked promoters could get away with their activities was that there were few firms specialising in the new-issue business. In general, the method of issuing shares had changed little in over 100 years and tended to be conducted in an almost amateurish manner.

The 1929 crash and the Depression

The Depression that began in 1929 is most commonly associated with the Wall Street Crash in October of that year; however, separately, the UK also experienced its own crash in the value of the shares traded on the Stock Exchange. On 3 September 1929, the UK stock market reached an all-time high, but in the weeks that followed prices began to decline. The 1929 financial crash was followed by an economic depression which contributed to the outbreak of the Second World War. The main question in the history of financial and business journalism is how the financial and business journalists at the time interpreted what was happening. Were the journalists of this period any better at spotting the impending crisis than their modern counterparts in 2007–8?

Significantly, the financial newspapers of the period did not see the collapse of share prices in September and October 1929 as anything out of the ordinary, and certainly not the harbinger of a wider economic crisis. In fact, quite the reverse. The fall in share prices was regarded as normal stock market activity, a necessary corrective to the record high prices of September 1929. There is actually an interesting parallel between the newspaper editorials of 1929 and 2008 (see Chapter 7).

In the UK, the October crash was preceded in September 1929 by the collapse of the business empire of Clarence Hatry (Robb, 2002). Hatry's activities have a now-familiar ring to them: a fraudulent company promoter builds a business empire on the back of credulous investors. However, when the company inevitably collapses it is found that there was nothing of substance at its core; the whole enterprise had been nothing more than a fraudulent sham. Following Hatry's business demise, the *Financial Times* said there was a 'Need for calmness', stating that 'it is desirable in the highest degree to realise that the ramifications and consequences of an isolated breakdown justify no general adverse reflection upon the business of the City as a whole' (quoted in Kynaston, 1998: 108).

A *Daily Mail* of 21 September 1929 said: 'The worst of such incidents (such as the Hatry) ... is the general uneasiness which is thereby created. Confidence is shaken and months or years may be required to restore it.'

In their analysis for the reasons why company share prices had fallen on the London Stock Exchange both the *Financial Times* and *Financial News* reflected and expressed conventional economic thinking – they could not see that this was the beginning of a crisis that struck at the fundamental nature of capitalism. On 22 October, for example, in its leader entitled 'Pros and Cons of Wall Street', the *Financial Times* argued that not too much should be read into the recent falls in share prices because, in terms of the US economy as a whole, 'there is little evidence of any all-round falling off in prosperity' (quoted in Kynaston, 1998: 108). Both the *Financial Times* and *Financial News* regarded what was happening as a temporary and necessary correction in the value of shares and a normal function of the stock market. The *Financial News* called it a 'temporary setback' that must happen occasionally (Kynaston, 1998).

In early November, the *Financial Times* actually attempted in one of its columns to find 'Signs of Strength' in the situation:

> Once Wall Street has assessed its losses – and the Hatry tangle has been sorted out – and established a new basis of trading the period of tension should come to an end, and the sane investor should have scope to display his enterprise. Optimism and pessimism each have their innings, and the latter's wicket is now due to fall. (Quoted in Kynaston, 1998: 109)

'The striking thing about the stock market speculation of 1929 was not the massiveness of the participation. Rather it was the way it became central to the culture' (Galbraith, 2009). The number of people involved in share-dealing activities was never large in the USA, for example; only 1.5 million out of a population of 120 million were active in trading on the stock market in 1929 (Parsons 1989). However, the rise and fall in the prices of stocks and shares had assumed a central place in determining whether the economy was doing well or not. Newspapers encouraged speculation on the market through share tips, news on companies floating and being sold. Stories along such lines provided a cultural and ideological background by suggesting that anyone could play the stock market and win, encouraging what Galbraith called 'casino capitalism'.

The popular belief that people could make easy money from stock market speculation was as strong in 1929 as when Grant had been writing in 1871, and the media played its part in encouraging the dream. It was not just the financial and business pages that subscribed to and fed the myth; in the USA it was endemic in a range of popular publications as well. Demonstrating Galbraith's point about how deeply it was embedded in the culture is an article that appeared in *Ladies Home Journal* in 1929 in the United States. In an article called '*Everybody Ought to be Rich*' John Jaskob[1] claimed that by investing $15 a month in stocks and shares it would be possible to make $80,000 in twenty years. The interview with Jaskob has become notorious because it appeared on news stands just two months before the crash in October 1929 (Farber, 2013) and demonstrates the lack of awareness of most of the commentators of the time. Another investor, Will Payne, stated in 1929 that it had become so easy to make money on the Wall Street Stock Exchange that it had ceased to become a gamble. Advances in technology and the availability of more or less instant news and information all added to the belief that anyone could participate. This was 'popular capitalism', and the magazines and newspapers, boosted by the advertising revenues that came from market activity, all played their part in encouraging it.

Keynes and the challenge to economic orthodoxy

John Maynard Keynes first came into the public consciousness with the publication of his book *The Economic Consequences of Peace* (1919), which criticised the peace treaty at the end of the First World War. His book was no obscure and aloof academic treatise intended for consumption by other specialists, but a populist polemical argument through which Keynes hoped to influence people and change policy. Keynes deliberately chose to air his arguments through the popular media of the day, as he believed that policy decisions should not be settled by theoretical debate between academics and politicians, but debated in public. The media was the means through which such debate should be undertaken.

Throughout the 1920s and 1930s, in newspapers and magazines such as the *Nation and Athenaeum* and the *New Statesman*, he contributed to the debate over future policies by criticising the economic orthodoxy of the time and putting forward alternative policies. His journalistic output was huge, consisting of around 300 articles for all kinds of newspapers and magazines (Parsons, 1989). He was a regular contributor to the *Daily Mail* on the few issues where they were in agreement, such as tariff reform.

As the stock market crashes in both the UK and USA evolved into a depression, the debate started over what policies should be pursued to get out of it. The scale of the problems facing the policy makers was huge, and, in the beginning at least, the financial and business media showed the same myopia as they did before the crash.

In 1929 alone industrial production fell by 30% in the USA, 25% in Germany and 20% in Britain. There were 5 million people unemployed in USA, 4.5 million in Germany and 2 million in Britain. Commodity prices collapsed in the industrial world, wholesale prices fell by 15% and consumer prices by 7%. Keynes alone seemed to recognise the severity and depth of what was happening. In two articles in the *Nation and Athenaeum* on 20 and 27 December 1930 he wrote,

The world has been slow to realise that we are living this year in the shadow of one of the greatest economic catastrophes of modern history. But now that the man in the street has become aware of what is happening, he, not knowing the why and wherefore, is as full today of what may prove excessive fears as, previously, when the trouble was first coming on, he was lacking in what would have been a reasonable anxiety. He begins to doubt the future. Is he now awakening from a pleasant dream to face the darkness of facts? Or dropping off into a nightmare which will pass away?

He need not be doubtful. The other was *not* a dream. This *is* a nightmare, which will pass away with the morning. For the resources of nature and men's devices are just as fertile and productive as they were. The rate of our progress towards solving the material problems of life is not less rapid. We are as capable as before of affording for every one a high standard of life – high, I mean, compared with, say, twenty years ago – and will soon learn to afford a standard higher still. We were not previously deceived. But today we have involved ourselves in a colossal muddle, having blundered in the control of a delicate machine, the working of which we do not understand. The result is that our possibilities of wealth may run to waste for a time – perhaps for a long time.

This was populist writing, intended to have an impact and bring economic debate back down to its roots in the community. The two articles were published as a book, *The Great Slump of 1930* (Keynes, 1930: 135).

Keynes argued that following conventional economic policies to try to resolve the crisis would actually make the situation worse. Traditional, conventional micro-economic policy as epitomised by Marshall[2] argued that businesses should reduce all their costs, including wages, in order to make products more competitive. Reduced costs would bring prices down, which would lead to increased sales, and this in turn would create more jobs as production increased to meet demand. Keynes argued that such a policy might well work in one country; however, the problem was that if every country pursued the same policy at the same time, then the effect would be devastating. The combined impact would suck demand out of the world economy, leading to further downward pressure and even more misery. And as all the major Western countries in the 1930s were pursuing such policies, this is exactly what happened. The result was a deep and severe recession.

Keynes, in sharp contrast to the supporters of conventional economics, believed that in a recession the economy should be made to grow and unemployment reduced through increasing government spending and reducing interest rates.

The debates that Keynes and his ideas stimulated also mark another stage in the evolution of financial and business journalism. Following the publication of Keynes's *General Theory of Employment, Interest and Money* (1936), for the first time we see issues about economic policy discussed in national newspapers, along with a new factor, the role and influence of the state in determining and shaping micro-economic policy. While governments had influenced economic activity by passing legislation such as, for example, the Corn Laws and the various Companies Acts, *laissez-faire* economists and their political supporters believed that the state had no place in attempting to determine or influence economic policy. From this point onwards the state began to be involved in, and started to determine, economic policy, culminating in the economic programme of the 1945 Labour government – possibly the most interventionist government in UK history. Until this point, 'economy' in newspapers had largely been synonymous with discussion about the household economy; after Keynes, writers discussed the 'national economy' (Parsons, 1989).

The ideas of Keynes were disseminated not only through his own writings but also by his supporters in the 1930s financial media. Nicholas Davenport in the *New Statesman*, for example, referred to himself as Keynes's 'City correspondent', while Francis Williams in the *Daily Herald* believed Keynes to be a 'genius whose ideas would save the world' (Parsons, 1989). Significantly, as the economic situation worsened and the inadequacy of conventional economic thinking became clear, Keynes came to enjoy support not only in Left-leaning publications but also from traditionally conservative papers and magazines as the realisation grew that conventional economic policies would not and could not provide the answers. Writers began to criticise traditional economics from a Keynesian perspective, arguing that a new approach was needed (Parsons, 1989; Kynaston, 1994). The UK's most influential economic and financial commentator of the time, Paul Einzig of *Financial News*, eventually gave his support to Keynes.

It was a significant event when, in 1943, even *The Economist*, the bible of free-market economics said,

> *The Economist* gives an ungrudging blessing to certain wide extensions of the state control for precisely the same fundamental reasons as led to Wilson and Bagehot to advocate the maxim of laissez-faire a hundred years ago, because that seems to be the surest way of serving liberty and the common good. (www.economist. com)

Not everyone succumbed to the wave of Keynesianism. On 20 December 1937 the *Daily Mail*, in an editorial 'Quack Remedies', attacked Keynes and Sir Arthur Salter for 'flourishing their ancient prescription' that the government should prepare plans for large-scale public expenditure to avoid a recession. Such plans and schemes, said the editorial, are a 'hoary delusion that the Government can keep everyone employed by disbursing huge sums for public works most of which are unproductive and unnecessary.'

At the heart of Keynes's alternative policy was the belief that government action could have a positive economic impact. What made this argument stronger was that the UK supporters of Keynes could point to examples where state action had reduced unemployment. The federal government in the USA had introduced the New Deal programme where, through infrastructure investment in such schemes as building dams, unemployment had been reduced. Even the German road-building programme in the 1930s was evidence that actions by the state to get people into work, spending money and paying taxes had a generally beneficial impact on the economy.

Many of the 'Keynesian' journalists and economic writers in newspapers and magazines in the 1920s were also active in the Labour Party and were to play a part in creating the interventionist economic and political policies of the 1945 Labour government. For example, in 1937 Douglas Jay of the *Daily Herald* was a persistent and perceptive critic of Governor of the Bank of England Montagu Norman's deflationary measures (Parsons, 1989). He was a keen advocate of the New Deal in the USA and a campaigner for economic expansion on Keynesian lines. He became a Labour MP in July 1946 and went on to serve in Harold Wilson's 1964 government as the President of the Board Trade. In an ironic twist, his son Peter Jay would play a significant role in challenging the Keynesian paradigm his father had helped to create (see Chapter 10).

Structurally, this period saw the introduction of a new section in the financial and business pages, the economic columnist or commentator – a move that helped to establish the credibility of financial journalism. It could no longer be accused of simply being about promoting companies that had taken advertising space in the paper. These columnists were determined to be independent in what they said, maintaining their freedom from the commercial pressures and temptations which had done so much in earlier decades to lower the standing of financial journalism (Parsons, 1989). The modern economic columnists are a crucially important part of the fabric of the newspaper, reflecting and also influencing the views and opinions of readers. These columnists also have influence in helping to shape political opinion.

6

The emergence of modern financial journalism

At the end of the Second World War business and financial journalism in the UK faced very different economic circumstances, forcing the papers to refocus their activities. The 'normal' reporting on public companies which had formed the bedrock of company news reporting was severely limited, due to the restrictions that the Labour government imposed on dividend payments. The lack of new company flotations after the war badly affected newspapers' business news sections, as advertising income fell (Jeremy, 1998). With overall corporate activity flat, the business sections in most newspapers focused on an ideological battle with the Labour government (see Chapter 10).

The Labour government imposed restrictions on the dividends that public companies paid to shareholders, arguing that any spare finance they had should not be spent on dividends but instead should be reinvested by companies in new capital equipment to help improve long-term productivity.

All newspapers faced resource problems at the end of the war, and with a scarcity of paper and other materials, space was maximised. This forced newspapers to adapt layouts and designs which had many similarities to the pre-new financial journalism of the 1880s. Much of the company reporting after 1945 also reverted to a dry, uninspired style of writing which commented on results.

Economic change

After the Second World War a consensus emerged among Western politicians of all mainstream political parties that the economic problems and policies that had contributed to the outbreak of the war should, if at all possible, never be repeated. In order to prevent this they built institutions which they hoped would address economic problems. Internationally this led to a series of interventionist schemes like the Marshall Plan and the creation of institutions such as the United Nations, the World Bank and the International Monetary Fund (IMF). The rationale for creating the World Bank and the IMF was that they could directly intervene in a country's economic policies, assisting them when they were in trouble. It was hoped to prevent local problems from turning into major crises. Ironically, however, by the late 1970s and 1980s the policies of both the World Bank and the IMF became the main conduits for the type of free-market economic policies which had caused the economic problems of the 1930s.

In the UK the Second World War had demonstrated that the state could act effectively to mobilise resources and production. Many of the mechanisms used during the war were utilised after it to try to stimulate economic activity, and economic policy was founded on attempting to maintain full employment. Many Conservative and Labour politicians had personally witnessed the devastating impact that mass unemployment had on society and were determined this should be not repeated. What became known as the 'post-war consensus' was a commitment to maintaining full employment and was at the heart of both Labour and Conservative post-1945 governments in the UK. Adopting such a policy also tacitly acknowledged that Keynesianism had replaced free-market Marshall-based economics as the dominant economic paradigm.

One of the first acts of the 1945 Labour government was to nationalise the Bank of England, in 1946, in order to demonstrate that the government was now in charge of economic policy, and not the Governor of the Bank of England (Ahamed, 2009). It was no longer believed appropriate that a private bank should have such power over the economy. The Labour government pursued policies that attempted to revitalise the economy, with the state undertaking investment when the private sector was either unwilling or unable to do so. The government also believed that where the private sector was failing the state should run industry directly. In an ambitious nationalisation programme, coal, gas and water industries, parts of the transport infrastructure such as railways, most of the wharves and docks, London's buses and underground railway, and later road haulage, all became state owned (Wilson, 1995). By 1951 approximately 20% of the national economy was controlled by the state and employed around 2 million people (Jeremy, 1998).

This programme was fiercely resisted by the majority of the economic commentators in the mainstream newspapers. The criticism of the Labour government and Labour Party was hostile, vicious and unrelenting. The tone had been set before the 1945 election with attacks on the party: 'The Labour Party chairman, Harold Laski was labelled a communist by the *Daily Express* and subjected to a "press feeding frenzy" as the Conservative-supporting press attacked every Labour proposal, including its plans to build millions of council houses to let, as a threat to individual freedom' (Temple, 2008: 52).

Faced with scarce resources, lack of corporate activity and falling advertising revenue, the *Financial Times* and *Financial News* merged in 1945. The new *Financial Times* opposed the Labour government at every opportunity. Brendan Bracken, an Irish-born businessman who had been Winston Churchill's Minister of Information from 1941 to 1945, emerged as the main force at the new paper. Bracken understood the power of propaganda and became one of the key ideological opponents to the measures. In a statement to the company's shareholders in July 1947 he said that it was his task to 'try to produce a paper which never falters in the fight for free enterprise' (Kynaston, 1994: 172). While there had been pragmatic support for Keynesian approaches to stimulating the economy in the pre-war crisis, the actions of the 1945 Labour government were regarded as being of a different nature altogether, striking, so it was believed, at the very heart of capitalism. Bracken in his weekly newspaper column was vituperative and vitriolic in his criticism. In April 1947, following a fuel crisis, Bracken believed that the tide was turning his way:

> The fact is that there has been too much defeatism about resisting crackpot socialist schemes, dating from the time when the Socialists arrogantly behaved as if they were to be in office for half a generation. But in the last two years the Socialists have proved themselves to be a Cabinet of all the incompetents. I never doubted that these puppets of Transport House would lose their nerve when they came up against real difficulties. (Quoted in Kynaston, 1994: 173)

The *Financial Times* argued that nationalisation was ultimately irrelevant to the country's needs:

> It is not the substitution of one owner, public or private, for another that can put British industry, or any part of it, on its feet again. That is a matter of organisation, of the infusion of large doses of new physical capital, of enterprise and planning in the widest sense. When nationalisation has been carried out, all the essential reorganisations will remain to do, and meanwhile the Labour programme will have delayed it. (Quoted in Kynaston, 1994: 153)

Increased Affluence

During the 1950s, when post-war austerity ended, a different type of economy and society began to emerge. This was one orientated towards the production and consumption of consumer products. Innovative mass-production methods brought prices down to levels that ordinary consumers could afford (Jeremy, 1998). During the 1950s there was a boom in the ownership of cars, televisions, refrigerators and washing machines. The consumer demand was fuelled by a new, emerging advertising industry that exploited new forms of media such as TV. By the end of the 1950s the UK was experiencing full employment, along with rising real incomes for a working class employed in a range of new industries.

Newspapers reflect the prevailing social and economic conditions, and business and financial journalism mirrors these changes. At the end of the war *The Times*, *Daily Telegraph* and *Daily Mail* maintained their reporting on company news and expanded their coverage of economic matters in their campaign against government policies. Middle-market titles such as the *Daily Express* and the *News Chronicle*, both of which had a high proportion of small investors among their readers, also maintained their coverage of company news for investors. However, newspapers such as the *Daily Mirror* and the *Daily Sketch* had little coverage of business or company news, reflecting the reality that for the majority of their working-class readers there was little surplus cash available to invest in stocks and shares.

In 1960 this changed and, reflecting growing working-class affluence, the *Daily Mirror* appointed its first City Editor. Derek Dale wrote every

Wednesday about stocks and shares because 'The *Mirror* recognises that there has been a revolution in the savings habits of Britain. No longer is the City the exclusive domain of Big Money' (quoted in Porter, 2000: 9). This was a significant appointment for the *Daily Mirror*, which with daily sales of 4.5 million copies, was the UK's largest-circulation newspaper. Traditionally a left-wing newspaper, it was now actively championing the right of the working classes to own shares and questioning why the financial benefits of owning shares should be restricted to middle-class investors. 'When Oliver Stutchbury, managing director of Save and Prosper, declared in 1965, that nobody with less than £20,000 should open a personal portfolio, the *Mirror* City editor Derek Dale mounted a vigorous defence of the little guy who wanted to "think big" rather than "play it safe", using as an example a Ron Regan, a Portsmouth dock labourer, who had amassed £10,000 since the war by backing his own judgment' (Porter, 2000: 13).

As in the late Victorian boom of the 1880s, in the 1960s we find arguments being advanced that investing in shares was not only about making a bit of money but also about advancing social mobility. However, echoing the approach taken by the *Daily Mail* in the 1880s, the *Mirror* believed it had a responsibility to help and guide its readers in making investment decisions. Dale agreed with Charles Duguid that people new to investing needed guidance on what to invest in, and also that they should be addressed in a language they could understand. 'Dale did not "talk down" to his readers but he sensed that many of them required some fairly basic information. A particular strength of Dale's journalism was his ability to make links between the remote science of investment and the everyday experience of *Mirror* readers ... It was important to demystify finance, to convince *Mirror* readers, male and female that the City was for them' (Porter, 2000: 10).

Personal finance journalism

Share ownership, however, was not the only option for those who had surplus cash to invest, as a new range of savings and pensions products emerged to compete with investments in equities. Rising personal wealth encouraged a range of new and innovative financial products such as pensions, savings and mortgages schemes: these were all attempting to entice individuals to defer current pleasures and spending for future benefit (Porter, 2000). Papers such as the *Mirror*, with its high circulation, were an attractive advertising proposition for companies such as M&G and Save & Prosper, looking to break into this new market to a new and as-yet untapped audience.

The emergence of these schemes and products also marked the start of a major structural shift in share ownership. From the 1960s investing in shares by personal investors started to decline as they moved from direct investment in company shares to indirect investment through pension schemes. Eventually the major investors in public companies would move from retail/individual investment to institutional investors such as the pension funds and insurance companies.

As the range of these products grew along with the number of companies offering them, financial and business journalism found a new role. This was to provide guidance and advice to the potential purchasers of pensions, mortgages and savings schemes, and to help readers decide on what offered the best buy. This was not, however, simple altruism on the part the newspapers: financial products and services opened up a new advertising market for them and it became commercially lucrative for them to cover the sector. Advertisements for these financial products and services began to replace new company flotations adverts, and this financial advertising remains one of the print media's most important sources of income.

The first dedicated financial services section in a UK newspaper was launched by the *Daily Mail* on 28 September 1928. *Money Mail* set the standard for similar pages and supplements that were subsequently developed by all newspapers keen to capitalise on the new source of advertising revenue. In the column, 'This Is Where We Come In', in the four-page supplement its rationale was explained. 'One secret of making a fortune is to find a need and meet it. A great need in Britain is for advice about Money, how to save it, how to use it, how to spend it and how to avoid paying too much tax on it. The aim of *Money Mail* is to fill this need' (*Daily Mail*, 28 September 1966). Significantly, the supplement also contained advertisements from Norwich Union, M&G savings and others keen to reach the *Mail*'s readers. Another popular financial supplement, launched in April 1968 by the *Daily Telegraph*, was 'Family Money-Go-Round', closely modelled on *Money Mail*.

Personal financial journalism took off after the liberalisation of financial markets and the financial services industry in 1989. Following 'Big Bang' (see Chapter 9) the buying public were confronted with an often-baffling range of products, with banks offering mortgages and pensions and former building societies able to provide current accounts. In addition to well-established names, there were new entrants attracted to the market, including foreign ones with little or no track record. Making the wrong choice could have expensive consequences, so reliable and independent advice was required. The personal and financial sections became among the largest sections in the newspapers. This became the role of specialist financial journalism, which has eventually developed into its own separate role.

Modern personal financial journalism is a hybrid – a mixture of journalism and counselling – with readers often turning to personal finance reporters and commentators for help in sorting out their financial lives. In many cases readers want assistance from them to right the wrongs they have suffered; it also continues the tradition of offering guidance on what can still be a baffling array of products as the market and companies respond to changing economic conditions. Personal finance journalism now covers a range of topics including investing, pensions, mortgages, tax planning, credit cards, student loans and retirement planning.

The emergence of the modern business and finance pages

In 1961 the *Daily Telegraph* launched the *Sunday Telegraph*, providing a much-needed boost to financial journalism at the time. 'Before the launch of the Sunday Telegraph, a newspaper's City pages were considered arid and unappealing pastures by the general reader' (Farndale, 2011).

In 1964, in another landmark development, the *Sunday Times* launched its *Business News*, the first stand-alone business news and features section in the UK. The success of *Business News* demonstrated the commercial importance of business news, mixing as it did news, hard investigation, profiles of companies and successful people in business (Fay, 2011). In the late 1970s Peter Stothard joined *Business News* and he provides the following insight into the newspaper at the time: 'It was combative, a vivid atmosphere. There was a clash of cultures between left and right, pro and anti-business. At least half the people on *Business News* were anti-business. This was the start of Thatcherism, and the story of politics and business was the hottest ticket in town' (quoted in Fay, 2011).

During the 1960s and 1970s financial and business journalism was in a transitional state. While company news resumed the by now-established pattern of comment on the results of public companies, it was still limited in its overall scope and ambition. The development of personal financial pages helped to breathe life into the financial sections, which were now composed of three elements: the economic pages and commentary, personal finance and company news.

The tone of the advice in this period is illustrated by the instructions given to the new City editor of the *Daily Telegraph*, Kenneth Fleet, by its then owner Lord Hartwell. Fleet joined the *Daily Telegraph* as deputy City editor in 1963, and was told by his new boss on his appointment at the *Telegraph*, 'Fleet, your job is to tell my readers how to make money' (German, 2000). This injunction was a direct continuation of the type of journalism that we saw with Marks at *Financial News* and Duguid at the *Daily Mail*, that the purpose of financial journalism was not to critique the nature of business or the way that companies did their work, but instead to provide help and guidance on how to make money. In fact other developments were taking place which suggested a different direction for company news reporting, rather than simply providing share tips.

In 1966 Fleet returned to the *Daily Telegraph*, this time as City editor. He broke with *Telegraph* tradition by taking complete charge of his section, where he brought in a more vigorous type of writing. He was not, though, at his best in dealing with old-fashioned management, or with senior editors, who regarded him as an upstart.

Fleet treated the important stories of the time in incisive fashion. He brought *Telegraph* readers tales of the thrusting young Jim Slater, commented saltily on Robert Maxwell and scrutinised the Wilson government's pledge to bring industry 'kicking and screaming' into the twentieth century.

The *Sunday Telegraph*'s first City editor was the future Conservative Chancellor of the Exchequer Nigel Lawson. He appreciated that news about takeover bids for companies and boardroom battles were not simply dry business stories but contained human-interest angles that would appeal to readers. These were major events that would affect people's lives, whether for good or bad, and not simply about accounting procedures.

Kenneth Fleet of the *Daily Telegraph* also understood that there was more to company news. The key to Fleet's ability was that he understood and identified with his readers, who were predominantly small shareholders and not City grandees, and wrote for them. He believed that his role was to articulate their interests, especially during takeover battles, when small investors were often the last to be considered.

Fleet also believed that companies should do more to communicate with the outside world and be far more open in their communication. This was a period when there was little or no obligation for public companies to provide any more information other than the limited formal announcements required by Stock Exchange regulations. Fleet, however, knew that his readers wanted and needed more information from companies, and in the days before financial public relations (PR) became a major industry he encouraged company chairmen, chief executives, merchant bankers and stockbrokers to be a more open in their communication.

City-based business and financial journalism was in this period a closed, insular world, with business being conducted by people who shared the same social and economic background. Fleet's great rival at the time was Patrick Sergeant. Personal contact was the means through which stories were sourced, and typical of this was the way Patrick Sergeant, who became one of the most influential City editors at the *Daily Mail*, used his background. He had started out in stock broking and, when he became a journalist, he used this background to gather information from both brokers and jobbers. And, as we have seen with other journalists such as Alsager and Sampson, those that had the 'right' social connections were trusted and became the preferred and chosen channels of communication. Because of his background, Sergeant was trusted by the brokers and regarded as a safe and reliable conduit through which information about companies could be filtered.

In the 1980s the Conservative government of Mrs Thatcher fulfilled the ambitions of its neoliberal supporters and unleashed a series of economic changes and reforms at the heart of which was the attempt to turn the UK into a nation of share owners. In the business and financial pages the ground would be laid for the intellectual justification of economic policies that would lead to the current dominant neoliberal economic paradigm. The task of reconnecting people to speculating in shares was the responsibility of financial and business journalists working in company news, and many of them took to it with missionary zeal.

'City Slickers'

Nowhere was this type of journalism exemplified better than by the so-called 'City Slickers', as the City columnists Anil Bhoyrul and James Hipwell of the *Daily Mirror* were known.

'Pile in' and 'hear the lion, roar baby' were typical of their colourful exhortations to their readers to go and buy shares. Their type of journalism in many ways epitomised the function of the individual share tipper – sharing their knowledge of the market with their readers to give them an opportunity to get rich on the information. Their main concern was making money. There was no concern about how that money might be made – what mattered was making profit. Their style was given a further veneer of credibility because they wrote as if they had access to the boardrooms of UK businesses and were sharing intimate management secrets with their readers. This was highlighted in their first column, where they stated: 'If you fancy a punt why not have a few quid on JJB sports ... Slicker reckons JJB shares can only go up. Why? Because this was based on what appeared to be an unguarded tip by the chairman of JJB, Dave Whelan, who had told them that, "The new Brazil (football) shirt is selling like hotcakes".' (Quoted in Porter, 2000: 23)

However, they did not get this information from attending the standard corporate press briefings. They prided themselves that their information came from 'carousing at Stringfellows, picking up tips from inebriated brokers and corresponding with anonymous gossips through internet chatrooms' (Walsh, 2005).

The column developed an enthusiastic following with its personal and engaging style. Although they were writing at the end of the 1990s and the start of the 2000s this was still the time when personal greed was epitomised by the Harry Enfield character 'Loadsamoney'. Bhoyrul subsequently described 'City Slickers' as 'A monster that was out of control – every time I tipped a share, the price shot up between 30% and 100%.' He also claimed that amateur day traders appeared outside his house looking for tips and he was occasionally threatened. On one level, this is a twentieth-century version of the condition that Albert Grant was describing in 1871 – an obsession with getting rich quickly. The problem was, however, that they were not only tipping shares for the *Mirror* readers – they were also benefiting from the transactions themselves. A Department of Trade and Industry investigation found that Bhoyrul and Hipwell had abused their column by artificially inflating share prices. There was, according to the report, a consistent pattern of 'first buy, then tip, then sell' (Bowers, 2005). Over a six-month period the investigation found that Bhoyrul made £14,000 from share dealings and Hipwell £41,000. *Mirror* colleagues, including the then editor Piers Morgan, their stockbrokers and relatives also dealt. Their share ramping involved forty-four separate incidents between 1 August 1999 and 29 February 2000. Their activities also have parallels with the share ramping carried on by Harry Marks at *Financial News*.

According to former trader Seth Freedman, however, what they were doing was just another example of a common practice at the time. Share ramping was also carried out by city traders who deliberately used the press in order to push the shares they had an interest in. 'There were financial journalists who were just as deeply in the pockets of the industry and broking figures. If the morning papers carried reports of bid rumours for a stock, you knew that whoever was the source of this had already loaded up on stock for themselves' (Freedman, 2009: 78).

Freedman describes an almost virtual circle in which both parties gained; once journalists had reported the story, their readers would see the way the shares they had tipped rose during the course of the day. Companies might, if the story continued to run, have to put out a press release in response to the media speculation and either deny or confirm that they were indeed in bid talks. If the latter, the shares would rise and those holding them would be laughing.

If the story was false, chances would be that the price would spike initially as the so-called 'mug punters' piled in, giving those who'd bought the day before the chance to offload their stocks. And by the time the company denied the bid the only people left holding the baby were those sucked in by the papers' eager reporting of the rumours.

Either way, the journalists played as an important a part as anyone in the ramping of the share prices, which is why they were treated with such deference by brokers and company executives alike.

(Freedman, 2009: 87)

7

The 2008 financial crisis

We now understand what caused the financial crisis and how it developed into the worst recession since 1929 (for example, Tett, 2010; Lewis, 2011; Ferguson, 2012). We know that what has become known as the 'sub-prime lending problem' was created by unscrupulous lenders in the USA selling mortgages to people who could not afford them. At every stage in the process somebody was adding to the problem; estate agents, for example, who sold the houses were incentivised by financial institutions through huge bonuses, and house buyers were tempted to buy properties they could not afford by teaser mortgage rates. These offered low interest rates for the first few years which then became financially punitive as the loan term progressed. When interest rates rose on the loans after the end of the introductory period, defaults on the mortgages increased.

We also know (Tett, 2010; Lewis, 2011; Ferguson, 2012) that investment bankers used these mortgages to create complex financial products which were packaged together in ways that they believed had no risk associated with them. Their argument was that risk had been removed from the products because any risk was spread so widely among the world's financial institutions that it was virtually eliminated. European banks and financial institutions bought these so-called Collateralized Debt Obligations (CDOs), believing they were safe investments, especially as they were given the highest, AAA, rating by the credit rating agencies[1] and were also insured by large insurance companies such as US giant AIG.

At the time the financial, business and even specialist banking correspondents who covered the beat either did not grasp what was happening or did not understand the seriousness of what was unfolding in the USA sub-prime market and what the impact could be on UK financial institutions. Dan Bolger, a former managing editor of the

Financial Times (FT) offered the following explanation as to why the crisis was not spotted:

> We believed the bankers when they said derivatives [the products that the sub-prime loans were packaged into] were making the world safer by spreading the risk. But in reality it became a game of pass the parcel and the parcel ended up in the hands of those who least understood it. We take our share of the blame for that. Why didn't we spot it? Unfortunately, financial journalists – and the FT has better trained financial journalists than others – don't really understand this stuff, and they join a long list of people that starts with bank regulators, central bank regulators and money managers. (Quoted by Fraser in Mair and Keeble, 2009: 52)

Bolger's comment brings us to the heart of a fundamental issue about the relationship between the financial sector and the journalists who report on the institutions. Was the relationship between the two so close that it prevented a real investigation into what was happening? It also questions the relationship that financial and business journalists have with the business sources who provide them with many of their stories. As we explore this issue later in the chapter we shall see how the balance of power currently appears to favour corporate interests at the expense of journalism, and this seems to be part of a wider problem affecting the whole industry.

Not all journalists, however, missed the 'sub-prime' story, the most notable exception being Gillian Tett of the *Financial Times*. A former social anthropologist, Tett, as the paper's capital markets editor, consistently raised concerns about what was happening. Unfortunately, her articles were usually hidden away in the back pages of the newspaper and did not receive the wider attention they deserved. However, while the *FT*'s editor, Lionel Barber, ruefully conceded during his evidence to the Parliamentary Select Committee in February 2009 that Tett should have been given more space, Tett herself argues that the lack of interest shown in her work was indicative of a wider problem facing financial journalism. Too much financial and business journalism concentrates on reporting equity markets through public companies and there is too little analysis or understanding of the debt market (Tett, 2010). Equity markets (i.e. news on and about the trading of shares in public companies) form the mainstay of company reporting in the financial pages.

Financial and business journalists should not, however, be judged on whether they did or did not miss the significance of the sub-prime crisis in the USA. After all, they were not alone, with most economists and politicians also failing. For a better understanding about the role of finance and business journalism, we need to analyse how two key issues that contributed to the crisis were reported. The first is the print media's relationship with the property market, the situation that produced the sub-prime problem in the first place. Second, how did financial and business journalists, and specifically the specialist banking correspondents, cover financial institutions such as RBS and HBOS *before* the crisis emerged? The issue here is whether the closeness that sector correspondents have with their corporate sources inhibited the way they reported on the banks, and also whether the corporate sources controlled the message in the media.

The media and the property market

The roots of the 2008 financial crisis lay in the almost mystical belief in the importance of property ownership that exists in the UK and the USA. For a number of years the combination of rising property prices and a range of lenders ready to invest in the expanding property market was both welcomed and used by politicians of all political persuasions during both Tory and New Labour governments. In June 1987 the average house price in the UK was £45,809. In April 1992 it had risen to £64,509. In May 1997, when Tony Blair and New Labour came to power, it was £68,085. By August 2007 and the beginnings of the financial crisis the average house price had risen to £199,612. In 2008, as the crisis unfolded, the price had fallen back to £160,142.

On the back of rising house prices, Conservative and New Labour governments pursued their policies of either tax cuts or increased spending and were happy for the property boom to continue, welcoming the revenues that the financial services industry contributed to the economy. The UK gorged itself on a rising tide of personal debt, building new conservatories, buying new cars and taking expensive holidays.

Judgement about the effectiveness of the financial press needs to be based not only on whether it did or did not spot the problems that

CDOs might create for European financial institutions, but also on how critical they were of the property market and society's relation with debt. And on this there was and continues to be a collective industry failing.

While a number of experienced individual journalists such as Robert Peston, Jeff Randall (Sky News and the *Telegraph*), Alex Brummer (*Daily Mail*), Will Hutton, William Keegan (*Observer*), Martin Wolf (*Financial Times*) and Christopher Fildes *(Daily Telegraph)* consistently warned about the problems we were creating by having too much personal and business debt, the majority of financial and business journalists were content to go along with and participate in helping to boost the growing property market. Property and property-related advertising (such as mortgages and savings schemes) became a lucrative and important source of revenue for many national and local newspapers. Peston (in Mair and Keeble, 2009: 16) highlights the problem that journalists had: 'How do we (the media) have the courage and the insight to go against the mainstream and against the powerful vested interests? Some parts of the media did their bit to pump up the property bubble. Newspaper property supplements and television property shows, for example, illustrate the greater risk for the media in reporting so many issues, but especially business and finance.' In this situation it is unlikely that even if Gillian Tett had been on the front page of the *Financial Times* every day, warning about the problems of the debt market, it would have made any difference to the eventual outcome, given our collective addiction to the property market.

'It was difficult for the press to criticise the rising property market as the housing boom seemed to be enriching millions of individuals. Indeed, the press played a central role in promoting the UK property boom, which made the rising house prices the obsession of the personal finance pages of the newspapers' (Steve Schifferes, quoted in Schiffrin, 2011: 153). The fact is that what was happening to property and debt was not new – financial bubbles based on rising property prices occur regularly – yet we still seem to be surprised when they happen. As we have seen in earlier chapters, it is in the nature of a capitalist economy to produce these 'bubbles', situations where asset prices rise, reach a peak and then fall. From the South Sea Bubble in 1720 onwards, the media has played an important part in contributing to the sometimes febrile and heady atmosphere surrounding financial bubbles. The media helps to create and then sustain a heightened sense of expectation and anticipation. Pre-2008, it was not critical enough. As Robert Peston argued, 'Let's be under no illusion: the media did too little to challenge the consensus that the world had entered a scenario of continuous low-inflation growth – or at least not until it was too late' (Peston in Mair and Keeble, 2009: 15).

Reporting the banks

In looking at the role of the financial press in the pre-2008 situation we also need to consider how key companies associated with the crisis were reported. We need to understand whether the values that financial and business journalism support were complicit in encouraging the banks and ignoring the problems. This can be explored through two issues: firstly, by analysing the way that the takeover of ABN AMRO by Royal Bank of Scotland (RBS) was reported; secondly, by examining the relationship that specialist banking correspondents have with the banks and whether this relationship helped or hindered our understanding of what was happening in the sector.

ROYAL BANK OF SCOTLAND TAKEOVER OF ABN AMRO

In 2007, in a deal worth £49bn, RBS concluded its takeover of the Dutch Bank ABN AMRO. The timing was disastrous for RBS: the UK and US financial systems were seizing up because of the developing financial crisis and RBS found that it could not finance the obligations it had entered into. This proved to be a deal too far for the ambitious, acquisitive bank under the leadership of chief executive Sir Fred Goodwin.

The 2012 Kay Report highlighted the RBS takeover of ABN AMRO as an example of poor decision making by a company management. After the government bail-out of RBS the financial and business media joined in universal and wholesale condemnation of both the bank and Sir Fred Goodwin for going ahead with the takeover. However, the key question should focus on how RBS and Goodwin were reported in the media before and during the takeover. Were the financial journalists, and especially the specialist banking correspondents, critical of the takeover, or did they support it? Did they identify any of the poor management decisions highlighted in the Kay Report? Or did they collectively accept the logic of the company's argument that in order to enhance shareholder value the company had to grow?

A basic principle of Anglo-Saxon capitalism[2] is that in order to build shareholder value a company must grow. This can either be achieved organically, through internal activities such as growing company sales, or growth can be achieved through buying other companies. For the City, companies that grow organically year on year are 'boring', because growth rates can be quite modest. The City, with its focus on short-term profits, wants to see high growth rates. There is also another reason why so many companies are pushed into acquisitions by their financial advisers, despite evidence from KPMG that the majority of takeovers do not work. Takeovers (or mergers and acquisitions) generate huge fees for the advisers – the accountants, merchant banks, lawyers, investment banks and PR consultants.

While finance and business journalists might take sides in declaring support for one party or another in a takeover, they rarely question the rationale for it. This is reflected in the coverage of the RBS acquisition strategy. Alex Brummer, City Editor of the *Daily Mail*, for example, is an experienced financial journalist and a consistent critic of the executive management of many public companies, with their excessive pay and pension provisions. On 2 February 2004, in an article which epitomises the frame through which many financial business journalists write their stories, Brummer explained 'Why Fred Must Keep Growing'.

> RBS has choices. It can do the complacent thing, which is to preen itself on how successful it has been and buy back its own shares. The risk is that it will be seen as no more than a British regional bank with a few add-ons, and be bought up by an American predator. Or it can continue on its expansion path, ignore the consumer barbs about super-profits and move more deeply into the businesses in which it has been expanding. These include east-coast banking in the US and general insurance which, through Direct Line and Churchill, have become a cash-generating machine. (Brummer, 2 February 2004)

Analysts and City correspondents expressed similar sentiments about HBOS after the merger between the Halifax Building Society and the Bank of Scotland, arguing that HBOS had to grow and could not afford to stand still.

At the time, there was very little criticism about the *rationale* for the deals. While there might have been criticism of particular aspects of how they were structured, the main focus of the analysis was on whether the deal was good for the shareholders. In none of the articles we have analysed was there any attempt to put the RBS takeover of ABN AMRO into a wider economic context. It was instead treated as just another deal.

Before RBS completed the takeover of ABN AMRO, Barclays Bank had also been interested in buying the same institution. The way that a newspaper accepts the company line that its purpose is to increase shareholder value is illustrated in an article by the *Daily Telegraph*'s banking correspondent, Philip Aldrick (23 April 2007), when considering the rival Barclays offer. The management of ABN AMRO, he wrote, has 'wrung out more value than its shareholders had expected'. The competing Barclays offer was described as being as '[c]ompelling an offer as could be expected for both sets of shareholders', even though at 1.25 a share it was more than analysts thought the British bank could afford. It was accepted because the 'Barclays' management is, after all, highly respected'.

Aldrick wrote that the 'real losers are the 23,600 staff[3] who will lose their jobs in order that Barclays hits its cost saving targets', for the benefit of shareholders. The argument that it might be better to keep staff and reduce the targets was not put forward, because in the final paragraph of his article Aldrick wrote that the 'biggest threat' to Barclays was from its own shareholders, who would need to be convinced that the cost savings 'are achievable and the team will be able to integrate the bank properly'.

The Barclays deal fell through because RBS offered ABN AMRO more cash to its shareholders, whereas the Barclays offer was for cash and shares in Barclays. The RBS offer was therefore seen as the better deal, as it delivered more value to shareholders. We shall explore in Chapter 9 how this type of reporting serves an ideological function by normalising one way of doing business.

TOO CLOSE FOR COMFORT?

In 2002 journalism won an important victory over the European Union and its proposals to regulate financial journalism through the Market

Abuse Directive. One of the profession's arguments against further regulation was that 'financial journalists fulfil an important watchdog function in relationship to corporations and that [the proposed] regulations would impede playing such a role' (Tambini, 2010: 3).

Arguably, leading in such a role would be the specialist correspondents who cover specific sectors. Being close to an industry and companies should enable them, so the argument goes, to identify problems and issues that are arising. In respect of the 2008 crisis, what role did banking correspondents play – were they successful as watchdogs or, as a report from the Reuters Institute suggests, were they lapdogs for the corporate PR?

An illustration of the way that corporate communications can control the media is demonstrated by the coverage of RBS during 2007 and 2008. According to research by the Reuters Institute (Picard *et al.*, 2014), RBS started off 2007 with 'strongly positive coverage'. The report notes that the media adopts a less negative tone when its own national business sectors are in trouble because of the 'often close relationship between reporters and their sources'.

> When the Royal Bank of Scotland was undergoing convulsions, its public relations people would speak to British business journalists. While it was impossible to ignore the bad news, i.e. the fact that one of Britain's biggest banks had almost failed, the close contact between reporters and public relations officers meant that much newspaper coverage in Britain contained background and context on the Royal Bank of Scotland on how it grew rapidly in the late 1990s and overstretched itself under the abrasive management of its former chief executive Fred Goodwin. (Picard *et al.*, 2014)

At the end of the year, when RBS won its bid for ABN AMRO and expanded in the USA, even though there was criticism of the takeover this was outweighed by the positive coverage the bank continued to receive. As might be expected, as criticism of the whole banking sector grew in 2008, so did criticism of RBS. However, it was only at the start of 2009, as the record losses were revealed, that the tone became more critical. Significantly, this was also when the bank's Chief Executive, Sir Fred Goodwin, was not only being criticised but pilloried in the media (Picard *et al.*, 2014: 22).

The RBS has received some of the most 'extreme' media coverage, both positive and negative. The bank began as a high street operation with high ambitions to become a global player. Its rapid growth did, initially, generate positive media coverage. As the bank ran into financial difficulties, the media appeared to change their tone, arguing that the rapid expansion was in fact a sign of hubris, not ambition as they had initially reported (Picard et al., 2014: 23).

Sector correspondents tread a fine and often difficult line between competing interests; they need to get and remain close to a company and its PR advisers in order to be given exclusive information and the inside line. To do that they must inevitably be seen as 'trusted' by the company. However, if they are 'trusted', does this compromise their ability or capacity to write critically about a company? If, for example, a journalist writes an article that the company does not like, she risks being cut out of the 'off-the-record briefings' and chats to the chief executive. Journalists inevitably weigh up such considerations and may decide that closeness rather than criticism is the best answer. It is, after all, a question of their professional careers. As we have seen, the history of financial and business journalism is littered with journalists who have been 'trusted' by companies and used as safe conduits to transmit information. On occasions this relationship has had disastrous consequences, with journalists being seriously compromised, and it demonstrates the dangers for journalism of getting too close to certain sources.

Standing up to strong corporate interests is difficult. Alex Brummer, for example, believes that too many financial journalists are bamboozled by the 'manipulative' PR operations of big companies and some are too fearful that they will lose access if they are too critical. 'The duty of a journalist is always to be sceptical. But they are up against very powerful institutions who lie and cheat' (Brummer, quoted in Mair and Keeble, 2009: 38–40).

Jane Fuller, a former financial editor on the *Financial Times* and co-director of the Centre for the Study of Financial Innovation, quoting the French sociologist Pierre Bourdieu (in Mair and Keeble, 2009: 89), describes the way journalists act in such situations as a 'complicitous silence' which 'captures the most dangerous trap that journalists fall into, although it credits them with too much guile to imply that the complicity is deliberate. The reasons for journalistic omission tend to be innocent and mundane: humility, lack of time and laziness.' Fuller believes that the answer is relatively simple: 'Journalists need to relearn the old habits of scepticism, fearless questioning, digging for information, spotting connections and taking pride in their independence.'

HBOS: MANAGING THE MESSAGE

An interesting, and worrying, insight into the way that corporate public relations can shape editorial perception is provided by HBOS, the other major financial institution the government had to rescue with a bail-out following the 2008 crisis. The financial crisis of 2008 impacted on a number of institutions: the former building societies, for example, Northern Rock and Bradford & Bingley, which used capital markets to finance their mortgage lending, were forced to close. It was, however, the government funding of RBS and HBOS which created the greatest economic impact, because of the amount of money required to save both institutions. At HBOS, the UK tax-payer injected £85bn, with Lloyds Banking Group providing a further £20.5bn for HBOS when it took it over. The bank also received a further £12bn from the tax-payer just weeks after the HBOS £12.5bn merger with Lloyds TSB.[4]

By the time of the merger in September 2008 and the infusion of tax-payer funds, HBOS was virtually on its knees. However, in the newspapers at the time there was little critical comment on the management or its strategy. The media repeated the company line that the problems at HBOS had been caused by the seizing-up of the world money markets, which no one could do anything about. This was the line taken by both the HBOS chief executive, Sir Howard Crosby, and its chairman, Lord Stevenson,[5] when questioned by the House of Commons Treasury Select Committee in 2012. In the subsequent, excoriating and brutal criticism of the bank by the Parliamentary Commission on Banking Standards in its report, *An Accident Waiting to Happen*, the HBOS explanation was dismissed: 'We are extremely disappointed by the attempts of the most senior leaders of HBOS at the time to attribute the scale and the consequent losses principally, or in significant measure, to the temporary closure of wholesale markets' (Parliamentary Commission on Banking Standards 2013: 10). While the critical report led to Sir James Crosby handing back his knighthood, Lord Stevenson did not feel obliged to resign his peerage.

According to the report, from the beginning of the new bank, the management strategy at HBOS has been flawed: 'The strategy set by the board from the creation of the new group sowed the seeds of its destruction' (Parliamentary Commission on Banking Standards, 2013: 8).

HBOS set a strategy for aggressive, asset-led growth across all divisions of the Group [which] created a new culture in the higher echelons of the bank. This culture was brash, underpinned by a belief that the growing market share was due to a special set of skills which HBOS possessed and which its competitors lacked. The effects were all the more corrosive when coupled with a lack of corporate self-knowledge at the top of the organisation, enabling the bank's leaders to persist in the belief, in some cases to this day, that HBOS was a conservative institution when in fact it was the very opposite.

The group's strategy was based on 'aggressive expansion across all divisions' (Parliamentary Commission on Banking Standards, 2013: 10).

Asset growth had been concentrated on areas of 'higher risk'. While the report drew attention to problems in all of areas of the bank, it had been the expansion in its corporate sector under Peter Cummings, chief executive of the corporate division, that had exposed the bank to the biggest problems. The policies pursued by the corporate division were described in the report as 'reckless'. HBOS planned to use the Bank of Scotland corporate expertise and the Halifax branch network to expand its market share among small and medium businesses, particularly in England. The stated ambition in 2001 was to 'break the mould' and mount 'a strong challenge to the four clearing banks' (Parliamentary Commission on Banking Standards, 2013: 10).

In 2004 the Board of HBOS said that its plans were to make 'significant in trade into the market' although the 'Big Four had extended, valuable positions' (HBOS, 2001: 24).

With failings on this scale, the question must be asked why the journalists, and the banking correspondents especially, failed to identify the weaknesses at HBOS.

Typical of the unquestioning and uncritical type of reporting that characterises too much business reporting was an article in the *Daily*

Telegraph, 'The heart said yes: the head said no' (*Daily Telegraph*, 19 September 2004) by Grant Ringshaw, the then Deputy City Editor of the *Sunday Telegraph*. Ringshaw went on to be the City Editor of the *Sunday Times* (September 2006 to March 2008), before treading what has become a well-worn path for financial and business journalists by moving into financial PR. Ringshaw joined the financial PR company Citigate Dewe Rogerson in March 2008, where he now holds the position of executive director.

The background was that in 2004 the Spanish bank Santander made an £8bn offer for Abbey National. HBOS expressed interest in making a counter bid that was expected to top Santander's. In September 2004, HBOS announced that it would not be going ahead. The interview with the *Daily Telegraph* was meant to clear the air; the City had been keen on the bid and Crosby was being criticised for not going ahead with it.

According to Ringshaw, 'James Crosby has gained the reputation for being something of a bold dealmaker.' Significantly, the *Telegraph* said it had revealed 'seven weeks ago that HBOS was considering a rival bid to agreed £8.5bn takeover by Banco Santander'. This is an ideal example of the kind of information that financial journalists rely on; the *Telegraph* in this situation is the 'trusted conduit' for the reliable dissemination of information that we have seen before in financial journalism, where the paper colludes with the company. While the newspaper will pride itself on gaining an exclusive source of information and breaking the story before other journalists, in fact it is being used by the company. The information will have been deliberately leaked to the newspaper in order to test the waters and gauge reaction about what is being intended.

Crosby wrote that the deal was called off because 'The fact of the matter is that we could not get a deal together in our minds which meant that our investors were acquiring Abbey on terms that enhance shareholder returns.' The article enabled Crosby to outline the company's long-term strategy. '"No there is not an issue on growth," Crosby insists. "I think we are in a wonderfully privileged position strategically because you have the four largest players who have some quite strong leadership in some markets and not in others. We are the best diversified of the banks".'

Ringshaw expands, 'Crosby argues that HBOS has scale and strength in all its markets – a market share of 10 per cent to 12 per cent in both credit cards and investment products, and 9 per cent in general insurance.'

An interesting insight, reading between the lines of the article, is the suggestion that the City was keen to encourage a more aggressive growth strategy at HBOS through an acquisition. 'However, some investors have asked whether HBOS should look at overseas acquisitions, given its UK focus and limited international interests ... One target is thought to be the Irish businesses of National Australia Bank' (Ringshaw, 2004).

The City was also in favour of the merger between Santander and HBOS, as it would give the company the type of growth rates it wanted. Crosby, though, appeared to outline a different course of organic growth and used the *Telegraph* to reassure investors. 'Having set himself a tough new hurdle, Crosby must convince shareholders he can deliver much more organically than through an Abbey deal. He is under no illusions that he is surrounded by sceptics in the City. "They are pretty sure we can't deliver, given the share price rating," he says. "But at the end of the day they are going to be wrong"'(Ringshaw, 2004).

The overall picture of the company that emerges from Ringshaw's article is of an ambitious, well-run financial institution that has a clear, well thought-through strategy and a management team able to carry it out – exactly the type of image that HBOS wanted to get across when it was facing widespread criticism. It was not that Ringshaw was short of critical material; he could, had he had the inclination, have asked some difficult questions of Crosby because even at that stage there was plenty to work with. Ringshaw, for instance might have asked about the fine of £1.25m imposed in January 2014 by the Financial Services Authority (FSA) for the bank's poor internal auditing and lax anti-money laundering controls. The FSA said the breaches were so serious that it had considered whether criminal prosecutions were appropriate. He might also have asked about the way the FSA had criticised the pace of HBOS's expansion, arguing that it was, 'an accident waiting to happen' and that the 'group's growth outpaced its ability to control risk'. This was all a matter of pubic record.

Of course, Ringshaw might well have wanted to ask such questions, but this was a 'trophy' interview, one agreed with the HBOS corporate PR team, who would define what would and would not be acceptable subjects to cover and questions to ask. It was aimed at the sceptical City institutions Crosby refers to in the interview. For journalists, these are prize interviews, and just as easily as they can be granted access to such sources, so also access can be denied. This is also a reason why the hard questions are avoided – their fear of being cut off from such contacts in the future.

At the heart of the apparently successful HBOS attempt to control the media message was Shane O'Riordain, the bank's communications director, described as 'the best PR guy in Britain' (Cave, 2008) in a survey of banking correspondents.

The 2008 survey demonstrates the close relationship that a corporate communications team can have with the specialist correspondents who follow the sector. Despite the difficulties that HBOS was having by then (2008), the press coverage was still largely neutral and, significantly, contained what we know was the key message the company wanted to transmit – that the bank's problems were the result of the 'seizing up the wholesale money markets'.

Evidence of the lack of critical coverage can be seen in the press coverage HBOS received before its emergency rights issue in August 2008 as it was defending itself against takeover rumours. Sixty-four per cent of newspaper coverage about the bank was neutral (Cave, 2008); the remaining 36% was negative. This appears to have been media management by the company of the highest order.

One senior banking journalist said: 'HBOS are the best UK bank at media communications simply because they have the best PR man in Shane O'Riordain'. Another correspondent added: 'HBOS are brilliant at communications but there are some fundamental problems at that company that not even brilliant communications can overcome' (Cave, 2008).

However, there were some concerns that too much rested on O'Riordain's shoulders. 'HBOS's problem is that it is pretty much all down to one bloke,' said one banking journalist, while another added: 'HBOS has been very clever over the years at having a pop at other banks but the bank has struggled to address the criticism it has faced in recent weeks. They probably hoped it would just go away but instead it went in the other direction' (Cave, 2008).

MEDIA CONTROL

While O'Riordain was not responsible for the banking problems at HBOS, it is a testament to his skills in managing the communication process and the lack of critical investigative skills on the part of some financial and business journalists and banking correspondents that while the bank was having so many problems most of the press comment about it was neutral. Only Lloyds TSB, which had little exposure to the US subprime market and produced decent interim profits, had a similarly high proportion of neutral press comment at the time.

Explaining the relationship between the in-house practitioner and the specialist correspondent, Katherine Griffiths, banking editor of *The Times*, says she prefers to speak to an in-house senior PR, rather than an external PR adviser, as she feels the company employee will provide more relevant information and background. 'Mostly, I have a good relationship with senior public relations people. I don't always get the information I need from them, but I do trust that the information they give is truthful. I would not expect a senior PR person to lie to me. I would expect them to refuse to tell me things or be obstructive. Some more junior PR people do lie sometimes, but not often' (Picard *et al.*, 2014: 27).

The control of the media extended to the way the sector was reported following the crisis. The banks having plunged the economy into the worst recession since the Second World War; there were many calling for and expecting some form of retribution against them, or at least measures to ensure it could not happen again. In 2009, as RBS announced the largest loss in banking history, causing a collapse in the share prices of all banks, the number of negative stories about banks was at its highest. However, even during this crisis, newspaper coverage was not as critical as it could have been. 'Most of the coverage did in fact retain a neutral tone. In 2007, 50% of the stories about banking were neutral. In 2009, this figure slipped to 44% and the proportion of negative stories increased, but the proportion of neutral stories climbed back up to 50% the following year' (Picard *et al.*, 2014: 19).

Following the immediate crisis of 2008, the banking industry began an aggressive fight-back to restore its reputation and credibility. The British Bankers Association (BBA) was headed by former Conservative MP Angela Knight. By 2009 she was on the front foot, arguing that enough was enough and it was time to stop criticising the banks. They had learned their lesson and if the banks continued to be 'demonised', then Britain would lose its place as the leading centre of the world's financial services industry (Treanor, 2009). Her comments were well received by the financial and business commentators, who issued dire warnings of the consequences if we let our desire for revenge have a wider impact on the banking sector.

The efforts of the BBA were complemented and supported by other activities of the financial services industry. One of the leading organisations was The CityUK, which in 2011 had a budget of over £3m.

> One of its central tasks was to make the interests of the City if not synonymous with, then relevant to, ordinary people around the country. Its purpose is to help restore the reputation of the financial services sector within the UK. This is the financial services industry promoting a message that almost directly contradicts what most people would understand as reality. In Britain debates about what we want from our banks have been dominated by the City's framing. With a well-coordinated and well-rehearsed campaign, it has succeeded in controlling the ground. It has monopolised the speaking parts over regulation, sold the line to politicians and consequently inhibited real change. The extent to which we have taken on their messages has so far restricted our collective ability to think through alternatives. (Cave and Rowell, 2014: 68)

However, despite all the sophisticated lobbying and PR events, criminal activity in the banking industry continues to be revealed. Anger over the LIBOR fixing scandal turned to incredulity when, in November 2014, six UK banks were hit by record fines of £4.5bn over attempts to rig foreign currency exchange rates. This led to a series of front-page headlines such as the *Daily Mail*'s, 'Why aren't crooked bankers in prison?' and the *Independent*'s, 'Shame in the City leaves London's reputation in tatters'.

As the financial crisis of 2008 unfolded, financial and business journalists were accused of making the situation worse by the way they reported events. Robert Peston of the BBC, in particular, was accused of 'irresponsible' reporting about Northern Rock,[6] helping to create the panic that brought it down. These accusations were brought to a head in the House of Commons Treasury Select Committee when the Chairman, Labour MP John McFall, asked whether Peston could have delayed reporting Northern Rock's troubles in September 2007 for long enough to prevent the run on the bank.

In 2009 Peston, defending his approach, said:

> At the beginning of the week of 10 September 2007 I was informed through sources that Northern Rock's liquidity problem was such that it would almost certainly need assistance from the Bank of England. I did not report this immediately because I wanted as much detail as possible before broadcasting. It is however, not just the number of listeners that is important, it's also the authority of the programme and the commentator. The timing the piece appears and its context will also provide a context. (Peston, quoted in House of Lords, House of Commons, 2013)

Peston described how the story developed,

> It was crucial that I obtained every relevant fact and would not be vulnerable to the charge of being sensationalist or sloppy ... I first broke the story at 8.30 p.m. on 13 September on the News 24 channel. It was repeated throughout the night and I also put together longer pieces for the Ten O'Clock News, Radio 4 and other radio channels. I also wrote about it in my blog. In the reports I said two things: one, it was hugely damaging for Northern Rock's reputation that it was running out of liquid resources and needed access to emergency funds from the Bank of England. Second, I didn't think depositors should panic, because the Rock did not at the time appear to be suffering serious losses on its assets (its mortgages). In my original reports there were no inflammatory images and no use of language such as 'bank run'. (Peston, quoted in House of Lords, House of Commons, 2013)

Some newspapers such as the *Daily Mail* used this as an opportunity to attack the BBC, asking, 'Does this BBC man have too much power?' because during the autumn of 2007 he appeared to be constantly on the news, reporting on and interpreting events. What in fact his evidence demonstrates is the responsible way that he reported the event, conscious that what he said could have an impact. This is in fact a characteristic shared by other financial and business journalists writing not just on specific companies but about the state of the economy. In many cases financial journalists, aware that their writing could have an impact and create unintended problems do exercise restraint and limit themselves in what they write.

Unfortunately, RBS and HBOS are not the only examples of where financial and business journalists have colluded with a company and missed a story. One serious case when financial and business journalists also failed to identify a story was the collapse of Enron in 2002, which at the time was the largest corporate collapse in US business history. Andrew Gowers, a former editor of the *Financial Times*, argued that the warning signs about Enron were there for everyone to see in anomalies in the company's annual report for the previous year. However, despite all that, 'The press blindly accepted Enron as the epitome of a new post-deregulation corporate model, when it should have been more interested in probing the company' (Gowers, cited in Doyle, 2006: 433). At the end of 2001 it was revealed that Enron's financial condition was sustained substantially by an institutionalised, systematic and creatively planned accounting fraud. Enron has since become a well-known example of wilful corporate fraud and corruption.[7]

Regular failures to spot what are broadly similar problems would suggest that this is a systemic failure of financial and business journalism. Analysing why this might be so requires a more detailed examination of the structure and content of the financial and business pages, and these issues are explored in the next chapter.

8

The structure of modern financial and business journalism

Research carried out at the Huddersfield Centre for Communication and Consultation Research[1] (HCfCCR) provides a detailed analysis of the content of business sections and supplements in some of the UK's national newspapers. In addition to analysis of the newspaper content, a number of financial and business journalists were interviewed, ranging from business correspondents of regional newspapers to business editors of national newspapers. The results of the research offer an insight into the pressures faced by business and financial journalists.

The structure of financial and business pages

The financial and business pages of the modern printed newspaper and its online version are composed of several sections, each of which has a different purpose.

Economic news and analysis: Stories in this section include articles and comments covering the overall macro- and micro-economic issues; typically, as well as describing and analysing government policy, they will include, for example, news about globalisation issues (including covering the work of bodies such as the World Trade Organisation and the World Bank). These sections also include comment by the newspapers' influential economic commentators.

Financial news: This section covers news on and about issues concerning national and international fiscal policy, such as interest rates and inflation. An important subsection is the personal finance section, covering news about banking and mortgage products, loans, savings accounts and insurance policies. The personal finance sections are among the most important in the financial and business pages, firstly because of the advertising revenue they generate, and secondly because of the link they provide with the newspaper readers.

Business news: This is the section covering company news, with news stories and features about businesses and their financial results, such as whether the company has made a profit or loss. A subsection is the newspaper's market news column details how the shares of public limited companies (plcs) have performed during the previous day's trading on the Stock Exchange.

Business news coverage

During the research period in July 2012 the *Daily Telegraph* had the most business and economic news coverage (expressed as a percentage of the overall number of pages in the paper).

Telegraph	26%
Times	14%
Independent	11%
Guardian	7.5%

This content was then broken down into economic news and company news.[2]

	Telegraph		*Independent*		*Times*		*Guardian*	
Total number of business stories	224		141		175		92	
Economic news	128	57%	26	18%	30	17%	34	37%
Company news	96	43%	115	82%	145	83%	58	63%

This is not a consistent pattern followed daily. Overall, though, the consistent trend is that the *Daily Telegraph* contains more news on companies, while the *Guardian* has more economic coverage and analysis.

A number of different factors influence the daily balance between economic and company news stories, as on some days there will be more of one type and on others the reverse. Monday, for example, is a quiet day for company news, as few public companies report their results at the start of the week. Accordingly, all newspapers carry more stories about economic issues on Mondays. Monday is also usually the day when the columns of the newspapers' main economic commentators are featured. During periods of economic upheaval there are also likely to be more economic-themed stories. Coverage on the economy and economic issues also increases around the time of regular economic events, such as the monthly interest rate announcement by the Bank of England; or the release by the government of statistics and information about the economy such as the rate of inflation or the monthly unemployment figures. Which economic events are chosen and the manner in which they are written about often reflects the ideological position of the newspaper. During the research period, right-wing economic commentators were commenting on the threat of the 'Greek debt' crisis. Their analysis supported the UK Coalition government's argument that Britain needed to follow an austerity programme to avoid falling into the same situation as Greece.

Public companies dominate company news

The HCfCCR research demonstrates how news on or about public companies dominates the company news sections of national UK newspapers. Public companies, sometimes referred to as quoted companies or plcs are divided into what are known as 'large cap' or 'small cap' companies, 'cap' being shorthand for 'capitalisation', which is the market value of a company's issued share capital.[3] The value (the market cap) is worked out by multiplying the total number of shares issued, divided by the current share price. Companies are ranked as being large-cap, mid-cap and small-cap depending on their market capitalisation.

Overall in both the economic and company news sections, the HCfCCR research demonstrated that 45% of all stories were on or about public companies. Of these, 41% were about large-cap companies, while only a staggeringly small number (4%) covered the small-cap companies. While one explanation for this might be that only large-cap companies were reporting their results during the research period, it is also indicative of a consistent trend that has been apparent for a number of years. Small public companies struggle to gain media attention. There are many vibrant, successful small-cap companies, but they receive limited media coverage. Most of the media coverage is about companies who are listed on the Main Market – the Stock Exchange index for large, long-established companies, which includes both foreign and UK companies. There are approximately 1,005 companies listed on it, with a combined equity market value of £2,0884bn (www.londonstockexchange.com/statistics/ftse/ftse.htm).

The Main Market is the best-known of the Stock Exchange indices and the one that is always referred to in, for example, the broadcast news bulletins when the day's share price is commented on. This is the home of the FTSE 100,[4] a list of the largest UK public companies according to market capitalisation. Whether a company is in or out of the FTSE (pronounced footsie) matters to a company's reputation and prestige. The FTSE 100 index fluctuates as firms leave or join depending on company performance. In September 2013, for example, the sports retailer Sports Direct joined the FTSE 100 for the first time, marking a remarkable turnaround in the reputation of the company established by the Newcastle United owner Mike Ashley in 1982. The company floated in 2007 and Ashley made £929m after selling a 43% stake that year at 300p a share. However, the company's initial performance as a quoted company was a disaster, in part because of its poor communication with the City. The share price fell, highlighting one of the most important rules for a quoted company – it must keep the City informed about what is happening, whether good news or bad. However, by September 2014 the situation had changed and Sports Direct's market cap value had risen to £42bn.

In reality, being a member of the FTSE 100 is more window dressing and a matter of company pride than an indicator of financial benefits. Falling out of the index suggests that the company is failing and that its performance is no longer as good as it once was, while entering suggests that the company is growing and should now be regarded as among the country's business elite.

The companies in the FTSE 100 index also reflect the way UK business changes as the economy grows and develops. Where at one time it was dominated by manufacturing companies, now there is a more diverse spread of companies, ranging from retailers such as JD Sports, Tesco, M&S to property companies such as British Land. There are firms such as G4S and Serco, beneficiaries of the new outsourced economy; drug companies such as Glaxo; and mobile phone companies like Vodaphone.

The FTSE 250 and the FTSE 350 indices, as suggested by their names, cover the next 250 and 350 largest companies in size. Companies in all the indices are placed in different sections on the indices according to their business type, such as banking, pharmaceuticals etc.

During the research period the newspapers covered the following sectors. The figures signify the percentage of stories in all newspapers:

Retail	12%
Banking/financial	12%
Manufacturing	11%
Minerals/mining	3%
Computers	2.5%
Land/property	1.5%
Telecommunications	1.5%
Publishing (media)	1.4%
Brewers	1%

One reason for the dominance of a sector on any day in the newspapers is that companies in sectors tend to have similar reporting periods and so all the firms produce their financial results around the same time. This is why in any period some sectors will feature more prominently than others. The media dominance by the largest businesses shapes our perception about what matters to business and what is in the 'interest' of the business community. The interests of big business may not, however, be the same those of as medium or small businesses.

There is, however, some justification for focusing on large companies. For one thing, they employ large numbers of people, so their activities have an impact on the wider economy. Employment practices at JD Sports, for example, raised issues about the use of zero-hour contracts which might not have attracted such attention in a smaller private company.

However, there are also more prosaic reasons why large companies dominate the media: with more resources available, they tend to have the largest PR departments. They can and do put more resources and effort into communicating with journalists, who in the current environment are becoming increasingly reliant on such external resources for information. For the twenty-first-century financial and business journalist, access to this information is both a blessing and a curse. While it makes their job easier, it also raises questions about the validity of editorial which is largely drawn from corporate sources and therefore likely to contain the view the company wants to promote.

As an illustration of which sectors receive most coverage in the newspapers, research from PRIME (Picard *et al.*, 2014) analysed front-page stories during 2008, looking at how coverage of the banking sector translated into front-page coverage and also which FTSE sector commanded the most attention. Almost 40% of first-page features allocated to the top FTSE companies were about the banking sector. Other sectors covered on the front pages were retail, raw materials, airline and aviation and telecommunications (Picard *et al.*, 2014).

Public company communication

Being a listed company on the Stock Exchange brings with it an obligation to communicate fully and openly to shareholders and potential shareholders equally and at the same time. The management of this communication function is largely controlled by companies that specialise in handling the financial results and communication with a company's financial audience, including journalists. As intermediaries between companies and the media, financial PR firms are in a powerful position to shape and influence perceptions about a company. In Chapter 9 we consider in detail the historical development of financial PR, how it operates and its relationship with financial journalism.

While the growth of financial PR would appear to be the result of an attempt by public companies to control the media agenda, our research suggests that there might be other reasons for its growth. As society has demanded more openness and transparency from public companies we have (through our regulators) imposed more regulations about what they can and cannot do. This, according to one senior section editor at the *Guardian*, provides an explanation for why financial PR has grown.

With over twenty years' experience in business journalism he has seen a 'dramatic increase in the amount of PR generated material that business journalists have to deal with'. And he identifies society's demand for increased transparency from business as one of the main reasons for this: 'The government [regulators] in response to a series of scandals and transgressions have increased the requirement for companies to produce more information. The growth of the Internet and the development of social media sites have also enabled individuals and pressure groups to access information and views on a company and this has led to companies needing to make more information available. Investors, potential investors, employees can now get access to company information from a number of different sources and companies have to respond to this by providing information. The demands of the Stock Exchange also require companies to communicate and again the provision of information to serve the needs of this is important' (Butterick, 2012a).

According to Richard Lambert, a former editor of the *Financial Times* and Director General of the CBI, 'Financial PRs have become central figures in the game ... their clients need guidance through a jungle of highly competitive and sometimes hostile news media. And journalists need information that's suitable for their audience, and which comes in a timely and readily digestible fashion.' He also goes on to say: 'The old system of business journalism, based on a system of implicit favours between the reporter and the reported is not to be lamented. Competition helps to keep people on their toes and honest' (quoted in Mair and Keeble, 2009: 63).

Tambini (2010: 22) quotes a business editor who also says that the rise of financial PR is the most important development in recent years:

> In the last twenty years the biggest change has been the rise of the financial intermediary, financial public relations services. They are putting up barriers to information. I think they were always around but they've developed and become much more sophisticated. When I first came across them they were really kind of press cutting services. But they are now really strategy advisers. And there are some company directors that do not talk or answer phone calls without consulting them. And they have enormous power. In many ways, they set the agenda. They are the access point. They are making these people available for interviews or they don't make them available. Things are very controlled. The consequences are the free flow of information has been interrupted and the kind of information we get can be very sanitized. It's very hard to get to the bottom of a story.

PR content in company news

The growth of corporate public relations and the influence of financial PR has had a major impact on financial and business news. How much, has been the subject of speculation, with some estimates suggesting the PR content in financial and business pages could be as high as 75% (Davis, 2002). The HCfCCR research provides the first comprehensive analysis of the volume of PR material in financial and business pages.[5]

During the HCfCCR research period there were 419 company news stories in the newspapers analysed. Of these, 65% were clearly PR sourced. This was established by analysing each story and identifying whether it had originated in a company press release.

The HCfCCR research complements the findings of the Cardiff Study (Lewis *et al.*, 2008). The first detailed analysis on the working practice of journalists was provided[6] by the 2008 Cardiff University study which analysed 2,207 stories from five newspapers. The survey looked at two separate weeks of domestic news coverage (one in late March 2006 and one in late April 2006). The newspapers analysed were the *Guardian*, *Independent*, *The Times*, *Daily Telegraph* and *Daily Mail*.[7] Most of the stories (71%) were standard news articles, while the remainder were largely small news-in-brief items (Nibs).

The study found that 'nearly one in five stories were verifiably derived mainly or wholly from PR material or activity' (Lewis *et al.*, 2008: 7) and concluded that 'Even in a sample based on the UK's most prestigious news outlets, journalists are heavily reliant on pre-packaged information, either from the PR industry or other media (notably agency services) ... 60 per cent of press stories rely wholly or mainly on pre-packaged information, a further 20 per cent are reliant to varying degrees on PR and agency materials. Of the remaining 20 per cent only 12 per cent are without discernible pre-packaged content and in 8 per cent of cases the presence of PR content was unclear' (Lewis *et al.*, 2008: 14).[8]

While the HCfCCR research demonstrates the high proportion of PR-sourced content in the financial and business pages, when we presented various business editors with the figures for their newspaper an interesting difference was revealed in how source material is interpreted. One business editor, for example, readily acknowledged that by his own estimate approximately 10% of the business news editorial in the paper was PR sourced; another editor said that its use was minimal in his newspaper. Significantly, none of the editors we spoke to recognised our figures for their newspapers! The difference between the HCfCCR figures and the editors' interpretations is, however, not down to their unwillingness to admit a high PR content in their newspapers, but due to their refusal to acknowledge the source of the copy that forms the basis for the majority of the company news stories in their publications.

For example, the editor who admitted to 10% PR content acknowledged using both the Press Association and Stock Exchange announcements as a source for stories. He did not regard copy provided by the Stock Exchange as being PR sourced, identifying it instead as another 'agency' source. This was a point echoed by a business reporter with responsibility for following public companies and writing stories on their results: 'My day starts with checking RNS (Regulatory News Service) to see what companies have reported. Of course for the large companies we know when they are going to report [their results] as the first official announcement is through RNS and then we begin to look at the results. That is the Stock Exchange announcing these results' (Butterick, 2012b). While there are several Stock Exchange-approved communication channels through which companies can distribute their information, the most popular is the Exchange's own channel, Regulatory News Service (RNS).

RNS has a direct input that companies use to deliver announcements to the Stock Exchange electronically which are then distributed to Stock Exchange subscribers and market audiences.

Katherine Griffiths, banking editor of the *Times*, says, however, 'I don't prioritise RNS. If you cover banks you will find your stuff other ways. If you cover markets or smaller companies maybe you need RNS' (Picard *et al.*, 2014: 26).

While company news is issued by the Stock Exchange it does not produce the stories, as some seem to believe. This is the responsibility of the company and its PR adviser and should therefore be considered as PR sourced. The Stock Exchange simply acts as the distributor of information in order to fulfil the principle that any information about a company which might impact on the share price must be shared with all financial audiences at the same time. Whichever distribution channel a company uses, the key is that in terms of the relationship with the newspaper, it is the company that produces the information, and not the distribution channel.

It might be argued that Stock Exchange-originated copy has to be considered a special case and not part of a company's PR output because it is responding to the demands of the Stock Exchange and the regulatory authorities, which require the information to be produced.

In addition to releases generated by public companies, financial and business journalists are on the receiving end of more press releases than any other newspaper section. Bernard Ginns, the business editor of the *Yorkshire Post*, for example, receives around a thousand e-mails a day offering stories and information (2012).

Corporate and business-to-business PR practitioners target the financial and business press because they work for companies that are attempting to sell a product or service and hope that financial and business journalists will write about it. Their product or service will then be in front of key decision makers. Davis (2000: 283) argues that this strategy of focusing on business news pages is 'aimed at influencing other mostly corporate elites rather than general public'.

Like many modern business and financial journalists, Ginns accepts the reality of PR: 'Working with PR is a fact of life in all types of journalism. There's no point hoping that one day they are going to disappear and let us get on with our job. They're not so we have to get used to it. There are good and bad PRs and I'm happy to work with those that I trust. The bad ones and the bad practice is where they try to phone you up and sell you a story or ask why their press release is not being used' (Ginns, 2012).

Another journalist highlights the pressures that some PR practitioners put journalists under: 'If PR gives it to you it means they want something. I don't particularly like it. If people give me stories I will be happy but I will stand them up. I try not to be used or manipulated. I don't want to be used. A lot of PR companies try to trade with journalists so it is always very subtle. They say "we will give this now" then they might want something nice written about their clients. It does happen. But I don't like it' (Tambini, 2010: 22).

While most contact with the business and financial journalists will be through press releases, the senior section editor discussed above has also been subject to what he described as the 'darker side' of PR. This is attempts by financial PR companies, for example, to 'Correct misapprehensions. It is incredibly easy to get sucked into the corporate mind-set for seeing things from their point of view, they will criticise, flatter, use tempting corporate hospitality, interviews with chief executives – all sorts of means

– all of which is intended to suck you into their point of view' (Butterick, 2012a). There are those in the PR industry who recognise that this type of pressure may be counter-productive. The senior section editor quotes the chief executive of a PR company who believes the dilution of critical editorial standards can actually be bad for business: 'If a video goes on a website unedited or a press release goes into the newspaper without any editing then people don't take it as seriously as if it were the subject of a critical piece of writing. A stamp of independence doesn't therefore have any credibility or effectiveness.'

Declining revenues, reduced resources

Print newspapers in the twenty-first century face an uncertain future as they work out how to respond to a number of different and serious challenges. Many of these challenges are changing journalism practice and affecting the way journalists do their jobs, which, as we saw in Chapter 7, had an impact on journalists' ability to identify the causes of the 2008 financial crisis. Financially, the traditional business model on which newspapers have been based has broken down. Newspapers were always a dual product, a combination of editorial which attracted readers and an advertising platform which attracted advertising because of a newspaper's circulation. However, falling circulations have reduced their attraction for advertisers, which has resulted in falling revenues and cost-saving measures.

Faced with declining revenues and the challenge posed by digital delivery platforms, newspaper owners have responded by cutting costs. As the most expensive element of a newspaper is the editorial, it is journalists who have borne the biggest brunt in terms of lost jobs. In the USA, for example, some 20,000 editorial jobs were lost between 1992 and 2009, with a similar story in the UK. Employment in the UK's mainstream print sector shrank by between a quarter and a third from an estimated baseline of 55,000–60,000 jobs in 2001 to around 40,000 in 2010 (Nel, 2010: 10).

Most newspapers now produce an online edition of their paper and, according to many observers, this is the future of newspapers. Currently newspapers produce both a print and an online version and meeting their joint demands has led to an increased workload for journalists.

The Cardiff Study interviewed forty-two journalists from national newspapers, major broadcast news companies and the Press Association. In terms of their workload the conclusion was stark: 'Today's editorial employees are, on average, expected to produce three times as much content as their counterparts twenty years ago' (Lewis *et al.*, 2008: 11).

> The average number of stories produced in a day by our respondents was 45. More than two thirds of those surveyed (30 out of 42) declared they believed that journalists were now producing more stories than they were a decade ago (split equally between those who said they were generating 'considerably more stories', and those who said 'a few more stories'). (Lewis *et al.*, 2008: 45)

A journalist working for a national newspaper expressed her concerns about how the combination of new technology and scarce resources was affecting her workload:

> I'm exceptionally busy. Part of that is down to changes in technology, for example I now get perhaps 150 emails a day on top of a foot of post, and there is no one but me to sort these. Journalism has always required investment in time for contacts but invariably these are now made on my own time. (Lewis *et al.*, 2008: 45)

According to an industry correspondent at the Press Association, 'I'm definitely busier and write more stories these days. I average about 10 a day. When I first joined PA 25 years ago I used to write no more than three a day. The main difference has been the growth in 24-hour news stations which need stories all day and night, so there is no peace for an agency journalist ... I don't usually spend more than an hour on a story, otherwise I wouldn't be able to write so many' (Lewis *et al.*, 2008: 46).

If fewer journalists are producing more copy, then this must inevitably impact not only on the quality but also on the accuracy of the final stories.

Fiona Walsh, online editor of the *Guardian*, said the economic pressures have forced newspapers to prioritise and change their coverage. 'Because of the reporting timescales we tend to cover companies reporting their results, all we can do these days is report results, analysis takes longer and is more expensive. There are more demands on the journalist and less time to actually do the checking. This is going to get far worse because of the economics of the media industry' (2011).

Due to the increased volume of work and the limited amount of time available to produce stories, journalists have changed from hunter-gatherers of stories to data processors, processing information they receive. Increasingly, this means that journalists are having to rely on external sources for both the source of the stories and their content.

A veteran journalist and section editor at a national daily newspaper said: 'The volume of stories we produce in a day has increased a lot. When I started out, in the days before the electronic revolution, I was producing one or two stories a day. Today it's not uncommon to be knocking out 5 or 6 in a day – and when you're doing that you rely more on the wires[9] and on PR than you did before' (Lewis et al., 2008: 46). An assistant news editor on another national daily stated: 'There is no doubt that fewer journalists are producing the same amount of stories, placing extra pressure and meaning longer hours for those in the newsroom' (Lewis et al., 2008: 46).

These changes have also impacted on financial and business journalism. The HCfCCR survey found that the number of journalists working on business sections had been cut at all newspapers, typically by half.

Churnalism or journalism?

With such a high level of PR-originated content in the financial and business pages, are business and financial journalists collectively guilty of 'churnalism'? The term was originally used by the *Guardian*'s Nick Davies, based partly on the findings of the Cardiff survey and partly on his own observation of the work practices of his colleagues at the *Guardian* (Davies 2009). He saw that journalists were going out less to investigate stories and relying more on external sources such as press releases for their information. Churnalism has now become a shorthand definition for poor journalism and bad practice by modern-day journalists who 'churn' or recycle news stories from PR sources and news agencies without appropriate critical investigation. At its worst it is simply reproducing a press release in the newspaper without any intervention or comment by the journalist.

While it cannot be denied that there is a high volume of PR-generated content in the business press, this needs to be set in context. If, for example, a journalist is using a company's financial results issued through the Stock Exchange, this will be regarded as being PR originated. Yet the journalist has no alternative but to use this as a source. Nor does it necessarily mean that the journalist cannot be critical. There are many examples every day where, for example, as companies report their financial results, individual journalists are critical of the company's performance and/or its management. Financial and business journalists have not held back from making harsh criticism of the banks, for example, or the excessive levels of chief executives' pay. It is perfectly valid to use PR material as a foundation for stories: a press release is a legitimate source of information, while rewriting that release and looking for additional comment on it is all part of normal journalistic activity. What is of more concern is that as financial and business journalists are having to produce more stories they are having to rely on a limited number of sources for comment and context.

Digital platforms and financial and business journalism

The biggest challenge to the printed newspaper format is how to respond to the digital challenge as increasing numbers of readers access news online rather than through the printed newspaper. Although newspapers have adopted different strategies, the common problem is that, so far, none of the solutions is commercially viable. Currently, there are two different financial models. The first is to keep access to online content free of charge to the reader. The rationale of this approach is that this will increase the number of visitors to the online site and, because of the larger number of visitors, the advertising revenue will increase. The second model is the so-called pay to view, which charges visitors for accessing a site (McCabe and Sydney-Smith, 2013).

The importance of developing new lines of revenue for newspapers is demonstrated by estimates suggesting that by 2017 advertising spend on newspapers will have fallen to 11.2% (£1.9bn) (McCabe and Sydney-Smith, 2013). TV advertising will also fall from 25.6% in 2013 to 22.5% by 2017. However, there will be a rise in advertising on the digital platforms which by 2017 will, it is estimated, have nearly 54% of market share. 'Digital will account for over 10 per cent of national newspapers' revenue for the first time in 2013, double the share in 2010, though this also reflects continuing decline in print' (McCabe and Sydney-Smith, 2013).

The two main free-to-view online newspaper versions with the largest digital audiences are the *Daily Mail* or *Mail Online* and the *Guardian*. While the online version of the *Guardian* closely resembles and follows the printed version, the *Mail Online* is different from the printed version, with a high concentration and focus on celebrities. 'The *Guardian* has been the most vocal champion of the free model. Its digital strategy has been to broaden its international appeal (especially in the USA and Australia) and has been helped in this by a commitment to and increase in its in-depth news coverage' (Enders, 2013: 31). It was estimated that in 2013 digital advertising would rise by 35%, amounting to about £175m in revenue or 15% of all national newspapers' advertising income.

The pay-to-view model charges online readers for accessing content and has been adopted by *The Times*, the *Sunday Times* and the *Sun*. Currently the *Times* papers have a combined 150,000 digital subscribers and more than 200,000 print subscribers. In 2013 over 600,000 people paid to access national newspapers' digital editions, an increase from 450,000 in 2012. This subscriber base generated an estimated £108m or 7% of revenue in 2013. The most successful of the UK newspapers charging for access to online content is the *Financial Times*, which has more than 380,000 subscribers; the income generated from its digital activity accounts for more than half of its revenue, suggesting that niche publications which contain 'must have' editorial will perform better than the traditional newspapers. At the *Financial Times* digital subscriptions range between £5 and £7 a week on various packages. There are 455,000 online subscribers and 220,000 print buyers, which together has produced a 13% rise year on year (with mobile growth accounting for nearly 50% of total traffic).

Increasingly, newspaper groups are recognising that the business pages can offer a defining characteristic that could attract both potential subscribers and advertisers. Fiona Walsh, the *Guardian's* business web editor, for example, argues that while the online edition is having a negative impact on the sales of the printed newspaper, it nevertheless offers opportunities that she believes will improve coverage of business and economic issues: 'The *Guardian* online punches above its weight and the business website has a big following. I believe it has re-invigorated business coverage because you can respond more quickly to issues and interact with readers by asking them what they think on an issue. We can also provide links into stories to provide readers with a wider perspective' (Walsh, 2011).

Online editions of the newspapers have real attractions for financial journalism. It is now possible, for example, to track reactions to company announcements during the course of a day, enabling the readers to participate by making their own comment. 'The internet has opened up access to customers and employees and could democratise financial journalism, lessening the influence of the PR machine. But whatever form it takes, the need for top-quality, independent financial journalism has never been greater' (Walsh, 2011).

Local newspapers and business journalism

Business news in local newspapers once played an important role in helping to raise funds for new enterprises and in building links between businesses and their local communities. We saw in Chapter 2, for example, the impact that local newspapers had on the building of the UK's railway network. Most morning and evening daily local newspapers had their own business editor or correspondent. Now, with a few notable exceptions in the larger metropolitan areas, this is another specialist role that, in common with many other roles at local newspapers, has largely disappeared. Coverage of business issues, however, is still important to local communities. Often, for instance, it is only in local newspapers that employment issues at local firms are considered and discussed. The local media can be the one direct link between a company and its customers, but with the decline in local newspapers it is a connection that is rapidly weakening.

Commercially, business coverage can attract advertising and one regional business editor believes this is why the owners of his newspaper have invested more resources in the business section. 'There is no doubt in my mind that our business coverage does attract readers for the regional coverage we give, the focus on companies in the area. People like to associate with that and the profile of our business readers, largely owner managers of businesses. It is important for them to read about the success of other businessmen and women in the region because it encourages them. The business editor of the *Yorkshire Post* also has an important linking role with the business community, I represent the paper and speak at various awards and then of course we have our *Yorkshire Post* Business Awards. These are very prestigious and are regarded as a real mark of distinction and honour for the winners. All of this helps to provide the business community with a sense of identity and focus' (Ginns, 2012).

Local town- and city-based newspapers have been badly affected by closures, mergers and, in many cases, the changes from daily to weekly publication. Only the largest newspapers serving cities like Liverpool, Glasgow, Birmingham and Derby now have designated business editors.

When asked about their role, one disillusioned business editor of a large city newspaper replied said that his job now largely consists of 'Rewriting press releases from local companies who have some new product or service. We have neither the time nor the experience to analyse the significance of the press release; but if it is bringing jobs and money into the area then that is good news for all of us. We do see it as our job to encourage local businesses and entrepreneurs so we want to celebrate their success' (Butterick, 2012e). This function of providing coverage of and encouragement for local businesses and showcasing their products and services should not be dismissed as simply a PR activity. Reading about the success of a company can help staff morale and provide a community with a sense of identification with local businesses. However, the downside to this is that such an approach can restrict a newspaper's capacity to be too critical of businesses if timings start to go wrong.

Background of financial and business journalists

In his testimony to the House of Commons Treasury Select Committee, Alex Brummer, City Editor of the *Daily Mail*, said that one of the reasons why journalists had failed to identify the crisis of 2008 was that young journalists covering the sector were not aware of the danger signals occurring in front of them. They lacked the experience and foresight to see the possible connections, or to understand that when one institution gets into trouble it could also spell trouble for others. Speaking before the Treasury Select Committee on 4 February 2009, Brummer said,

They [the young journalists] had been brought up in a period of non-stop output and growth. I cut my teeth as a financial journalist in the white heat of the 1976 financial crisis, when 25 banks went under. Having lived through all of that you learned a [crisis] spreads from one institution to another and [governments] need to do something very quickly to stabilise the system. (Treasury Select Committee Q1533, 4 February 2009)

The HCfCCR research explored the background of financial and business journalists. Significantly, perhaps their only common characteristic was that few of those we interviewed actually wanted to be business journalists when they began their journalism career. Of the seventeen journalists we interviewed working on local and national newspapers, 86% said they did not consciously choose to be a business journalist but pursued it because at the time it was the only career option available. A business editor of a major regional newspaper summarised what must be the experience of many journalists: 'I sort of fell into it, really I wasn't uninterested in business or financial matters, just that I did not think that I would end up in it. To me this is only a stepping stone on to another job in journalism' (Butterick, 2013c).

Ian King (2011), Business Editor of *The Times*,[10] however, is one of the minority who used his background as a logical career progression: 'I started in banking but always wanted to be a journalist, business journalism seemed therefore like a natural choice.'

Fraser argues that few business journalists have the necessary professional qualifications that would enable them to understand the 'fine print of the complex deal-making' they cover and this contributed to not identifying the problems before 2008. 'This problem is more acute in Britain with its long-established elitist tradition at the quality newspapers and the BBC which have preferred to hire generalists from Oxbridge. While the American media's professional model can be criticised, it finds at least some justification in MA level training at top journalism schools' (Fraser in Mair and Keeble, 2009: 52).

Doyle (2006, 440), in her analysis of financial journalism and the lessons learned following the collapse of Enron, also found that 'Whereas numeracy and basic skills in financial analysis are taken seriously in specialist publications such as the *Financial Times*, surprisingly little commitment to training is available to support journalists working on the business sections of many mainstream newspapers in the UK (where the skills of financial reporting have to be learned "on the job").' We shall see later how this lack of experience and inadequate analytical financial skills impacts on the way that financial and business journalists write. To their general lack of financial awareness we should also add a limited historical awareness that capitalism produces regular crises and that business and financial journalism can play a role in encouraging these.

9

Ideology, business discourse, news values

News values

The question of how and why some events are included in news pages while others are excluded applies just as much to the financial and business pages as to the news pages. Journalism theory states that news stories are not chosen at random but according to certain criteria or 'news values'. The initial analysis that news went through a filtering process was first developed by Norwegian researchers John Galtung and Mari Ruge (1965: 65–71); in attempting to understand why some overseas events did or did not become news in the Norwegian papers they identified twelve factors that they regarded as influencing the selection process: frequency, threshold, unambiguity, meaningfulness, consonance, unexpectedness, continuity, composition, reference to elite nations, reference to elite people, reference to persons, reference to something negative (bad news is good news).

While initially regarded as being a definitive explanation of how news is selected, with the passage of time, technological developments, changes in tastes and differing social and cultural values, these news values became less relevant. Harcup and O'Neill (2001) in their empirical study of the UK press produced a more contemporary set of news policies. A potential news story becomes an actual one if it (generally) satisfies one or more of the following requirements:

- The power elite: stories concerning powerful individuals, organisations or institutions
- Celebrity: stories concerning people who are already famous
- Entertainment: stories concerning sex, show business, human interest, animals, an unfolding drama, or offering opportunities for humorous treatment, entertaining photographs or witty headlines

- Surprise: stories that have an element of surprise and/or contrast
- Bad news: stories with particularly negative overtones, such as conflict or tragedy
- Good news: stories with particularly positive overtones such as rescues and cures
- Magnitude: stories that are perceived as sufficiently significant either in the numbers of people involved or in the potential impact
- Relevance: stories about issues, groups, and nations perceived to be relevant to the audience
- Follow-ups: stories about subjects already in the news
- Media agendas: stories that set or fit the news organisation's own agenda. (Harcup and O'Neill, 2001: 279)

While there has been little work done on business news values there are suggestions that they may be similar to 'ordinary news values'. Tumber (1999: 351), for example, argues that the news values of the business news pages reflect 'The media's normal pre-occupation with the lives of the rich and famous'. Doyle (2006: 435) quotes a city editor on the rationale for such stories: 'Focusing on people and personalities is a much easier way to bring readers in than focusing on say technological trends or industry structure or gearing histories.'

Harcup and O'Neill, quoting Franklin, point to the developing trend for 'journalists to entertain as well as inform', 2001: 277). Fiona Walsh (2011) says the purpose of business journalism is to 'inform and entertain'. However, this need to 'entertain' has contributed to distorting the way that business news is reported and helps explain why a great deal of business coverage is through the eyes of a personality.

This reflects mainstream news where we see stories about powerful individuals, celebrities, organisations and institutions. In business journalism the comparable stories are about the size of the company, with large companies being discussed more often than small ones. One financial journalist explained the rationale for this: 'You tend to think about the size of the deal involved – numbers. When you're talking about multi-billion pound deals then that is considered very sexy indeed. The other thing that would be considered of great value is if the companies involved are household names. And that's why retail companies get an awful lot of coverage – because everyone knows them.' The same source also speaks of the personal aspects: 'If there is a personal aspect – directors and pay-offs – then that can be helpful. People have been interested over recent years in reward for failure and "fat cat pay" stories' (Butterick, 2012c).

Such personality-driven journalism in business news has, however, become a controversial aspect. Critics argue that the concentration on individuals diverts attention away from more important and substantial issues such as analysing a company's performance.

Jesse Eisinger, a former financial columnist for the *Wall Street Journal*, looking at the role of business journalism in 2008, believes that business journalists were clinging to outdated formulas and at the heart of this was the focus on personality-driven stories. This was one reason why the story about the impending crisis was missed. 'There was no deconstruction of balance sheets or figuring out risks the companies were taking. Stocks were the focus, when the problems were brewing in derivatives. We were following the old model' (Starkman, 2009).

Jon Talton, economics columnist for the *Seattle Times*, also raised the issue about personality-driven journalism, blaming it for ignoring more substantial issues. 'The reality: we committed journalistic malpractice on a grand scale. We wrote accounts of the heroic masters of the universe, epitomized by endless reverential profiles of the likes of Jack Welch of General Electric, and, until the roof fell in, Ken Lay of Enron. We asked far too few questions about derivatives and risky changes to the banking system, instead following mergers and slick new securities like star-struck sports writers. We helped pimp the stock market as working Americans were giving up their pensions and embarking on a risky – and now ruinous – experiment' (quoted in Schiffrin, 2011: 7).

By focusing on company chairmen such as Ken Lay at Enron, reporters missed deeper underlying problems. 'One business reporter stated that the failure of journalists to detect financial problems at Enron 'is not surprising and it would not be surprising to see this happen again. I would always see this as being about resources. It's not that there is any disinclination to do stories like this. People at a morning conference are going to get far more excited about the story of an Enron collapse than Enron new figures ... But if I got a tip-off that (Company X) was massively cooking the books and asked for a week off to follow it up then it would be very hard – people would be highly sceptical' (Doyle, 2006: 442).

The focus on the company chief executive (CEO) attracts two different arguments. The first recognises that the CEO is important to the company, an argument supported by a 2008 study by FTI Consulting which found that the reputation of a chief executive is a critical factor when investors decide to buy or sell a company's shares. According to the survey, nearly a third of investment decisions are based on perceptions of the CEO. In contrast to their influence, the survey found that the media has only a limited impact on potential investors, with only 27% saying they invested because of media recommendations. Ironically, though, their perceptions about the competence and ability of the CEO will be mediated and framed by the media.

The counter-argument to this is that concentrating on the chief executive gives the impression that they alone are responsible for the fortunes of the company. It distorts the picture by suggesting that in an underperforming company simply removing the chief executive will be like replacing a football manager and the company's performance will improve as a result. It ignores the systemic structural problems in a company.

There is another editorial function of writing about business personalities: business people like reading about the success (and failures) of others; their stories can provide lessons on what others thinking of following in their footsteps should and should not do.

Fred: wise after the event?

The concentration on personality journalism at the expense of considering underlying problems and issues can also be illustrated by the coverage devoted to RBS chief executive Fred Goodwin. Following the government bail-out of RBS, that the media, along with politicians, were all keen to blame him personally for the bank's problems is indicative of this personality-driven focus at the expense of the systemic issues. Clearly, Goodwin was a powerful, dominant personality who micromanaged and bullied his staff (Martin, 2013), but the point is that he operated and functioned within a system and that system was as much to blame as Goodwin personally. However, before the takeover, were there any criticisms made about him? With few exceptions the answer is no. Goodwin became an adept media player; he was valorised, feted and applauded by the media because he was seen as a success in building shareholder value and a global bank of which the UK could be proud. While some journalists might have found Goodwin personally arrogant, brusque and overbearing, what mattered was that he performed – that is, he delivered an increase in shareholder value.

In one of the few studies of how business news stories are chosen Doyle (2006: 436) found similar criteria in use as in the selection of conventional news stories.[1] '[Business] news selection procedures are not dissimilar from many other areas of journalism. However, judgements among financial reporters about newsworthiness are very strongly governed by perceptions about utility and levels of financial literacy amongst target audiences.' A *Financial Times* journalist stated (Doyle, 2006: 436): 'We're very conscious of who we are writing for. We're writing for investors such as city fund managers. Our role is to inform educated, professional investors.'

News values and ideology

Stuart Hall argues that news values should not be seen in isolation from society's cultural values, arguing that they 'Are one of the most opaque structures of meaning in modern society. Journalists speak of "the news" as if events select themselves. Further, they speak as if the "most significant" news story and which "news angles" are most salient are divinely inspired. Yet of the millions of events which occur daily in the world, only a tiny proportion ever become visible as "potential news stories" and of this proportion only a tiny fraction are actually produced as the day's news in the news media. We appear to be dealing, then with a "deep structure" whose function as a selective device is un-transparent even to those who professionally most know how to operate it' (1973: 181).

Furthermore, Hall argues that the choice of news stories reflects society's dominant ideology (Hall *et al.*, 1978: 54), 'Thus, for all the apparent diversity of the media and taking into account various exceptions, the routines and practices of journalists *tend* to privilege the explanations of the powerful and to foreclose discussion before it strays too far beyond the boundaries of the dominant ideology.'

Davis, Harcup and Richardson, however, argue that this is too mechanistic a view of journalism as it rules out the choices, actions and decisions of the individual journalist. Richardson (2007) states that ideology is a 'contestable concept' between different parties and there is therefore 'little point to describe what it (i.e. ideology) "really" means'. While Harcup states (2006: 171): 'the suggestion that newspapers have an ideological content is controversial. News reporting is supposed to be objective, reporting on facts that are there for all to see.'

A 'fact', however, is rarely isolated, but appears in a context or frame. How facts are framed and their context can change their meaning and nature. In company news, for example, we can report on whether company 'A' has produced pre-tax profits, but the context in which the information is used will determine whether this is regarded as 'good' or 'bad' news. The rise in profits, for example, may be good within the specific context of company 'A' but 'bad' when compared with other companies in the same sector. Trying to ensure that the figures are interpreted in the right way by the media is one of the functions of a company's financial PR company (see Chapter 10).

While domestic and foreign news may or may not contain ideological elements the situation is different in business and financial news. It is my contention that ideology in financial and business news is manifest in several different ways. Company news expresses the application of neoliberal thinking to business, and this is that the sole function of a company is to enhance shareholder values. We have already had some examples (Ringshaw's interview with Howard Crosby) where a company executive clearly states that increasing shareholder returns is their purpose.

Newspapers have their own individual style, language and phrasing; the same story in different newspapers will be described using different phrases and nuances reflecting the unique character of the paper. The language of financial and business journalism, however, has its own distinct language and terminology, transcending the stylistic differences of newspapers. While most of the language of the business and financial sections uses most of the technical language and terms used by public companies in their Stock Exchange announcements, there is also a language which reflects the prevailing culture and values that are endemic within business.

Davis (2000) argues that the use of this technical language disadvantages ordinary newspaper readers who do not use such language as part of their everyday discourse. With most business and economic discourse occurring in broadsheet newspapers and not the popular newspapers, this only reinforces the position of the corporate elite.

However, while this might be the ambition of the corporate elite, as we have seen on several occasions in this book, an important characteristic of the most successful financial and business journalists has been (and continues to be) their ability to demystify technical phrasing. This assumes that they see their role as being on the side of the ordinary investor and want to communicate with them, which is not always the case.

One aspect of how prevailing social attitudes are expressed in business news is explored by Koller through analysing the highly stylised nature of business and financial discourse and identifying how, for example, in company takeovers the language and imagery used often involves martial or sporting metaphors. 'It can be seen that in media discourse on marketing and sales, the WAR metaphor is most frequent and most entrenched, followed by the SPORTS metaphor[2] and third, GAMES' (Koller, 2004: 86). 'As the three main contenders push forward, others must move quickly to avoid becoming also-rans' (Koller, 2004: 84). While Koller's work is based on US business magazines, it is supported by HCfCCR analysis which shows that the language used in UK newspapers in situations such as takeovers is broadly similar.

Koller believes that the largely masculine-orientated language in many of the metaphors used in financial and business reporting is neither a creative production nor accidental but reflects the reality that business is still largely a masculine domain. The language inevitably reflects this: 'The obvious explanation as to why journalists focus on the WAR metaphor so much lies in its masculinised nature: emphasis on that metaphor characterizes marketing discourse as a male arena and thus reifies the power of male readers.' One manifestation of this in the real world, for example, is the lack of women in senior positions on the boards of UK public limited companies (plcs).[3]

Ideology in financial and business news

Financial and business journalism has an ideological function because it accepts and helps to sustain a neoliberal view of business. At the heart of this is the almost universal acceptance that the sole function of a company is to enhance the value of its shareholders. This is neoliberalism in business. The ideological component in financial and business news discourse has two effects. Firstly, it helps to establish the ideological hegemony of free market capitalism; and secondly, and related to the first point, it underscores the argument that the Anglo-Saxon model of capitalism has no alternative. The ideology becomes manifest in a number of different ways, from the choice of companies whose results are reported, to the vocabulary used in the company news stories. Phrases and words that are regarded as a 'normal' part of business discourse have ideological functions and roles and, as they are used every day, have become embedded in our ordinary language. On a trivial but significant level, for example, this is manifest when virtually every BBC radio news bulletin seems to end, 'finally in the City today the FTSE closed down (or up) ...'. The inflection and tone in the news reader's voice suggests a rising share price is a 'good' thing and a falling share price a 'bad' thing. The audience is invited to participate in the City news about share prices as an issue about which we should all be concerned. This is just one small example where we normalise our acceptance of 'the market' discourse to reinforce the belief that the success of the market is fundamental to all our economic well-being.

Shareholder value paradigm

The actions of all executive directors of quoted companies are underpinned by a belief in the necessity to enhance, improve or increase the returns that the company provides to its shareholders. This goes under a number of different titles: 'shareholder value', 'shareholder primary' – whatever it is called, it is neoliberalism. It has become so entrenched that many cannot conceive of any other alternative.

However, crises like that of 2008, and continuing corporate excesses, reveal not just the intellectual weaknesses of this stance but also how the sole pursuit of shareholder value, with no wider considerations, can be bad for the wider economy. UK companies pay more generous dividends than their US counterparts (Stout, 2012). In fact, maintaining a level of dividend payment that the shareholders are happy with often becomes the defining feature of a company. Even companies that are in financial difficulty have to maintain the all-important dividend payment or risk a falling share price. Ironically, companies often experience a fall in share price because of the falling dividend payment and not necessarily because of their overall performance.

'There is one and only one social responsibility of business – to use its resources and engage in activities designed to increase its profits. So long as it stays within the rules of the game, which is to say, engages in open and free competition without deception or fraud' (Friedman, 1970). In his famous newspaper article Milton Friedman set out shareholder value theory, which in essence states that the sole function and responsibility of the public company is to make a profit – not to engage in corporate social responsibility programmes, as such activity dilutes the money that should have gone to the shareholders and is an irresponsible use of resources. The company contributes to society by employing workers who then pay their taxes; the profitable company also pays taxes, which are then collected by the government. It is the responsibility of the government to use those taxes to deal with society's problems.

In his analysis of the 1995–96 takeover battle between Granada and Forte, Davis illustrates how both sides in the takeover concentrated on the importance of shareholder value: 'The simple message that both sides wanted to communicate was that they would offer "more value to shareholders"' (Davis, 2000: 296). Phrases such as, 'The City/the market knows best' are continually reinforced. 'Articles frequently use such phrases as "City opinion believes …" "Market sentiment dictates …" "Analysts have determined that …".' These are common phrases that can be found in the business pages of any national newspaper. In his analysis of the coverage Davis also looked at who was referred to, which illustrates who communication is aimed at.

Shareholders/investors (usually refers to institutions)	63.5%
'The market'/ 'the City' (as in 'The City backs Granada')	39.8%
'Analysts' (e.g. 'Analysts think bids should be raised')	21.4%
'Takeover panel/takeover rules'	12.2%
Employees	7.1%
Private investors	4.2%
Customers	4.2%
(Total number mentioning one or more of these three	13.4%

(Davis, 2000: 296)

The way that the market is described in financial and business pages makes it appear as an absolute, a law of nature, unchallengeable, like an angry god to be satiated when disturbed. This was illustrated in the early days of the Coalition government, when the deficit reduction programme was justified because 'the market' demanded it. The clear message was that if the government's policies were not followed 'the market' would react and we would then be in an even worse economic situation than we were already in.

The Kay Report commented on the 'almost magical powers' attributed to 'the market':

> Anthropomorphisation of 'the market' in phrases such as 'markets think', or 'the view of the market' is common usage. It should hardly need saying that the market does not think, and that what is described as the view of 'the market' is simply some average of the views of market participants. 'The market' knows nothing except what market participants know, although it is of course possible that the average of a range of competing views may be a better estimate of fundamental value than the opinion of some (or conceivably all) individual market participants. The assessment of 'the market' is therefore only as good as the quality of the analysis done by asset managers and those who advise asset managers. (Kay Review, 2012: 41)

High pay of chief executives

As we have already seen, the financial and business press has been compliant in promoting the 'cult of the chief executive', which has led to these managers being accorded an almost mythic status in corporate culture which has enabled their pay and remuneration packages to balloon way out of control. There is, though, another angle to this – CEOs' high pay is another manifestation of neoliberal business philosophy.

The growing gulf between chief executive pay in public companies and that their workforce has also become one of the most potent issues in contemporary business life and a symbol of the increasing gap between rich and poor in society. In 1984 equity-based compensation accounted for zero per cent of the median executive's compensation at Standard & Poor 500 (the American equivalent of the FTSE 1000) firms. By 2001 this figure had risen to 66%. In 1991 the executive of a large plc received compensation approximately 140 times that of the average employee. By 2003 the ratio was approximately 500. This has, however, not happened either by accident or chance and is entirely consistent with shareholder value theory. 'The shareholder primacy (stock-based compensation) ensured that, by the close of the twentieth century, managers in US companies had stronger personal incentives to run public corporations according to the ideals of shareholder value thinking than at any prior time in American business history' (Stout, 2012: 21).

The media interest in the issue is demonstrated by the number of articles in the UK national press discussing 'executive pay', which rose from fewer than 550 in 2006 and 2007 to 832 in 2008 and more than 1,000 in all subsequent years (Gregory-Smith et al., 2014). It has become a controversial and political issue in the UK, particularly in the aftermath of the 2008 recession, and has been another of the issues that has given some businesses a bad name or a poor reputation. The average FTSE 100 CEO was paid £4.3m in 2012, nearly double the amount they received in 2002. Over the same period, the average UK worker did not experience a real-terms pay rise at all. CEOs are now paid around 160 times the average worker's salary. In 1998 it was about 50 times, and in the early 1980s CEO pay packages around 15 or 20 times the average salary were commonplace. *Capital in the Twenty-First Century*, the best-selling book by economist Thomas Piketty, highlights the growth in pay of so-called 'super-managers' as a key contributor to the pay gap between the super-rich and everybody else that has widened since the early 1980s (High Pay Centre, 2013: 11).

Average CEO pay for the companies analysed in 2013 stood at £4.5m – this represents an increase of around 5% compared to the FTSE 100 average of £4.3m recorded by Manifest/MM&K in 2012.

> The new rules on pay do not appear to have had a significant effect in terms of reducing executive pay packages from around the £4 million mark, a level more than 150 times that of the average UK worker. (High Pay Centre, 2013: 11)

Perhaps in response to the media and political attention, in 2008 some institutional shareholders started challenging the high rates of pay, in what the media began to refer to as the 'shareholder spring'. However, despite all the optimism, Gregory-Smith, Thompson and Wright (2014), in a study of the UK's highest-paid company directors, found that there has in reality been no change – institutional shareholders are still inclined to approve the pay of top directors, just as they were before the 2008 crisis. This demonstrates how entrenched is the neoliberal belief that the sole function of a company is to enhance/increase shareholder value.

In a way, it is naïve to expect public companies just to 'do the right thing' by society. A public company's ultimate responsibility is not to some abstract notion of 'society' but to its shareholders, and if this means that it tries to minimise, for example, its corporate tax bills by using offshore tax centres and this results in its being able to pay more dividends to its shareholders then, according to shareholder value theory, it is acting responsibly.

Despite the campaigns against high pay and the many individual examples where journalists have been critical of public companies, generally speaking, business and financial journalism have colluded with the growth of this ideology because is easier to report results rather than to analyse and criticise. Stout (2012) argues: 'Shareholder primacy rhetoric also appealed to the popular press and the business media. First, it gave their readers a simple, easy-to-understand, sound-bite description of what corporations are and what they are supposed to do. Second, and perhaps most important, it offered up an obvious suspect for every headline-grabbing corporate failure and scandal. If a firm ran into trouble, it was because directors and executives were selfishly indulging themselves at the expense of the firm's shareholders.'

Militancy and markets

The ideological dominance of the free-market economic paradigm in financial and business news is reinforced by the choice of contributors who are regularly quoted in company news reports and, equally significant, those who are not quoted. The HCfCCR research showed that 65% of all company news stories studied during the research period contained a quote or comment from a stock market analyst.

News reports on a company's financial results often include a quote that attempts to put the story into a wider market context or provide a rationale for why the results are either good or bad. Most of these comments are provided by stock market analysts, and because they are quoted as 'experts' they shape our perceptions of the story.

Stock or securities analysts research and examine financial data on quoted companies in order to advise their clients on where to invest. They are employed by banks, stockbrokers and insurance companies. Economic commentators and analysts are also extensively used in various broadcast business news bulletins on BBC news such as *BBC Breakfast* and the *Today* programme. These 'expert' commentators are able to make contentious and unchallenged statements that range from, for example, the assertion that it is time that the banks were 'rehabilitated' to the 'economic madness' of Ed Miliband's energy policy. Such comments are made with apparent authority and, while they appear to be objective, are actually ideologically loaded because they are pro-market and reflect free-market opinion. Far too often the presenter of the show does not or will not challenge the expert's comments, either because they agree with them or because they do not feel sufficiently confident in their knowledge of the subject to challenge the perceived expert.[4]

Doyle believes that one of the reasons why journalists use analysts is to cover up their own shortcomings due to their inadequate training. One business news editor explained that 'Journalists certainly rely on analysts to do the interpreting for them of the performance of companies and of economies ... [and] for off-the-peg opinions and quick reactions to the things where we feel they are better briefed than we are' (2006: 441).

Analysts are sector specialists and it is their responsibility to know as much as possible about the companies they follow and the industries in which they operate. Analysts compete with analysts from other companies, all of whom are looking for that key piece of information about the company that will give them an edge on their competitors. They follow a only limited number of companies. As their research work is expensive; it is only therefore cost-effective for their employer if they focus on larger companies. Their research is used to inform the purchasing decisions of institutional and retail investors.

Large companies on the Stock Exchange, the household names with turnovers in the billions, all have analysts who follow or report on them. It is less easy to get analysts to follow the smaller-cap companies, because of the associated costs. Companies need research in order to show to the outside world what they are up to.

Typical of how an analyst's recommendations are used in the media are the following extracts taken from the *Guardian* Market comment, 8 November 2013.

> **Rolls-Royce** rose 40p to £1210 as the aero engine maker said improvements in its defence and marine businesses would lead to better than expected growth in full year profits. Analyst Tina

Cook at Charles Stanley said: 'In our opinion, recent share price underperformance offers an attractive entry point for investors. Rolls Royce remains well positioned with a diversified business model, global customer base, earnings visibility and potential for margin improvement.'

The idea of **Vodafone** being a possible target for US telecoms group AT&T continued to gain ground, with two more brokers raising the prospect last week. At Berenberg, analyst Paul Marsch said: 'While rising political concerns over US eavesdropping may make European Commission approval of an AT&T move more challenging, if AT&T is serious about the European mobile opportunity, it is unlikely to be put off by such concerns. The prospect of 265p–275p per share remains enticing.'

Trade unions

The dominance of analyst comments in the newspapers contrasts sharply with that of organised labour. As highlighted in Davis (2000), analysts were mentioned or commented on in 21% of the stories, while employees registered only 7.1%.

Few national newspapers or broadcast media possess a dedicated industrial or labour correspondent. This was not always the case: in the 1970s every major newspaper had an industrial correspondent. 'Once upon a time, labour specialists were the media equal of political reporters in prestige and clout. They were a vital part of the national dialogue. But now? Virtually extinct' (Preston, 2011).

Kevin Maguire (2008), political editor of the *Daily Mirror* states: 'When I covered employment and industrial relations for the *Daily Telegraph* in the first half of 1990s there must have been thirty or forty hacks doing similar jobs across Fleet Street and the airwaves. Now there are three.'

Alan Jones (2013), industrial correspondent of the Press Association, said that in the early 1980s, when he joined, they had three labour reporters covering what was known as 'strikes and strife':

> Every newspaper had at least one labour correspondent and it was the top job, guaranteeing a front page story most days after several hours of standing outside offices of ACAS, or more

likely the nearest pub. Union leaders were almost as powerful as Government ministers and that power transferred to the reporters covering the patch. The miners' strike was the beginning of the end of that power – things were never the same again. Union power waned, the Conservative government introduced laws seen as anti-union, and the demise of the labour correspondents was well and truly under way.

In the twenty-first-century media the only time we read or hear about trade union activity is usually in a negative context, when, for example, industrial action is being taken by a union. This situation would appear to confirm a long-standing media bias and hostility against and toward unions and their activities (Glasgow University Media Group, 1976, 1980, 1982, 1983; Beharrell et al., 1977; Hollingsworth, 1986; Jones et al., 1985). Such actions are almost always portrayed as having a bad or negative impact on the rest of 'us' (the community): news reports will often focus on how normal life is disrupted by strike action, without considering the causes of that action. This is an attempt to pit the trade unions against the 'public interest' – an approach epitomised by the Conservative Prime Minister Mrs Thatcher, who infamously described the miners as 'the enemy within'. At the base of this attempt to marginalise the unions is a consensual view of society which is symptomatic of a type of reporting that assumes that we (society) all share the same interests (Hall et al., 1978).

In this context, reporting on industrial disputes and labour issues has moved from the business pages to the political pages (Jones, 2011). This in itself suggests that trade union activities are 'political' and not related to the pursuit of industrial causes. Many of the special labour correspondents such as the BBC's Nicholas Jones were sympathetic to the unions and moving the stories away from their industrial context symbolises a real distancing in tone and attitude. When industrial actions are reported in the context of public companies, invariably there will be a comment on how the industrial action has impacted on the share price. The implication is that the fall in the share price is bad not just for the company but for the whole community.

Mergers, acquisitions and takeovers are often justified because of the cost savings that it is claimed will be made. One of the justifications for the RBS takeover of ABN AMRO, for example, was that 20,000 jobs would go, all of which was deemed acceptable because it would produce a higher return for the shareholders. Where, however, was the voice of organised labour in this?

Although trade unions no longer possess the same power, and various governments have succeeded in emasculating and largely marginalising them, the media hostility towards them continues. Dr Matt Davies' (2014) exploration of the mainstream UK media, 'set[s] out to convince news consumers that being an active member of a trade union is tantamount to joining an underground terrorist cell, rather than working to protect the pay and conditions of the 65 million people who currently belong to one in the UK' (Davies, 2014: 19). Davies highlights front-page headlines such as from *Daily Mail*, 'The Union Challenge to our Democracy', 'Militant Agenda: Kill New Labour'; from the *Daily Express*, 'Strikes to Ruin Easter'; from the *Daily Telegraph*, 'Held to Ransom by the Unions'.

What, one wonders, what would the headlines have been had the trade unions been involved in the banking crisis that cost this country so much?

In a reverse of the way that the market and its values have become naturalised, trade unions and their activities have become demonised. Davies, in his empirical study, demonstrates 'That the majority of the news representation of trade union activity – especially strike action – ignores the grievances, aims and objectives of the action itself in favour of regularly associating it with violence and disruption, and that the use of the word "militant" plays a key role in these demonization strategies' (Davies, 2014: 20).

Davies analysed the way two high-profile strikes in the UK – the strike by BA cabin crew protesting about the reduction of cabin staff on individual flights, which would lead to redundancies (20 March–4 April 2010) and a public sector workers' strike against pay and cuts (29 June–1 July 2011) – were reported. Using the corpus linguistic software tool wmatrix to process 200,000 words on both actions, he analysed news reports, editorials and opinion columns from all the UK national newspapers.[5]

From the *Daily Mail* of 20 March (the first day of the BA strike) came the following: 'Millions of passengers face travel misery', 'In a further blow to the travelling public, the militant RMT union announced plans for the first national rail strike for 16 years, expected over Easter …'

'Discourse strategies included here which are designed to discredit the strike include: foregrounding the effect of the dispute on "passengers", rather than the grievances of the strikers ("travel misery"/"blow to the travelling public") ... One of the most consistent, and therefore presumably effective, strategies, however, is the persistent labelling of union activists as "militants" and union activity as "militancy" and associating this in the minds of newspaper consumers with violence and chaos.'

Davies found that, 'The transport strike data [the BA action] is topped by forms of "threat" ("threatened", "threatening") etc with 178 examples. This is followed by 119 examples of "militant" (including the plural version and "militancy"), "hit" (63) and "bullying" (31) ... The prominence of the "violent/angry" category seems to confirm my intuitions that the tendency of sections of the UK press to associate trade union activism with aggressive behaviour is a consistent phenomenon' (Davies, 2014: 22).

Davies also looks at the way the newspapers use the word 'militant' in reports about trade union activities, 'in ways which assume readers perceive "militancy" as a sinister activity'. By tracking militancy, 'The consistency therefore with which "militancy" has these associations in the UK press provides some fairly damning evidence of routine demonization of trade union activity, implying a media agenda to convince their readership that workers should be condemned for standing up for their rights' (Davies, 2014: 22).

10

Financial communication and financial PR

Professor John Kay, in his review of the UK equity markets (2012), describes the situation where potential investors have to rely on the company for the information they need in order to make informed investment decisions as one of 'information asymmetry' – where the balance of power lies with the company. Historically, from the South Sea Bubble onwards, the role of the financial press has been to provide a counterbalance to information asymmetry by providing the objective, independent advice that the potential investor needs. However, it is becoming increasingly difficult for financial journalism to sustain this important role, firstly, because of the problems affecting the newspaper industry; secondly, because of the increasing power of the corporate PR machine. If business cannot be reported on freely and critically, this will have serious implications for society's relationship with business.

One of the reasons for the growing imbalance between journalism and the media is the pressure on the resources that journalists have at their disposal to carry out detailed scrutiny and analysis. A combination of staff cutbacks and the demand for greater output has forced journalists to rely on more external, usually PR-driven, sources of information.

Company news in the financial and business pages is dominated by reports on public companies, and, in order to understand why, it is necessary to examine the communication obligations that a modern public company has to fulfil. These commitments are required by society and have, ironically, fuelled the growth in financial PR. Our analysis will also provide an explanation on the role that financial PR plays.

Being a public company

Public company communication falls into two distinct areas. Firstly, it fulfils the obligations a company makes when its shares are traded in public through the Stock Exchange; and secondly, it provides information on behalf of companies that are going to go public or about work undertaken during a company takeover.

The function of the twenty-first-century Stock Exchange[1] is broadly similar to earlier stock exchanges we discussed in Chapter 1. It brings together companies looking for money and individuals and institutions looking to invest in companies. While in the past such investors were largely individuals (or retail investors), nowadays the main investors are pension funds and financial intermediaries (Kay, 2012). Major structural changes are taking place in share ownership, with over half of all investments in quoted companies in the UK now owned by foreign shareholders (ONS, 2012). This shift in the ownership of shares will have consequences for the future of financial journalism (see Chapter 11).

While companies who need investors have always had to communicate with their shareholders and potential shareholders for marketing reasons, a modern public company now has legal obligations to communicate. Managing this communication process has become one of the most important functions of a company's management executive. Communicating information about a company's performance and operation is not about generating publicity for the company: ineffective communication can impact on the company where it matters most, on its sales and share price.

Stock Exchange announcements

The financial results are only one of a series of announcements that Stock Exchange regulations require public companies to make. The principle that governs public company communication is that any information that will impact on the share price has to be submitted to all interested parties at the same time.

These announcements include senior company appointments, such as changes to a company's directors, and notification of any company meetings. Directors also have to declare any directorships in other public companies, along with changes to the size of their shareholdings. We saw the problems this caused in 1720 when the directors of the South Sea Company sold their shares. It created panic among the other shareholders, who believed the directors were selling because they had inside knowledge of what was going to happen at the company.

News about any deals or transactions that the company has been involved in, along with operational updates such as a plant closure, also have to be communicated to the Stock Exchange, as these could affect the share price. If the shareholders believe that a significant capital investment in new plant and machinery means increased expenditure and therefore lower short-term profits, then the share price could fall as a consequence.

Financial results

Company news coverage in UK newspapers is dominated by the financial results of public companies. Currently, it is a requirement of the companies listed on the London Stock Exchange that they must report their financial results every six months; the results that are produced half-way through the year are known as the interims and the end-of-year figures as the finals. While this might appear to demonstrate financial transparency by a company, this six-monthly reporting cycle has been criticised because of the impact that it has on a company's performance. Changing to an annual reporting system was one of the Kay Review's (2012) main policy recommendations.

The main criticism of reporting results every six months is that it encourages short-term thinking by company executive directors, who, it is argued, become focused on producing short-term profits at the expense of long-term growth.[2] This could mean in practice closing factories and making employees redundant in order to boost profits as quickly as possible. Executive managers are under constant pressure to consistently and continually produce profits, and ideally a level of profit better than that of the previous six months.

The production of the financial results is not only an accounting exercise; the company also announces the next dividend payment it will make to shareholders. Shareholders of a public company make a return on their investment in two ways. Firstly, by an increase in the overall value of their shareholding in the company: if the company does well, so the value of the shares rises; secondly, through receiving a dividend payment on each share owned.

Managing the announcement process is a serious matter for a public company and its executive directors. If, for example, the share price falls when the results are announced, this can be accompanied by negative headlines in the financial press, which can impact on the financial value of a company. It is the role of the financial PR company to manage the announcement process and attempt to explain (or spin) the results to the media in as positive a manner as possible in order to prevent or minimise the negative headlines and reduce their impact.

The presentation of the results on the announcement day is a carefully choreographed, stage-managed process. The formal announcement is made through the Stock Exchange first thing in the morning; this is now picked up by the media and carried in the newspapers' online editions. This ability to carry up-to-date news is one of the positive aspects of online editions, enabling readers to track reaction to the story. Links to previous stories on the company and related issues can also improve a reader's understanding of the story. Online versions also enable readers to participate in the news story and add their own perspective and views.

The next stage in the announcement process is explaining the results to the various company analysts who follow the company. Where this was once done at a formal conference which everyone attended, now it can as easily be done through a telephone conference which might also include the media. The two most important audiences for a public company are the analysts who follow it and the fund managers of the institutions who own shares in the company. Depending on the company's explanation about the figures, the analysts will recommend their clients to either 'buy' or 'sell' their shares. If the financial results are not what the City has expected, then the executive directors – usually the chief executive and the finance director – have to explain why, and as positively as possible. The financial PR company acts as the intermediary between the reporting company and the media and will respond to questions from the media.

Arguably, the most difficult and contentious announcement a public company can make is a profits warning. Public companies, when they report their results, must also state what the expected level of profit will be when they report their next results in six months. This is not of merely academic interest, as a company's shares will often trade in response to or in anticipation of the stated profit/loss level. Making a profits warning is a serious event for a public company and hits right at the function and the purpose of the company. The City is an unforgiving master. Executive directors may get away with one profits warning; two, and the alarm bells will start ringing; producing three successive profits warnings suggests to the City that this is a company in trouble, and no amount of spin from the PR advisers will change that. Such figures will usually mean that the chief executive running the company could be in danger of being ousted by the shareholders. The Tesco chief executive Philip Clarke, for example, was forced to resign his position when the company announced a profits warning in July 2014. 'City' patience had run out with Mr Clarke, who in his three years in charge had consistently seen profits fall. Tesco's share price rose on the announcement of his departure.

An example of how a profits warning is handled on the day is provided by the Trading Statement on 4 October 2013 issued by the carpet retailer Carpetright. It was distributed through RNS at 7.00 a.m. and later that morning the story was already on the online versions of the newspapers, giving it an immediate impact. While traditionally the announcement would have been carried in the following morning's newspapers, by having the news in the online editions the printed versions the next day carried more analysis. The announcement said that the company was not expected to make its level of anticipated profits and that the company's chief executive was going to resign after only a year in the post. The trading statement issued through RNS, the Stock Exchange's news distribution channel, announced that a conference call for analysts was being held by the company chairman and founder, Lord Harris. The statement also provided details of where he and the finance director could be found later in the day. Alternatively, interested parties could contact their financial PR company Financial Dynamics. Unsurprisingly, on the announcement, Carpetright's share price fell.

Initial public offerings, mergers and acquisitions

While the financial calendar provides the staple work of a financial PR consultancy, reputations are made and lost on the activities associated with flotations (initial public offerings – IPOs) and mergers and acquisitions. In addition to being a staple of financial and business journalism since 1720, the advertising associated with IPOs has also been a valuable source of income for national and, on key occasions, local newspapers. IPOs tend to follow trends: when the economy is doing well and share prices are high, IPOs increase; when the economy is performing badly, there are fewer listings.

An IPO is when a private company offers its shares to the public for the first time. Usually these are growing companies looking for new capital to expand their business. This process, also known as 'going public' or 'floating' the company, radically alters the company's profile: it becomes literally a 'public' company and open to media and public scrutiny. It can be an intimidating experience and is not suitable for all companies. One of the main functions of the financial PR company before a float is to prepare the company's directors for the forthcoming media interest. For the first time they will be exposed to the media glare, where their every action might impact on the share price.

A financial PR company is responsible for all the communication activities of a company going through an IPO. The PR firm will be part of an advisory team which usually includes a stockbroker, corporate lawyer, accountants and sometimes, depending on the size of the float, a merchant banker. The aim of an IPO is to market the company shares to potential purchasers such as institutional investors and individual (or retail) shareholders. The target audiences for the IPO are potential investing institutions, including pension funds, unit trusts and their analysts, who recommend whether the shares should be bought or sold. Private individuals will be targeted through private client stockbrokers and the financial press, although nowadays buying through the internet has become an easier way to buy stocks and shares, as the IPO of the Royal Mail demonstrated.

Mergers and acquisitions earn financial PR companies, along with a company's other advisers, large fees. This is also where reputations are made and broken. Brunswick Public Relations, for example, is one of the UK's leading financial PR consultancies in the mergers and acquisitions field. In 2013 it led the Mergermarket[3] M&A PR league table. In 2012 Brunswick worked on 75 deals throughout the world, worth a combined £77bn.

The company's reputation and subsequent growth was based on the work it did in mergers and acquisitions. The company was established by Paul Parker, who began his career at Broad Street Associates (see below). His father, Sir Peter Parker, was a former chairman of British Rail and a City grandee with an extensive range of contacts. Parker initially ran Brunswick from the front room of his parents' home. The big break came when the firm worked for ICI and played a major role in preventing the attempt by the Anglo-American conglomerate Hanson plc to take over the company. In a clever campaign largely played out in the media, Parker used a range of stories that appeared to cast doubt on the credibility and integrity of the Hanson management. They highlighted, for example, how racehorses owned by Lord White, the Hanson chief executive in the USA, were being paid for by the company. A private letter from Lord Hanson critical of the way his PR advisers, led by Sir Tim (now Lord) Bell, had handled the PR war was leaked to the press. In it, Hanson claimed that Parker was 'running circles around us' (Blackhurst, 2000). What better publicity could a firm have than praise from a rival company?

The growth of financial public relations

Financial PR companies advise and manage the communication process for a public company not only with the media but also with a company's financial stakeholders. The significance that a financial PR company has for a public company is illustrated by research carried out by stockbrokers Corporate Synergy. According to the survey, public companies rated their financial PR advisers second only in importance to their stockbrokers, and more important than other corporate advisers such as lawyers, bankers and accountants (Synergy, 2006).

Joint stock companies and their modern successors, the public companies, have practised a form of financial communication with investors and potential investors since the earliest days of both the joint stock companies and printed newspapers. However, the modern financial PR firm where professional intermediaries act on behalf of the company, is a relatively recent development.

During the 1950s and 1960s the City was an insular, hermetic world where staff recruitment to the main financial institutions that traditionally define 'the City' (the stockbrokers and merchant banks) was largely done through the school old-boys' network. This was a world where social contacts and connections arguably mattered more than talent and where the boardrooms of many public companies were often filled with peers of the realm, not necessarily because they knew anything about business but because their social contacts opened doors for companies into the City. A peer on the board provided the company with the appearance of solidity and respectability (Jeremy, 1998). Although in the 1960s the pattern of share ownership started to move away from retail (or individual) to institutional investors, the way that the shares were bought and sold had changed little in over a hundred years. The stockbrokers who traded shares on behalf of their clients (the investors) were separate from stock jobbers who made the markets on behalf of client companies. A stock jobber acted as a market maker, holding company shares on their books. Brokers, acting on behalf of their clients, would buy and sell shares from and to the stock jobbers. Stockbroking firms were small in terms of the numbers employed and were structured as partnerships where the principle on which business was transacted was 'trust' – between the client and between the partners. As the partners of a firm were jointly and severally liable for each other's debts, the principle of 'my word is my bond' really mattered.

Stockbrokers charged a fixed commission for their services and, while this produced a good living for the small band of elite traders, it was an almost amateurish way of operating, with typical late starts at 10.00 a.m. and long, alcohol-fuelled lunches. The City of London was seen as an extended 'gentlemen's club',[4] accessed only by the socially privileged and the well-connected (Jeremy, 1998).

With fixed commissions being their main source of income, there was no incentive for stockbrokers to try to create corporate activity or to increase their fees by making deals through, for example, the takeover of one public company by another. While flotations did occur, they were relatively modest in size.

This was the background against which the UK's first financial PR company was launched. In an environment where personal relationships dominated, communication with the media was seen as neither relevant nor important for most established public companies. John Addey, who launched John Addey Associates in 1970, was the UK's first recognised financial PR practitioner, and the ideal operator for the clubbable network of pre-Big Bang City of London. A former barrister, he knew that to succeed in this environment he had to have the right type of image, and cultivated his meticulously. He was, for example, always immaculately groomed, employed a butler and drove to business meetings in a Bentley convertible. His style of doing business was also perfectly suited to the 'City way' and based on using his extensive, personal City and media contacts (Coyle, 2004).

John Coyle (2004), then a journalist, recalls how he first met Addey: 'The telephone call came out of the blue from a man I had never met nor spoken to before. In fact I had never heard of him. I was working as a staff writer for the financial pages of a national Sunday newspaper.

He said, "John, I am the public relations consultant to a well-known financier and would dearly love to talk to you about him. Could you spare some time to have dinner with me at the Savoy?"' As an intrigued Coyle had never met anyone in public relations before, he accepted the invitation: 'The dinner was lavish, the benefactor was enthusiastic and as I recall, the waiter was tipped £10 for doing little more than supply vast amounts of expensive alcohol.' An impression was clearly made on Coyle, as he went on to become one of the most important financial PR consultants in the UK in the 1980s.

Media coverage was not regarded as a high priority for public companies at this time and, with few regulatory obligations pushing them, public companies distributed only limited amounts of information to financial journalists. Press releases, for example, when they were issued, were delivered by hand to the journalists, who had little formal opportunity to follow up a release or ask questions of the company executives. There was limited contextual information available, as few stockbrokers provided research to enable comparisons to be made between the performances of different companies. The value and worth of a company could be assessed only through the published financial figures such as the profits it had made, the dividends paid out and the share performance over the long term.

This limited world was, however, ideal for a practitioner such as John Addey, who could and did shape media opinion through his personal influence and contacts with journalists. As the first financial PR company, John Addey Associates provided a foundation for many individuals who started their careers working for him.

Tim Jackaman of Square Mile Communications said of Addey, 'As far as I'm concerned, all the thoroughbred horses in this industry have come from one stallion and that stallion is John Addey. He really invented the whole genre of financial PR. He was a very successful chap, as sharp as anything and charming, too. Importantly, he had a good head for figures and ran a line between clients and journalists brilliantly. In his heyday he was a colossus' (Blackhurst, 2000: 15).

Big Bang

In 1986 the safe, comfortable, closed world of the City was shattered by a series of regulatory changes now known as Big Bang, an unintended consequence of which was to give the financial PR industry a major boost.

Big Bang is the collective name for a series of regulatory changes that affected not just the City but the whole financial services sector. Although Big Bang is principally identified with the Conservative administration of Mrs Thatcher, the idea that the City needed freeing from closed, restrictive practices had in fact been circulating among politicians for a number of years (Jeremy, 1998). The wide-ranging regulatory changes fundamentally transformed the financial services industry. Competition was introduced into the previously closed world of the building societies, enabling them to compete with banks by allowing them to expand their range of services by offering current accounts in addition to savings accounts. Banks were allowed to compete with the building societies in the home-buyer lending market by offering mortgages. Restrictions were also removed on the amount that could be lent and borrowed, and this would lead in the future to Britain having high levels of both corporate and personal debt. These are the real historical roots of the 2008 financial crisis (Hutton, 1995; Jeremy, 1998).

In the City, the restrictions that had separated the jobbers from the brokers were removed, allowing the development of so-called 'integrated' house banks, while other financial institutions were allowed to buy brokers and jobbers or establish their own. Probably the most significant consequence was that freeing up the market gave large foreign financial institutions the opportunity to buy into London firms. This would transform small firms into large ones and also (and of longer-term impact), change the culture and the way that business was conducted (Jeremy, 1998).

When the tumult created by these changes finally settled down, the result was that London's financial services industry was dominated by a small number of large, powerful banks largely controlled by US or Swiss financial institutions. Foreign ownership brought with it not only new management and funds to finance large transactions but, crucially, a different and more aggressive culture. Out, for example, went fixed commission remuneration, to be replaced by a bonus culture driven by personal motivation. Success in deals in such transactions as contested takeovers, mergers and IPOs was incentivised by bonuses, resulting in personal rewards of large bonus payments. The Kay Review (2012: 19) summarised the changes brought about by Big Bang: 'The norms of the City of London were significantly affected by the pre-eminent role established by US investment banks which favoured transactions and trading over relationships and whose style was imitated by their European counterparts. This cultural shift was associated with a rapid rise in share prices 1982–2000.' We need look no further than the crash of 2008 and the subsequent problems faced by the banks such as Barclays to see what the effect of a bonus-driven culture can be on an institution.

The privatisation of the former power utilities (such as the electricity and water companies) and the IPOs of former building societies helped to create a stock-market boom which encouraged more transactions. The combination of financial institutions which had access to larger amounts of capital and a rising stock market meant there was finance available for companies that wanted to do deals. As remuneration for executives at the City's merchant banks and stockbrokers became increasingly transaction driven, teams in the corporate finance departments of accountants, merchant banks and banks, became proactive. Instead of waiting for potential deals to come to them, they searched public and private companies looking for potential deals. They would then approach companies to try to 'sell' them the deal. The types of transactions included private companies going public through a stock market listing or existing quoted companies using their shares to expand by acquiring other companies through agreed or contested mergers and acquisitions.

The resulting flurry of flotations, privatisations or takeovers, whether contested or agreed, required management of the communication process. Contested takeover bids made excellent newspaper copy, enlivening the sometimes dry and repetitive copy of financial and business journalism. This was especially true when the fight was reduced to an assessment about the contrasting management styles of the two opposing chief executives. Stories were sometimes spiced with salacious personal details of the characters involved. The media became increasingly important in determining the outcome of these takeovers, which meant that controlling and managing this process could become crucial in determining the outcome of a bid.

As financial PR grew, specialists in different types of activity began to emerge. Some firms for example, concentrated on the flotations of the former utilities and large financial institutions such as the Halifax Building Society. These often required a great deal of investor relations management work (see below). Other firms, such as Brunswick, specialised in contested takeovers. The growing stock market during the 1980s also encouraged a number of smaller companies to float on the Stock Exchange, either to realise value for shareholders or to raise new capital to grow the business.

Such flotations produced their own specialists. Peter Binns for example, became the specialist financial PR consultant to smaller companies; at its height, his company, Binns Cornwall, founded in 1980, had 178 clients. Following a split in the firm, one of the companies that emerged, Buchanan Communications, remains one of the specialists in the IPO field.

The financial PR company that handled most of the privatisations on behalf of the government was Dewe Rogerson, which was responsible for approximately 90% of the privatisations. Starting with the British Telecom campaign, it went on to handle the privatisations of Britoil, British Gas, Trustee Savings Bank, British Petroleum, British Steel and the water and electricity industries. Many criticised the government for putting so much power into the hands of one firm, which was responsible not only for the financial PR but also for choosing the advertising agencies (Chapman, 2011).

Dewe Rogerson is now part of Citigate Dewe Rogerson, and although it now handles a broader range of work than IPOs, it continues to work on them, handling, for example, the flotation of the Royal Mail in 2013. In the argument about whether Royal Mail was undervalued at the time of the float, the following comment made by Chapman when reviewing a similar argument about the under-pricing of the floats in the 1980s is appropriate: 'It is probably too cynical to believe that the Thatcher government priced the issues at bargain basement prices to curry favour with the electorate. Each issue could have been priced at more than 15% more and still been highly popular. I prefer the conspiracy theory: that the city, ever ready to look at the short term, saw the opportunity of making a quick buck and seized it' (Chapman, 2011).

Investor relations

The flotations of the former building societies and their transformation into public companies, along with newly privatised companies such as British Telecom and British Gas plc, created companies with large numbers of shareholders. When the Halifax Building Society floated in June 1997, between spring 1996 and June 1997 it sent out 65 million separate communications. On its first day of trading 76 million people owned shares worth £18bn (Pugh, 1998). Communicating with large volumes of shareholders required specialist skills and opened up a new phase of financial communication and eventually developed its own field: investor relations (IR).

In the UK the Investor Relations Society defines the practice as 'the management of the relationship between a company with publicly traded securities and the holders or potential holders of such securities'. According to Marston (1996: 478), 'Investor Relations can be defined as the link between a company and the financial community, providing information to help the financial community and investing public evaluate a company.' While the growth of IR in the UK was driven by privatisation and IPO floats, in the USA, according to Hayagreeva and Sivakumar (1999), it was driven by the growth in social activism and the need for companies to respond to outsiders.

Originally, IR was carried out by a financial PR company, and while many firms continue to provide such a service, nowadays most investor relations departments, especially at large quoted companies, tend to be in-house. When the investor relations function is carried out in-house it is, significantly, often separate from the communications/PR department. The company senior executive in charge can be the chief executive but is more usually the finance director (Marston and Straker, 2001). Communication with a company's key financial audiences is achieved not indirectly through a channel such as the printed media but by more direct methods of communication such as roadshows and one-to-one conversations either in person or by telephone. Communication is also carried out electronically through the company website, webinars, webcasts and conference calls.

Hostile/contested takeover battles

Hostile or contested takeover battles are where when one public company attempts to take over another public company. In an agreed takeover the management of both companies settle on a price for the shares of the target company. A contested or hostile takeover bid is, as it suggests, very different. In the 1980s, as a rising stock market added value to the shares of public companies and financial institutions had money to lend, companies embarked on acquisition sprees. As deals became bigger by value, takeover mania seemed to grip corporate UK, sometimes involving the UK's leading companies. Many of these battles were fought out in the media glare, as the financial PR companies recognised that media support could influence shareholder perception about a takeover. Sometimes in a contested takeover battle the tactics used were to try to hurt the reputation of one company's management through placing damaging stories about it.

In 1996 Granada plc launched a hostile takeover bid for the hotels and leisure company Forte. Both companies had their advisory teams of stockbrokers, financial advisers, accountants and the by-now the essential PR consultants. Granada appointed Citigate, in addition to its own in-house team, while Forte used Brunswick and Makinson Cowell. 'As part of the conflict the two sides expended significant resources in trying to control communication channels and influence media coverage' (Davis 2000: 288).

However, despite both sides producing over 200 press releases, 'Most of the communications work was carried out in telephone conversations and private meetings with journalists, analysts and fund managers. Since the written output of respected commentators helped to influence shareholders (75,000 of them), every major journalist, editor and analyst also became a target. Both sides used favourable analyst quotes in their public documents and in the information sent to journalists' (Davis, 2000: 288).

Davis demonstrates the success of the PR advisers in turning the media attention to the perceived weaknesses of the management. Over 13% of the points and arguments of the stories raised personal points about Rocco Forte and his family, and Forte was accused of being a nepotistic, family-run firm. The focus of the Granada campaign was to attack the management style of Forte and the personalities of the Forte family. 'The Fortes, although well-connected in certain political circles, were poorly perceived in "the City" along with their anachronistic management practices ...' (Davis, 2000: 288). By placing stories about Rocco Forte's love of country sports pursuits such as shooting, the campaign attempted to paint him as a part-time, remote figure who was out of touch with everyday concerns. In contrast, actual arguments about financial issues focusing largely on Forte's poor returns to shareholders accounted for only 7.8% of the articles.

On the Forte side, the largest number (12.5%) of negative comments argued that the proposed deal had no industrial logic and that Granada was an asset stripper. Significantly, the majority of their articles (16.5%) focused on the returns to shareholders that had been made by the company by carrying out a number of disposals.

'Financial spin-doctoring began with the presentation of very different sets of figures [from the companies]. At every opportunity the Granada campaign compared Forte's poor results to Granada's own impressive ones' (Davis 2000: 284). Davis found that contributions from both sides dominated the newspaper coverage – out of the 425 articles/features/comments on the bid, 383 (901%) included contributions from Granada, Forte or both sides. The newspapers 'Included figures, quotations and/or arguments supplied by those companies or they discussed such contributions in comment pieces. Even where journalists showed scepticism about the information they received, they rarely offered alternative arguments or figures' (Davis, 2000: 294).

One of the most successful of the companies specialising in mergers and acquisitions in the 1980s was Broad Street Associates, founded by Brian Basham, a protégé of John Addey's. Basham had been a financial journalist at the *Daily Mail*, the *Daily Telegraph* and *The Times*, joining John Addey Associates in 1972 and leaving in 1976 to form Broad Street Associates with John Coyle (the journalist wined and dined by Addey). Broad Street itself eventually became a public company with an annual turnover of £15m. As Addey defined financial PR in the 1970s, so Basham and Coyle's Broad Street defined financial PR in the 1980s, developing a reputation for high-profile and aggressive PR.

Basham's 'trade mark was carrying out detailed investigations of his opponents' strengths and weaknesses which were then used in the takeover' (Blackhurst, 2000). As specialists in the hostile takeover, Basham and Coyle were involved in almost all the big deals of the time, such as the Hanson and United Biscuits' bid for Imperial Group and Argyll's unsuccessful battle with Guinness for Distillers. Basham's reputation and style were perhaps best epitomised by an incident that occurred after he had left Broad Street and set up a new company, Warwick Corporate, in 1991. The incident perfectly illustrates how some financial PR companies thought it perfectly legitimate to attack personally the management of the opposition company. Basham's client was British Airways (BA), for whom he had acted since the mid-1980s. In 1993 Virgin Airways boss Richard Branson accused BA of fighting a 'dirty tricks' smear campaign against his company, Virgin Atlantic. Basham, according to Branson, undermined his and the company's reputation in the City and the media by spreading unsubstantiated rumours. After the spate of suing and counter-suing for libel the case was settled in January 1993, BA paid Branson £610,000 plus costs, along with an apology, and ended its association with Basham.

The size of the deals and the fees that could be earned by the financial PR companies pushed some of them to use any tactics to achieve their ends. In 1995, for example, during a disputed takeover between the construction company Amec and the company bidding for it, the Norwegian shipping company Kvaerner, the financial PR company acting on behalf of Amec was censured by the Takeover Panel for leaking price-sensitive information about it to the media concerning profit expectations. This was in breach of the Takeover Code in operation at the time and served as a warning to other financial PR companies that they, like other advisers such as lawyers and accountants, were also governed by the Code.

One of the most notorious tactics used by financial PR companies was known as the 'Friday night drop'. Its purpose was simple: to try to influence the financial headlines in the Sunday newspapers, and especially the *Sunday Times* and *Sunday Telegraph*, as it was believed they set the media agenda for the rest of the week. The practice, which was eventually outlawed by the Financial Services Authority, involved a financial PR consultant phoning a newspaper contact on Friday evening and offering them an unaccredited exclusive. This could range from a favourable stockbroker's report on a client, to information on a possible takeover target. The rationale for this, rightly or wrongly, was that Sunday was the one day that key influencers actually had time to sit down and read a story, so getting favourable newspaper coverage would control the agenda. Sometimes the story used information that bordered on insider trading.

The modern financial PR consultancy

Most of the early financial PR companies were formed by former financial journalists because they had the media contacts, knew the language and style of the paper and could write stories that would get covered. At one time in the 1970s and 1980s financial PR was dominated by former financial journalists, who moved seamlessly from one field into another.

The modern financial PR consultancy is a more sophisticated organisation, offering a wider range of services than simply media relations, many of them reflecting the global ambition and reach of their clients. As the range of services offered by companies has grown, so has the range of skills required of employees. The changing employment pattern at a financial PR consultancy is demonstrated by research carried out by HCfCCR into employment at twelve of the UK's leading financial PR consultancies. While those with a journalism background are the largest single category (19%), this is followed by those with an investment/merchant banking background (11%), which illustrates the importance of the City as an audience. Talking to this audience is an important aspect of modern financial PR.

The former journalists are not, however, former hacks looking for a career in PR because there is no other career option available to them. They include high-profile former business editors of some of the UK's most prestigious newspapers. For example, the senior ranks in financial PR companies include two former business editors from the *Sunday Times*; a former *Guardian* City editor; a *Daily Telegraph* investment column editor, and also its former City news editor; four former staff at the BBC's Business and Economics unit; and a former editor of the *Sun*.

Having former financial journalists working in financial PR does have advantages for journalists. 'Understanding what we are looking for is very important. PRs need to know our approach and send us relevant and appropriate material, they have to understand how we might treat the story and what we can or cannot do' (Butterick, 2012d), said one business editor. While claiming that having a background in financial media does not necessarily mean that PR practitioners have any special privileges, it clearly makes a difference if you are approached by an ex-colleague with a story.

> Financial journalism is such a specialised area, all the London-based journalists for example know each other where they came from. Even if you are working on a rival newspaper you might spend more

time on a story with colleagues from rival news organisations. So if someone you know contacts you about a story then, yeah you are going to look at that before you look at what someone you don't know says. (Butterick, 2012d)

One significant trend has been the merger between financial companies, creating bigger companies that can provide a global level of service for their clients.

For the larger financial PR companies, their growth and development has reflected the global ambitions and aspirations of their clients. Global growth has been achieved either by opening their own international offices or through a merger with another company, which in addition to global reach also has complementary services. What was the UK's largest financial PR company, Financial Dynamics, was bought in 2009 by FTI Consulting and now terms itself a multi-agency management consultancy. In 2012 FTI Consulting topped the global table in terms of deal volume, working on 94 deals worth US$44bn. FTI Consulting now claims to have 700 'expert strategic communications consultants in more than 25 key markets around the world' (www.fticonsulting.co.uk).

In addition to international growth, financial PR companies have also expanded the range of services they offer. One of the most critical areas has been the linking of financial PR with public affairs, through either mergers or opening their own subsidiaries to offer clients a seamless influence in business media and politics, demonstrated by the increasing amount of pro-business legislation being passed by governments.

The first links between financial PR and public affairs were established by the powerful New Labour PR machine. Brian Basham claims to have taught Peter Mandelson, the Director of Communications at the Labour Party and a future cabinet minister, the benefits of leaking information to the media. 'I was the one who coached Mandelson, I had to explain to him that news and information had become a currency' (Jones quoted in Mair and Keeble, 2009). Jones (2002, 174) points out how, in a direct copy of the 'Friday drop', New Labour began to use the Sunday newspapers for its exclusives to try to set the weekly political agenda: 'A late breaking story in the Sunday evening bulletins suits the spin doctors because it helps build up interest and Sunday newspapers hope that the extra publicity might generate additional sales.'

What is emerging is a new power base: a metropolitan political and business elite linked by social and business ties which are just as close as the pre-Big Bang City. One firm, Finsbury, epitomises the growing connection between financial PR and corporate lobbying and the almost seamless connection that links the metropolitan elite of the corporate class to the political classes.

Finsbury was founded by Millfield and Oxford-educated Kevin Rudd in 1994. Rudd started off as a researcher and policy co-ordinator for the Social Democrat Party founder David Owen before moving into journalism. He worked at *The Times* and *Financial Times* before leaving to set up Finsbury. Through a series of mergers, this has now become RLM Finsbury, which, in a 2013 poll of financial journalists, was rated as the UK's leading financial PR consultancy.

When Britain's credit crisis began in late 2007 two of Rudd's contacts were to prove invaluable to another social associate. Robert Peston, the BBC's business editor, broke the story that the Northern Rock bank could no longer balance its books. Rudd was handling the bank's PR. A year later Peston got the scoop that Lloyds TSB, headed by Sir Victor Blank, was about to step in and rescue its foundering rival, HBOS. There had been fears that a run on the bank could wreck the deal. But Peston's exclusive saw the HBOS share price rally.

This connection between financial PR and lobbying serves only to strengthen the grip that business has. Through financial PR it can and does influence our perceptions of the way that corporates are viewed, and through its lobbying activities it can and does influence the political agenda.

11

Financial journalism: its role in the creation of economic paradigms

For over 200 years the business and finance pages of newspapers have played an important but largely unacknowledged role in the dissemination and discussion of different economic philosophies. In the early nineteenth century economic philosophers and writers used contemporary journals to debate new philosophical, social and economic ideas. The journals were an 'opinion forming' medium: 'The *Edinburgh Review* itself proved extraordinarily successful in transmitting to the British political class and to the educated public at large the central ideals of 'philosophical whiggism' (Parsons, 1989: 21). The *Edinburgh Review*, with a circulation of 50,000, was influential in spreading the economic doctrines of Scottish political economy. Some political economists were prolific writers. J. S. Mill, for example, wrote for a range of journals such as *Westminster Review, Edinburgh Review, Harper's Magazine* and the *Fortnightly Review*, expounding his economic and social thinking.

What characterised many commentators of this period was their ability to write on a wide range of issues, not only 'economics'. Writers such as Richard Cobden, David Hume and Jeremy Bentham were as much social commentators and political philosophers as they were economic theorists. This was a period of economic, political and intellectual flux and their writings reflected the huge structural changes that were taking place in society. While some commentators articulated the concerns and worries of the community, others attempted to explain, rationalise and justify what was happening as modern working practices were brutally and painfully imposed on both people and the landscape. 'The chief legacy of the political economists in terms of journalism was that of shaping the discourse of economic opinion rather than the diffusion of their economic theories' (Parsons, 1989: 22).

While by the mid-1850s Adam Smith's free market philosophy had established itself as the dominant economic paradigm, the writer who best articulates the worldview and outlook of the Victorian industrialist was the former journalist Samuel Smiles, author of *Self-Help*. Published in 1855, the book sold 20,000 copies in one year and developed the *laissez-faire* philosophy by recounting the lives of men who, through the virtues of perseverance, energy, thoroughness, honesty, thrift, self-reliance and common sense – in short, self-help – achieved their social goals. What made the book significant was that for many successful Victorian businessmen it described their personal path to success.

Socially, the impact of *laissez-faire* economic philosophy created an atomistic, individualist, self-help society where unemployment and poverty were regarded as the consequence of an individual's actions. The poor had in effect brought their condition on themselves. There was no commentary in the newspapers or journals on how economic forces impacted on society and thus on the causes of unemployment and poverty. The word 'unemployment', for instance, only entered the *Oxford English Dictionary* in 1888 (Parsons, 1989). By the 1880s the success of *laissez-faire* economic philosophy was further demonstrated to its supporters by the UK's worldwide dominance in industrial markets.

With *laissez-faire* established as the dominant economic paradigm, commentary in the newspapers began to change, moving away from general arguments about the fundamentals of economic philosophy. Comment instead became focused on specific events and issues that might affect the trading activities of companies. The aggressive form of new financial journalism as seen in the pages of the *Daily Mail*, *Financial News*, *Financial Times* and *The Times* had no room for debate about the nature of economic activity.

The effect of this was that, from the late 1880s, economics became disengaged from the wider community, becoming a largely academic discipline increasingly only practised and written about by those with a degree in economics. The Royal Economics Society was created in 1890, the London School of Economics opened in 1895 and the Cambridge Economics Tripos was developed in 1903. Such events mark the development of the 'professional' academic economist who, in true academic form, believed that academics should talk only to other academics. This 'professionalisation' encouraged the growth of academic journals to facilitate communication between academics. The *Quarterly Journal of Economics* was founded in 1886 and the *Economic Journal* in 1890. Economists largely disappeared from the popular press.

The most important economist at the end of the nineteenth century was Alfred Marshall, whose *Principles of Economics* (1890) became the main economic textbook in the UK for many years. While still holding firmly to the *laissez-faire* tradition, Marshall was the founder of a neoclassical economics at the core of which was the attempt to improve the mathematical rigour of economics and transform it into a more scientific profession. *Principles of Economics* concentrated on technical issues such as elasticity, consumer surplus, increasing and diminishing returns, and marginal utility.

Economics became less interested in macro issues and more concerned with a statistical, factual, detailed approach. Indicative of the way that economic debate retreated from mainstream newspapers to become the preserve of university academics was the approach of the so-called marginalists, who did not believe in debating issues in public. Significantly, the most successful magazine established to try to emulate the success of the *Economist* was *The Statist*, which used statistical information in economic arguments and objective, fact-based reporting.

The history of financial and business journalism demonstrates that a dominant economic paradigm begins to break down when it no longer appears to provide answers to economic problems. The dominant paradigm is questioned by alternatives, and during these periods the media becomes one of the key battlegrounds through which new ideas emerge. This was epitomised in the 1930s, when Keynes deliberately used newspapers and magazines to challenge and then proselytise his economic theories. We can also see how this occurred again in the 1970s as Keynesianism broke down and new ideas began to emerge.

The rise of neoliberalism

What we now call neoliberalism emerged in the late 1930s, becoming a shorthand term to describe an economic philosophy with several different strands. However, the core of all neoliberal thinking is the basic belief in the liberalisation of the economy through the privatisation of state assets, deregulation of rules, free trade and open markets, decreasing the size of the public sector and enabling the private sector to grow.

Keynesianism emerged as the dominant economic paradigm at the end of the Second World War, largely because the theory had been proved in practice. The theoretical analysis had been vindicated by the impact of the practical policies in solving economic problems. Everyone, it seemed, from ordinary people to politicians and economists, accepted that Keynes's analysis of the policies required to lift a country out of a recession had been correct. However, despite this almost universal acceptance there was an influential core of free market or *laissez-faire* economic theorists who refused to accept that either Keynesian analysis or the resulting policies had been responsible for solving any of the economic problems of the 1930s. They also rejected the Keynesian interpretation that the 1930s depression had been caused by the pursuit of conventional free market-based policies, arguing instead that it was the result of a massive contraction of the money supply. Furthermore, key neoliberal economists such as Milton Friedman and Friedrich Hayek argued that the New Deal had not been responsible for saving the US economy (Stedman Jones, 2012). In the UK, the free market economists rejected the post-war political consensus established by the 1945 Labour government and the subsequent 1953 Conservative government.

The basis of neoliberal opposition to Keynes and any form of state intervention in economic matters is a conviction that the state has no role at all in framing or shaping economic policy. What matters to neoliberals, above all other considerations, is individual liberty; any intervention or action by the state must inevitably infringe individual liberty.

Friedrich Hayek was an Austrian-born free market economist whose philosophy was to influence the governments of both Margaret Thatcher and President Ronald Reagan. In his book *Road to Serfdom* (1940), he argued that what he called 'well-meaning' socialist policies would inevitably lead to the curtailment of economic and individual freedom. Preserving individual freedom and liberty mattered more than economic hardship because the 'market' would, when left unhindered, eventually solve all economic problems (Stedman Jones, 2012).

During the 1950s and 1960s Keynesian policies remained a relevant and appropriate analysis of the economic landscape. With the UK economy performing reasonably well, and both employment and living standards rising, the post-war economic consensus held. The economic policy pursued, albeit with a different emphasis, by successive Labour and Conservative governments was based on full employment. State intervention either in providing funds or in nationalisation, where appropriate, would be taken as a corrective action when the market failed. Any decision on when to intervene was made on pragmatic rather than ideological grounds. Unemployment was regarded by all the main political parties as the economic problem that must be avoided at all costs. This consensus politics between the Labour and the Conservative policies was derided by the *Economist* in 1954 as 'Butskellism'.[1]

During this period, as the economy performed reasonably, neoliberalism was side-lined and ignored, remaining on the fringes of mainstream economic debate because it offered no solutions to the economic problems of the day. Hayek, however, did not intend to remain in obscurity, but he recognised that in order to gain influence, neoliberals had to influence and shape opinion, just as the Fabian Society had influenced Labour Party policies. In 1947 Hayek founded the Mont Pelerin Society, an international discussion group composed of invited academics and a few selected journalists and business people. The society was devoted to the advancement of neoliberalism. Hayek believed that prevailing political opinion (including the dominant economic paradigm) was influenced and shaped by what he termed 'second-hand dealers in ideas' which included journalists, academics, teachers, publicists and novelists.

> These individuals – who usually had no particular claim to expertise themselves – drew on what they took to be the most fashionable expert opinions and broadcast them to a wider audience. The key to changing policy, Hayek argued, was therefore to change the minds of this opinion-forming stratum. This was why the think-tank became such an important weapon for neoliberals: it was a crucial instrument for changing the climate of opinion by persuading journalists, commentators and politicians that what they had previously regarded as out-of-date and intellectually unfashionable was, on the contrary, at the cutting edge of political thinking. (Jackson and Sandos, 2012: 44)

A number of think-tanks were established on both sides of the Atlantic to advance the neoliberal philosophy; these were financed by businesses to shape and influence political and economic thinking. Business was in effect supporting economic policies from which it would ultimately benefit through the introduction of policies such as curtailing the trades unions, and encouraging the idea that the sole function of a public company was to make a profit. Free market ideas gained political prominence in the UK and USA because of 'A concerted effort, sponsored by sympathetic business elites, to disseminate these ideas through a complex international network of institutions' (Jackson and Sandos, 2012: 45). Neoliberal activists targeted four key groups: business, sympathetic intellectuals, journalists and politicians.

The Institute of Economic Affairs (IEA), set up in the UK in 1955, provided a platform for Hayek and his ideas. This was followed by other think-tanks such as the Adam Smith Institute (established 1977) and the Centre for Policy Studies (established 1974). These were, and continue to be, financed by sympathetic right-wing businesses, many of which have benefited financially from the subsequent economic policies introduced by different governments. Significantly, they found a ready and sympathetic ear in some influential sections of the media.

In the 1970s the Western economies faced new economic problems when the cheap oil that had subsidised them suddenly ended. The oil-dependent West was confronted with an entirely different economic reality as costs rose dramatically and an old economic worry returned: inflation.

In the face of such problems Keynesian policies no longer seemed either relevant or appropriate, giving rise to an opportunity for economic alternatives. The changing economic conditions of the 1970s also polarised political opinion, and the post-war consensus that had broadly held between the main political parties broke down. From the fringes and margins of economic debate, neoliberals such as Hayek and Friedman began to find a more receptive audience.

Neoliberal economic analysis appeared to provide an explanation for what was causing the UK's economic problems in the 1970s: a combination of rising inflation and low productivity. The neoliberals argued that the cause of the problems was the Keynesian policies that had been pursued to maintain full employment – an argument eagerly adapted by the newspapers that the neoliberals used to advance their case. In an article in the *Daily Telegraph* Friedrich Hayek explained that 'The responsibility for current world-wide inflation, I am sorry to say, rests wholly and squarely with the economists, or at least the great majority of my fellow economists, who have embraced the teachings of Lord Keynes. What we are experiencing are simply the economic consequences of Lord Keynes' (Parsons, 1989: 189).

Neoliberals argued that a policy of full employment had two major negative side-effects that damaged the economy. Firstly, the public sector became too large, squeezing out the private sector by denying it resources; a large public sector also created an anti-enterprise culture. Secondly, with full or close to full employment, those in jobs were in a powerful position to demand high wages, which in turn caused inflationary pressures to grow. The situation in the UK was exacerbated, they argued, because of traditionally strong trade unions which enjoyed a number of legal privileges. The restrictive working practices that the trade unions were able to impose in many workplaces also affected the country's productivity. 'Unions, in particular, were to blame for creating unemployment and pressurising [*sic*] governments to undertake an inflationary expansion of the money supply' (Jackson and Sandos, 2012: 52).

Hayek wrote frequently and critically about the trade unions, making large claims about their adverse economic and social impact. According to Richardson (1993), little of his analysis was based on empirical evidence: 'The conclusion is that he was morally so offended by the extraordinary legal immunities which the trade unions had acquired that his judgment deserted him, so that he descended into a series of wholly untenable empirical assertions. His significant influence on thinking and policy on industrial relations matters, at least in the UK, looks to have been based far more on powerful emotions than on science' (Richardson, 1993: 2). Despite the lack of evidence, the eventual marginalisation and subsequent defeat of the trade unions became a major triumph of neoliberal ideology.

Like Keynes in the 1930s, Milton Friedman understood that the media had to be used to spread ideas and influence policy. However, in the 1970s and 1980s Friedman had access to more powerful media to expound his views: TV and radio. 'Professor Friedman's success in Britain owed much to the way in which he skilfully deployed instances of economic failure to discredit Keynesianism and promote the idea of controlling the money supply as the only alternative to state interventionism' (Parsons, 1989: 172).

However, it was the influence of two leading newspaper economic commentators of the 1970s and 1980s, Peter Jay of *The Times* and Samuel Brittan of the *Financial Times*, that provided the decisive intellectual support for neoliberalism. Jay (the son of Douglas Jay, see Chapter 5) and Brittan helped to take neoliberalism out of the backwaters of academic debate and provided it with the intellectual credibility that it needed.

In Britain, politicians such as Keith Joseph and Margaret Thatcher became convinced of neoliberal ideas through the journalism of both Jay and Brittan. The former journalist Nigel Lawson and Conservative MP Norman Lamont, both later Chancellors of the Exchequer, were also both convinced by their articles. Andrew Duguid, a former civil servant and member of Margaret Thatcher's Policy Unit, said, 'I do think that both [Brittan and Jay] were very important. Peter Jay who had these articles in *The Times* in which he would ... convey thoughts and ideas that he picked up from somewhere else to a different audience, so he was a channel of communication and Sam Brittan ... used to write so many think pieces and everybody in government read those pieces. You know, it would be on the lips of everyone at lunchtime, what has Sam written today sort of thing ... So he was very influential. They were two really important sources for the transmission of ideas in the direction of Britain [from the United States]' (quoted in Stedman Jones, 2012: 233).

Neither Jay nor Brittan was a 'political conservative' but both were convinced by the economic argument of the neoliberals that the 'British disease' of low productivity and high inflation had made the UK the 'sick man of Europe'.

Jay was sent to investigate economics in the US by William Rees-Mogg, editor of *The Times*, because he believed that this was the direction of new economic thinking. In the US, Jay was introduced to right-wing free market economics by a friend at the British embassy. Jay said: 'My friend began to open my eyes to what the Chicago based people were saying: what Milton Friedman was saying. I visited the University of Chicago, the Hoover Institute in Stanford, the Federal Reserve in St Louis, the great centres of monetarism. I met Friedman. He's a very attractive character. He has that wonderful Jewish humour and intellectuality. He became a good friend' (BBC2, 2006).

According to Samuel Brittan (1995: 20), 'In the middle years of the 1970s, Peter Jay who was then economics editor of *The Times* and I were regarded by many in the British economic establishment as two terrible monetarist twins. The charge was that, because of the coincidence of two people with such views having prominent positions in two heavy-weight newspapers, half-baked journalism was undermining economics. Some of our articles were even given to students as set-pieces for demolition.'

According to Keegan and Pennant-Rae (1979: 140),

> At times the traditional Keynesians in Whitehall complained bitterly in private about the degree to which the responsible press was in the hands of the monetarists. There was an interplay between the views of these commentators and the financial markets, which seemed to reinforce each other. This public campaign hardly weakened the hands of the burgeoning monetarist school within the Bank of England. And while protesting all the way that they were in any sense 'monetarists', ministers and the official machine reluctantly appeared to absorb a large part of the Friedman/Brittan/Jay message.

Peter Jay used his columns, lectures and articles to promote a change of direction in British economic policy and institutions. 'Jay for example, wrote that the assumption of Keynesians that, to "put more spending power into people's pocket, whether by cutting taxes, increasing government spending or easing credit conditions through monetary policy was harmful and wrong"' (Stedman Jones, 2012: 234).

According to Brittan, 'Jay and I had slightly different starting points. Nevertheless ... Jay never flinched from the implications of the new (or rediscovered) ideas on the ultimate futility of traditional full employment policies – witness his role in James Callaghan's famous speech to the 1976 Labour conference in which the former Prime Minister delivered his much cited speech about governments being able to spend their way to prosperity' (Brittan, 1995: 20).

Jay was the economics editor of *The Times* (1967–77) and economics editor of the BBC (1990–2001). He saw the rise of economic journalism as 'the by-product of a literary lacuna in British intellectual and political life' (Parsons, 1989: 183).

The great heritage of political economy, as developed in this country by Adam Smith, David Hume, David Ricardo, John Stuart Mill, Marshall and Keynes, is essentially a literary tradition orientated to the illumination and solution of real problems. It was perhaps inevitable that as fewer of the limited store of discoveries remained to be made, the hankering of economists for a more strictly scientific reputation should have steered the subject further and further away from broad general truths and the real world ... economics has offered diminishing returns to policy-makers. (Parsons, 1989: 184)

He was appointed by his father-in-law, the Labour Prime Minister James Callaghan, as ambassador to the USA between 1977 and 1979.

Samuel Brittan had been a conventional Keynesian in his youth, believing in full employment policies, which could be achieved through monetary expansion and deficit finance. According to Brittan, 'It was Professor Milton Friedman who removed the scales from my eyes – not by his more technical views on money, but by his analysis of the effects of demand management on unemployment' (Kynaston, 1998: 368). Brittan had in fact been taught by Friedman when he was at Cambridge in 1957, when Friedman had been a visiting professor.

Articles with a Friedmanite influence began to appear in Brittan's *Financial Times* 'Economic Viewpoint' column, their main thrust not so much an adoption of Friedman's specific views on correct monetary policy as a 'conversion' to Friedman's tenet that 'the authorities have no more than a temporary power to influence output and employment' (Kynaston, 1998: 368). As Kynaston states, 'One way or another, his column was doing much to set the intellectual agenda for the next decade or more' (Kynaston, 1998: 369).

The IEA played an important role during this period – organising visits and media briefings for Friedman, Hayek and other leading neoliberal figures. While the Brittan–Jay axis was probably the highest-profile source of support for neoliberalism at this time, there were a number of other significant sympathetic journalists. William Rees-Mogg, the editor of *The Times*, threw his authority behind monetarism when it was adopted as a policy by the Conservative Party. Ronald Butt, *The Times*'s political correspondent was also a supporter.

The editor of the *Daily Telegraph* between 1964–74 was Maurice Green, who had a background in economic journalism, and during this period he moved the paper firmly towards neoliberalism. He also encouraged contributions from the think-tanks, with Arthur Seldon, the joint founder and President of the IEA, a key contributor enjoying regular access to the paper's editorial pages. Between 1966 and 1979 the *Sunday Telegraph's* City editor was Patrick Hutber, also a close associate of the IEA and a regular at its events. 'The *Telegraph* was the paper with the closest links to the IEA and one where the IEA's work made the greatest impact on its editorial line' (Jackson and Sandos, 2012: 55).

Undoubtedly the support given by some newspapers to the neoliberals was almost certainly influenced by the industrial background of the UK newspaper industry, which was also affected by the economic crisis. In 1973–74 as the oil crisis developed, advertising revenues fell, the cost of newsprint rose and wage costs were high because of the strong trade union presence in the newspaper industry. 'For some commentators union control over the printing presses threatened free expression. In these circumstances it is not surprising that proprietors, editors and journalists were receptive to neoliberal analysis' (Jackson and Sandos, 2012: 53).

From the mid-1970s the *Financial Times*'s editorial line was increasingly neoliberal, attacking the post-war consensus and supporting moves by the Conservative Party for a 'social market economy'. 'The experience of both Labour and Tory governments in the past ten years suggests that the expansion of State influence over the economy and industry, and the replacement of market forces by bureaucratic decision, almost always has harmful consequences' (Kynaston, 1998: 405).

While neoliberalism and monetarism came to define the Conservative Party of Margaret Thatcher, at one point it was regarded as a policy that could in theory be adapted by any political party. The intellectual end of Keynesianism, for example, was marked not by the 1979 election of the government of Margaret Thatcher, but by a speech by Labour Prime Minister James Callaghan to the Labour Party conference on 28 September 1976. In a section that was, significantly, written by his son-in-law, Peter Jay, he said, 'We used to think that you could spend your way out of a recession and increase employment by cutting taxes and boosting government spending. I tell you in all candour that that option no longer exists and, in so far as it ever did exist, it only worked on each occasion by injecting a bigger dose of inflation into the economy, followed by a higher level of unemployment as the next step' (www. britishpoliticalspeech.org).

The intellectual climate changed rapidly in the UK, from one where all the political parties agreed on the policy of maintaining full employment, to the belief that the main economic problem was how to deal with inflation. 'The speed with which Keynesianism and many other beliefs in government support for the economy were displaced in dominant economic thinking by monetarist and then other neoliberal ideas was extraordinary' (Crouch, 2012: 15). This was highlighted by the triumph of neoliberals in international economic thinking. In 1974, for example, Friedrich Hayek was a joint winner of the Nobel Prize for Economics, and in 1976 the prize was awarded to Milton Friedman.

At the heart of the new dominant economic paradigm was an understanding about how inflation had not just destroyed the German economy before the Second World War but had brought about the destruction of society.

In the UK the neoliberal philosophy was translated into political policies by Mrs Thatcher, a politician with the conviction to pursue policies because she believed them to be right. Mrs Thatcher also had the political skill to translate economic policies into clear, simple messages that resonated with ordinary voters.

The first Conservative government, of 1979, adopted monetarism, an untried economic philosophy which, with its apparently simple economic prescriptions, seemed to offer radical solutions to control inflation. The ideological belief that it was correct was more important than any evidence that the policies were right. In fact there was no evidence that this economic policy worked, but this did not matter to the ideologues. In the *Observer* after the election of Mrs Thatcher, J. M. Galbraith said: 'Britain has, in effect, volunteered to be the Friedmanite guinea pig. There could be no better choice. Britain's political and social institutions are solid ... British phlegm is a good antidote for anger; but so is an adequate system of unemployment insurance' (quoted in Keegan, 2010).

Monetarism as an economic policy did not succeed because, while it appeared to have reduced inflation, it was not how it had predicted. In the mid-1970s the annual rate of inflation, at its highest, was over 20%; by the early 1980s it had been brought down to just over 4%. However, this had been achieved through high interest rates (at one point they were as high as 17%), which devastated UK manufacturing. The Conservative Chancellor of the Exchequer Norman Lamont described the growing unemployment as a 'price worth paying' for achieving low inflation.

There is a tendency to assume that when monetarism was ditched by the Conservatives this marked the end of neoliberalism in the UK. In fact the economic and social policies carried out by Mrs Thatcher's and John Major's Conservative governments were the essence of neoliberalism. Both administrations enthusiastically embraced privatisation (a fundamental of neoliberal philosophy), combined with reducing the public sector's share in direct and indirect provision of goods and services to business and the community.

What needs to be remembered about neoliberalism is that it is more than an economic philosophy; it is also a social philosophy which aims to radically transform society. The policies pursued by successive Conservative administrations, including the Coalition government formed in May 2010, were to promote the role of market forces, encourage the mobility of capital and labour and stimulate global market forces. Cutting direct taxes expanded the scope for the operation of market forces through enhanced investor and consumer choice. While monetarism may have failed as an economic policy, neoliberalism, shrinking the state, privatising the public sector, decreasing the power of the trade unions – were all successful.

When Tony Blair famously said that ideology was dead, this might have been seen as an acknowledgement of New Labour's acceptance of neoliberalism. While there were distinct differences between the social policies of New Labour and the Conservatives, both pursued neoliberal policies. The modification of neoliberalism by the Labour government was to appease its own supporters, who were largely suspicious of its economic policies. New Labour adopted socially inclusive social policies so as to mitigate some of the harsher effects of those policies through state action. These social policies included the economic regeneration of marginalised communities and attempts to alleviate individual, family and child poverty through 'stealthy' redistribution measures –for example. Gordon Brown's efforts as Chancellor of the Exchequer to introduce the redistributive policies had to be made secretively and surreptitiously, because of the hostility of most of the media towards such measures.

From its time in opposition New Labour had attempted to win over the business community through what became known as its 'prawn-cocktail' offensive. A succession of shadow ministers were deployed to speak at meetings with business and financial leaders. The party also used organisations such as the Labour Finance and Industry Group to open up channels of communication and deployed businessmen such as Chris Haskins, the chairman of Northern Foods, to promote Labour policies. New Labour realised that while it could never completely win over the business pages, although the *Financial Times* did support it, it could at least command grudging respect for the change it had gone through.

A new economic paradigm?

With the distance of time it is easy to forget how traumatic the events of 2008–9 were. The collapse of Lehman Brothers and the seizing up of the financial markets were indicative of a deeper and wider malaise; there was a very real fear of a banking collapse with untold economic and social consequences. There was a popular response to the failure of capitalism. New protest movements such as 'Occupy' emerged in New York and London and quickly spread throughout the world as an expression of popular discontent with 'the system' that had so clearly failed. It really did seem at the time that a fundamental challenge to capitalism was emerging, such was the depth of anger at the activities of the banks and the system that had produced the financial crisis. Some saw or hoped that the 2008 financial crisis and its aftermath would be the 'apotheosis' of neoliberalism (Stedman Jones, 2012) and that the crisis that had been produced by an unregulated financial sector unhindered by state control would lead to a more pragmatic relationship between the state and industry/business.

Stuart Hall (cited in Davison and Harrison, 2015: 98) argues that 'There was a moment at the height of the financial implosion when questions were raised that went far deeper than the economic. They went beyond hostility to individual bankers – to touch upon, and question, the philosophy of greed and self-interest that underpinned their wealth and our crisis. Questions were raised of the wider ideological framing of life, and questions of ethics too. There were, for a moment, glimmerings of the possibility that the ideological underpinnings of the economy itself might be brought into the light and acknowledged.'

However, despite the dissatisfaction, just two years later in the UK, in May 2010, a Coalition government between the Conservative and Liberal Democrat parties took power following the general election. At the core of its programme was a commitment to reducing the government's national debt over the lifetime of the Parliament. This was to be achieved by a programme of massive cuts in government spending and increased taxation. The programme was presented as a tough but rational response to the huge debt incurred by the previous Labour administration, which had spent recklessly and irresponsibly. 'Cleaning up Labour's mess' was the mantra repeated *ad nauseam* by Coalition ministers on every media appearance. However, under this excuse what the Coalition government was actually enacting was a further phase of neoliberal social and economic philosophy, including the opportunity to launch an attack on probably the most important example of positive state activity: the NHS.

The financial and business pages played an important if not a key role in helping to provide an intellectual justification for the austerity argument. This is illustrated in the coverage of two main issues in the financial and business pages – both reflecting the rationale of the government. The first was on the need for the austerity to be pursued and how there was no alternative. This argument would often be bolstered by a supporting statement from a business source. The second issue was on the danger that the UK would lose its AAA rating by the credit agencies if austerity policies were not introduced.

Wren-Lewis (2015) describes the macro-economic coverage in the majority of the media as 'Mediamacro'. Among other things, he argues, it 'Puts much more emphasis on financial markets and on the views of participants in those markets and prefers simple stories to complex analysis. So after the 2010 election (and to some extent before it) mediamacro had bought with barely a murmur the view that reducing the government deficit was the top priority. It even bought a second story, which was that the previous Labour government had played a large part in creating the deficit in the first place.'

Although austerity has been presented as a rational, non-party political policy that all the mainstream parties should adopt, it is in fact deeply ideological and the continuance of neoliberalism under another guise.

Austerity is the 'policy of cutting the state's budget to promote growth' (Blyth, 2013: 2). It 'is a form of voluntary deflation in which the economy adjusts through the reduction of wages, prices and public spending to restore competiveness, which is (supposedly) best achieved by cutting the state's budgets, debts and deficits. Doing so, its advocates believe, will inspire "business confidence" since the government will neither be "crowding-out" the market for investment by sucking up all the available capital through the issue of debt nor adding to the nation's already "too big" debt.'

Reducing government expenditure and the overall size of government, which, it was said, was 'crowding-out' the private sector, and as a consequence reducing the opportunities for job creation, are all familiar *laissez-faire* /neoliberal arguments.

In considering why a new economic paradigm did not emerge from the 2008 financial crisis and the widespread dissatisfaction, we have to remember how long it took for neoliberalism to emerge and consolidate its position. Neoliberalism, as we demonstrated in the previous chapter, is now embedded into our common sense and our language. However, austerity and neoliberalism have not delivered the widespread economic benefits that were promised. Instead we have seen society become more polarised, and with wealth being held by fewer rather than the many, the economic benefits of neoliberalism are being questioned, with many business leaders questioning the growing inequality that seems to be the inevitable consequence of neoliberalism.

This dislocation and dissatisfaction with business might provide the seeds of a new more inclusive and just paradigm. Significantly, some business and financial journalists have played a key role in exposing and highlighting practices such as tax avoidance by major corporations that have helped to fuel the dissatisfaction. An analysis of this role in the next chapter will enable us to consider the key question: what should be the function of financial and business journalism – to act as an uncritical cheerleader for business or to adopt a more critical function? If the latter, then this could also lead to a new, more critical and questioning type of financial and business journalism.

12

The future of financial and business journalism

Financial bubbles and the financial media.

A number of writers and commentators have attempted to identify the underlying causes of financial bubbles and manias. For the earliest writer who attempted this, Charles Mckay, writing in 1852 in his *Memoirs of Extraordinary Popular Delusions and the Madness of Crowds*, the reasons were quite clear. It was a collective type of madness that could be found elsewhere; for him, the investors in financial schemes such as 'The Mississippi scheme, the South Sea Bubble, Tulipomani were possessed with the same irrationality as those who believed in and practiced, "alchymists", fortune-tellers, astrologers, Magnetisers and the "The Influence of Politics and Religion on the Hair and the Beard" Money ... has often been a cause of the delusion of multitudes. Sober nations have all at once become desperate gamblers and risked almost their existences upon the turn of a piece of paper' (McKay, 1852: 3).

John K. Galbraith (1993) identified a 'financial euphoria' common to episodes such as the South Sea Bubble, the crash of 1929, the original Ponzi scheme and investment frauds in the 1990s run by Bernie Caulfield and Donald Trump. Investors and financiers in such schemes, Galbraith argues, experience a

> Mass escape from reality that excludes any serious contemplation of the true nature of what is taking place [there is an] extreme brevity of the financial memory – financial disaster is quickly forgotten ... In further consequence, when the same or similar circumstances occur again, sometimes in only a few years, they are hailed by a new often youthful and always supremely self-confident generation as a brilliant, innovative discovery in the financial and larger economic world. There can be few fields of

human endeavour in which history counts for so little as in the world of finance. (1993: 12)

Kindleberger and Aliber (2005), in their analysis of the causes behind financial crises, argued that a distinction should be made between a financial crisis and a mania. A financial crisis has potentially devastating economic, political and social consequences on society. They follow a pattern starting with an invention or discovery which attracts businesses and entrepreneurs into a market looking to exploit it. To finance their business activities they borrow money, and often overstretch themselves by borrowing too much, which then precipitates a credit and financial crisis.

A mania, however, while dramatic, is infrequent and 'Associated with the expansion phase of the business cycle, in part because the euphoria associated with the mania leads to an increase in spending. The features of these manias are never identical yet there is a similar pattern to them. There is an increase in share and commodity prices or real estate; household wealth increases and so does spending. There is a sense of euphoria of "we never had it so good". Eventually asset prices peak and begin to decline' (Kindleberger and Aliber, 2005: 9).

Euphoria and excitement are, then, common elements surrounding financial bubbles, and in earlier chapters we have explored the role that newspapers have played in helping to create and encourage such an atmosphere. Sometimes this has been deliberately fostered by fraudulent publications and unscrupulous journalists keen to try to profit financially from rising share prices. More often, though, it has been by default – because the journalists writing about the situation have not understood how bubbles emerge and how they, the journalists, might, by a certain style of writing, encourage euphoria and excitement. The form of financial and business journalism most closely associated with helping to create such an atmosphere is share tipping.

The share tippers, market commentators, have long been associated with financial and business journalism and the two main approaches of this type of financial journalism illustrate the ethical pressures that they operate under. In 2008, Tambini's survey found that 'Some specialist business and financial journalists see their role entirely in terms of provision of information to investors and their primary responsibility in terms of helping them make successful investment decisions' (Tambini, 2010: 8).

On one side are the unscrupulous financial journalists, such as the *Daily Mirror* City Slickers with their advice to 'pile in and hear the lion roar', operating without any apparent regard for how their advice might impact on the readers. In fact there is evidence to demonstrate that modern financial and business journalists take their role responsibly, continuing the tradition of Charles Duguid, Derek Dale and Kenneth Fleet. This role and function is a serious one and should be exercised with responsibility; the share ramping epitomised by Harry Marks and the City Slickers would now be impossible because of the legal restrictions that financial journalists operate under. They believed it was the responsibility of the company news reporter to guide the investor. The imbalance of information asymmetry is now more heavily weighted in favour of the company, due to the combined influence of their in-house PR machines and their PR advisers.

Since the 1720 South Sea Bubble, 'information asymmetry', where the company possesses more information than the investor and therefore is in a better position, has been a problem. In the twenty-first century the imbalance appears to be growing and, ironically, one of the main causes is society's demands through its various regulators for more transparency and more information from the companies. It has been and continues to be one of the key functions of company news reporting to counter this information asymmetry.

The ethics of financial and business journalism

Arguably, financial and business journalists have to deal with more ethical issues and problems than do other journalists. The 2008 financial crisis demonstrated the ethical dilemmas facing financial and business journalists when reporting not just on companies but also on the economy. It was not only Robert Peston but many other financial and business journalists who were criticised, and accused that by writing about a recession they were helping to bring one on. By talking the economy down, they were damaging confidence and creating problems that did not exist. Writing in the *Guardian*, the former *Economist* editor Bill Emmott, in a column entitled 'What Pray Is All the Fuss About?' criticised the press: 'We risk talking ourselves into recession through media scaremongering' (*Guardian*, 3 January 2008). Sir Samuel Brittan of the *Financial Times* wrote: 'I feel like saying Buck Up ... There is no need to talk ourselves into a recession' (*Financial Times*, 1 February 2008). Anatole Kaletsky of *The Times* also played down the possibility of a recession in the UK. In a column entitled 'Slowdown, but Not Crash and Burn' (*The Times*, 10 January 2008) he wrote, 'My hunch is that Britain will avoid a recession,' adding that 'the global credit crisis, far from taking a turn for the worse, is almost over' (Steve Schifferes, cited in Schiffrin, 2011: 163) Nicholas Jones, a former industrial correspondent at the BBC, identified the pressures that the government attempted to put reporters under when discussing the national economy: 'We see that if we report [government figures] critically, we get loads of phone calls from the political people in the Treasury. Not only the political people but also the official press officers and civil servants who shouldn't have a political outlook on things but do. They say why are you reporting us so critically and aren't we doing well? There is, immediately, a [sense that] you're attacking the government' (quoted in Mair and Keeble, 2009: 64).

The reluctance to discuss the impact of the recession appears to have been widespread. An analysis of over 2,000 newspaper UK articles on the financial crisis between August 2007 and March 2009, carried out by Editorial Intelligence (Steve Schifferes, cited in Schiffrin, 2011: 162), showed that until March 2008 the newspapers did not want to describe the crisis as a 'crisis', preferring to use the term 'credit crunch', which 'implies a much milder, more manageable event which might not need massive government intervention' (Steve Schifferes, cited in Schiffrin, 2011: 162). They argued that the problems could be managed within the financial sector, rather than impacting on the wider economy. The analysis also found a difference in the way the events were reported by journalists and how they were then interpreted in newspaper editorials, which were generally more reassuring about the state of the UK economy.

'Thus while commentators such as Martin Wolf and Gillian Tett were warning about the credit crisis, on October 10th 2007, an editorial in their own paper, the *Financial Times*, asserted that: "the fact that loans are changing hands at all is reassuring and it is crucial to ensure that the summer's credit squeeze does not turn into a fully-fledged US credit crunch"' (Schiffrin, 2011: 162).

Schiffrin (2011) believes that many financial and business journalists were inhibited in the way they reported on the events of 2008 because the uncertainty about the future of the newspaper industry made many of them 'afraid' of their own positions. 'Business and financial journalists appeared to be pressured into not writing "depressing" economic or business related stories that might affect the business and economic mood' (Schiffrin, 2011: 5).

> Honesty in appraising bank losses from declining house prices would have presented a bleak picture of the economy's prospects. That would undermine confidence, further freezing consumer spending and making the economy weaker. Their [the journalists'] training requires them to cover the news no matter how bad it is. But they are afraid that their coverage will cause share prices to fall and consumer confidence to evaporate and will push the economy into a downward spiral.

While it is understandable that journalists should exercise care in the way they report, Tambini (2010: 5) wonders whether this is 'an unacceptable form of self-censorship'. 'Should the ethical standards of business and financial journalists differ from those of others such as political journalists' because of the effect their writing can have on companies and the economy.

Does this temporising and equivocating compromise the position of the journalists? This could lead down a slippery slope – if you comprise on this issue, why not comprise on a critical report about a company that is a major advertiser in the newspaper? Should not a journalist's responsibility always be to tell the truth? This is a difficult question to which there is no easy, neat or simple solution – in theory, of course, the truth should be pursued, whatever the cost and impact. However, this is not an abstract, theoretical debate but one that might impact on people's lives and fortunes. What this debate does is to illustrate the power and influence wielded by the financial and business press.

Safe conduits

The history of financial and business journalism is littered with many examples of where journalists have colluded with companies to produce editorial coverage that is more sympathetic to a company. We have described them as safe conduits who possess impeccable credentials and contacts who are trusted by business and become the channel through which their opinions are expressed. They are regarded as a safe pair of hands by the corporate PR team and become relied on not to ask too many difficult questions. At its worst this can seriously compromise the integrity of a story. We demonstrated in Chapter 7 how, even in a major crisis, a corporate communications team of a major financial institution can transmit its key messages and dominate the media agenda when there is an uncritical press which is prepared to play along.

The safe conduits have also been used by pro-business lobby groups and think-tanks to act as cheerleaders for political and economic causes that they argue affect business interests. Issues that were first raised in the financial and business pages, such as the so-called 'war on red-tape' and the 50p tax campaign, became political issues which were then translated into legislation. However, it has to be asked whether such an uncritical acceptance of business is either healthy or good for either business or journalism. What type of 'friend' is it that will not hold it to account even when it does wrong, often applauding misdemeanours and dubious practice as being essential business activity? That enables it to precipitate an economic crisis or seeks to excuse or apologise for behaviour that might elsewhere be regarded as criminal? If our newspapers reported on politics or politicians in such an uncritical fashion we would quickly dismiss this as propaganda.

Changing focus of company news

According to the National Audit Office (2014), the 2013 privatisation of the Royal Mail attracted 690,000 private investors who bought shares in the company. However, the popularity of this high-profile share issue that attracted a huge amount of publicity has to be seen against the long-term decline in company investment by retail investors, and to suggest that it is leading to a return to the halcyon days of privatisations is a mistake. The changing nature of share ownership and potential changes to the reporting requirements of a public company will impact on financial and business journalism and could offer a new role for the reporting of company news.

Fifty years ago, most shares in UK companies were owned by individuals and traded through stockbrokers who charged a fixed (and high) rate of commission for their services (Kay Review, 2012). The stockbroker would often know his client personally, and was probably also acquainted with the companies whose shares he recommended. A great deal of Stock Exchange activity that took place at this time was of a type that might today be regarded as insider dealing, with a hint or suggestion from a 'company source' leading to a stockbroker's taking action. Financial and business journalists had an important role to play in providing potential investors with information on the company, its prospects and management. Newspapers were regarded as sources where objective information could be found.

However, with the globalisation of financial markets, more UK equities are now held by foreign institutions. Current holdings by pension funds and insurance companies account for around 20% of the total (Kay Review, 2012). This contrasts sharply with non-UK equity holders, who now own over 40% of UK shares. At the end of 2012, UK individuals owned around 11% of UK equities, a slight increase from the record low in 2010, and halting the downward trend seen in recent years (ONS, 2012).

At the end of 2012, non-UK investors owned 53.2% of UK shares by value; fifty years ago this figure was less than 10%. In 1998 it was 31%, so there has been a steady and inexorable rise in the proportion of equity shares being held by foreign institutions and individuals of various kinds. This trend is likely to continue, especially as most of the mainstream political parties in the UK do not appear to believe there is anything wrong with foreign ownership of an increasing part of our corporates.

> The proportion of UK quoted shares (in terms of value) owned by 'rest of the world' investors has increased substantially since 1963, the large increases since 1994 partly reflect the growth in international mergers and acquisitions, and the [increasing] ease of overseas residents to invest in UK shares. (ONS, 2012)

Following the financial crisis of 2008 and the low levels of the FTSE, many institutional shareholders cut their equity stakes so that, for example, insurance companies held only an estimated 6% by value at the end of 2012. Pension funds had an estimated 5% (ONS, 2012), down from nearly 6% in 2010, which, as the ONS report drily states, is 'significantly lower than the levels seen in recent years'.

In such circumstances it is legitimate to ask, with the declining numbers of small investors, what impact this will have on company news reporting.

Company news reporting may also be affected if key recommendations from the Kay Report are eventually implemented. A weakness in current company news is the way it has to concentrate on reporting a company's financial results, leaving little room for analysis. The impact of these changes could substantially alter the focus and dynamics of how public companies are reported. Financial journalists argue that the pressure to report on a daily basis with fewer resources leaves little room for analysis. The Kay Review of UK equity markets might lead to the end of quarterly company reporting and the focus on short-term corporate performance. There are proposals to scrap the reporting requirements for big listed companies.

What is business and financial journalism for?

Tambini (2010) answers the question by placing the role of financial and business journalists in a legal setting: 'A simple way to understand this role is to see it as a framework which governs and shapes professional practice. In return for the social function they perform, financial journalists are granted professional privileges' (by this he means having access to price-sensitive information about a public company). This, however, only considers the journalist in the context of company news reporting and in too limited a role.

Following our historical analysis and research into the practice of modern financial and business journalism, what answer can we provide to the question of what the role of financial and business journalism should be?

The decline in the number of retail investors and possible changes to the way businesses report their financial results will change the nature of financial and business journalism. Tambini (2010: 172) argues: 'This could be the opportunity to revisit a broader debate about what role journalists should play in the overall framework of corporate governance: not only unearthing cases of fraud, but providing the balanced and sceptical news and comment that deflates bubbles and helps avoid market irrationality. In the current environment, pressures of time and resources are in danger of undermining business journalism in general, and the ability of financial journalists to find a way through the current impasse.' Company news reporting has never been needed more, for two reasons. Firstly, because the power of financial public communications to control the communication agenda is increasing the problem of information asymmetry, and secondly, because of society's changing relationship with business.

However, for it to have an effective role and function it must be prepared to be less of a safe conduit and more critical of business. As we have seen earlier in the chapter, business can believe itself to be in a sacrosanct, privileged position and above criticism, and it is precisely this arrogance which helped to produce the crisis of 2008 and continues to believe that business cannot be criticised.

To criticise business practices is not to be anti-business. Quite the contrary. But one of the dangers of attempting to be critical and questioning about business practice is to incur the accusation that you are 'talking business down'. Typical of this approach was the speech made by the president of the Confederation of British Industry at its conference in October 2013 when he said, 'Business is not the enemy' and criticised the way that anti-business sentiment seemed to be manifest in the wider community and in media coverage. Such criticism misses the point. It was not after all, those who criticised business who caused the depression of 2008, it was the businesses who believed that it is the right of the business to operate free from state control and lack of interference. This reluctance to rock the boat or criticise business because of the potential consequences was also apparent during the economic crisis.

Financial and business journalism is needed because of the way that our relationship with business has changed. Over thirty years of neoliberalism has reduced the power of those institutions, such as the state and the trade unions, that traditionally protected society from the predatory activities of business. At the same time, neoliberal policies have rebalanced the economy so that services once provided by the public sector have been outsourced to private companies such as Serco and G4S. Key sections of our infrastructure, such as waste management, energy and the railways are owned by foreign companies that are, sometimes ironically, owned by foreign governments. Prisons, probation services, even the NHS, are increasingly in private hands.

If that can go, why not then the police or the army? Many of these companies are multinational corporations owned by shareholders in offshore companies that are remote and inaccessible. These are the kinds of companies that are increasingly impacting on and affecting our daily lives through the services they provide.

We live and work in a global economy. Amazon, Starbucks, Google are major household names, and while we might welcome their services we have learned that these can come at a cost. As society suffers under the impact of government-imposed austerity, each individual taxpayer has had to contribute financially to the bail-out of the banks. There has been widespread public outrage at the tax-evasion schemes carried on by many of these global companies have no allegiances other than to their shareholders. It has been the financial and business reporters in newspapers who have been in the forefront of exposing their activities, and also demonstrating the importance and effectiveness of such reporting.

Society needs a strong, independent, financial and business journalism to explain what is happening. Yet this needs commitment, and understanding about its nature, and to have a mature relationship with business. In order to carry out this function it has to be critical, and at times a harsh critic. Business and politicians need to recognise that criticism will not lead to economic collapse. Journalists need to see it less as a stepping-stone to a future career and to understand that this is a battleground, and currently the most important type of journalism. In such an environment, where society is looking to redraw and redefine its relationship with business, financial and business journalism has a key role in bridging the gap and helping to come to a new and more healthy relationship with society.

Notes

Introduction

1 The actual cost is estimated to be £3,562.00 to each taxpayer. The exposure to the taxpayer was £26,562.50 at the height of the crisis. This was made up of the following:

- £76bn on the shares in RBS and Lloyds
- £200bn for liquidity support through the Bank of England (Quantitative Easing)
- £250bn in guarantees on banks' borrowings
- £40bn in loans to Bradford & Bingley and others
- £280 billion in providing insurance cover for banks' assets.

2 In his book, *Inside Job*, Charles Ferguson outlines a number of examples where criminal prosecutions could have been taken against American financiers. It would be useful to have a similar analysis for the United Kingdom. In the UK to date the 'roll-call' of responsibility includes: Johnny Cameron, the former head of RBS's division which had responsibility for investment banking, was singled out for criticism by the Financial Services Authority; Peter Cummings, in charge of the corporate division at HBOS and in charge of HBOS property lending, was fined by the FSA; Bob Diamond, former CEO at Barclays, was forced out of his position over the LIBOR scandal; Sir Fred Goodwin and Sir James Crosby lost their knighthoods. A few others have been forced out of various banks.

3 Muckraking. This refers to the 'muckrakers', a name given to American journalists by President Theodore Roosevelt in 1909. The muckrakers attempted to expose corruption in business and politics.

Chapter 1

1 To complicate matters, a private company whose shares are not traded publicly can call itself a plc if it has paid-up share capital of £50,000. This book deals only with companies whose shares are traded in public and we will therefore use the term 'quoted company'.

2 The basic purpose of a stock exchange is to bring together companies looking for finance and investors who are looking to invest in companies. The first recognised stock exchange was established in Bruges in 1309. The trade carried out in the Bruges exchange was generally in financial securities such as debts. The first stocks were traded on the Antwerp exchange.
 3 Trading houses still exist and the term is used to describe firms that specialise in facilitating transactions between a home and foreign countries. A trading house is an exporter, importer and also a trader that purchases and sells products for other businesses. A trading house advises companies involved in importing and exporting.
 4 McCusker (1991) suggests that Italian merchants may have also produced similar information earlier, but no records of these exist.
 5 The Fuggers were German bankers, and their network of subsidiaries spread throughout Europe. The Fugger Company also traded with India, South America and Africa. Its most famous customers were the various popes, the emperors Maximilian I, Karl V and Ferdinand I of Habsburg, the kings of Germany, Spain and Portugal, England and Hungary, as well as the Medici family of Florence.
 6 Sociologist Jurgen Habermas gave the London coffee houses a special place in journalism/media theory – for him they epitomised the 'public sphere', a place where open and free debate between citizens could and did take place.
 7 So called because they wrote their names under the terms of the insurance contract to show they accepted the risks associated with the policy.
 8 Huguenots was the name given to French Protestants. The Edict of Nantes (1598) gave them a number privileges, including widespread religious liberty.
 9 As evidence that we seldom seem to learn the lessons of history, or that later generations think they know better, South America features again in this book in two further economic collapses, in 1835 and 1890.
 10 A further factor influencing the demand for shares was the influx of foreign investors eager to make good the losses that many had made on the Mississippi company.
 11 Alarm bells should have been ringing following a similar earlier scheme based on building a colony in South America. What has became known as the Darien scheme was a colonisation project by Scotland to try to establish a colony called Caledonia in the isthmus of Panama. Financed by Scottish nobles and landowners, it was hampered by bad planning, epidemics and disease and was finally abandoned in April 1700.

Chapter 2

 1 Was this a 'low' circulation, as Temple suggests, or, given the distribution networks and limited education of the time, quite a high circulation? Copies of the paper would be read in coffee houses and subscription libraries,

which would mean that its actual readership could be two or three times its circulation figure.
2   The opposition of *The Times* and *The Economist* stands in contrast to those who opposed the spread of railways on the basis that they would destroy the social life of the country such as fox-hunting and, with it, the basis on which society's rules and order were established (Robb, 2002).

Chapter 3

1   Consols – short for consolidated annuities – were a form of government bond. They were first issued in 1751.
2   Duguid wrote this in 1897 for the Journal of Finance. He was no longer editor of the *Daily Mail* and was drawing on his by then considerable experience in financial journalism, working at *The Economist*, the *Pall Mall Gazette* and the *Westminster Gazette*.

Chapter 4

1   William Stead, as editor of the *Pall Mall Gazette* (a forerunner of the *London Evening Standard*), wrote a series of ground-breaking articles which exposed the reality of life for the poor and dispossessed in Victorian London. His stories about squalid living in the slums of London led a Royal Commission to recommend their clearance and the building of low-cost housing. He also campaigned against child prostitution and his articles on this topic in the *Gazette* proved so popular that copies of the magazine apparently changed hands for as much twenty times their cover price.
2   In fact many of these practices of charging companies for editorial are now standard at many specialised business publications.
3   'Guinea-pig' directors were 'decoy' directors rather than active ones, they received money (guineas) for attending board meetings (Robb, 2004 36).
4   These were so called because they were run by the more disreputable outside brokers, where the coils of tape showing the latest Stock Exchange prices would eventually fall into a conveniently placed bucket.
5   The Pactolus is a river in Turkey where, according to legend, King Midas divested himself of the golden touch by washing himself in the river.

Chapter 5

1   John Jaskob was, among other things, the builder of the Empire State Building.
2   Marshall had been his economics tutor at Cambridge and persuaded him to study economics.

Chapter 7

1 There are three main credit rating agencies: Standard & Poor's, Moody's and Fitch's. According to the Financial Crisis Inquiry Report (2011) for the US government, the credit rating agencies played an important role in the 2008 crisis. In one of its conclusions (p. xxv) it states: 'The failure of the rating agencies were essential cogs in the wheel of financial destination. The three credit rating agencies were key enablers of the financial meltdown. The mortgage-related securities at the heart of the crisis could not have been marketed and sold without their seal of approval. Investors relied on them, often blindly. In some cases, they were obligated to use them, or regulatory capital standards were hinged on them. The crisis could not have happened without the rating agencies.'
2 Anglo-Saxon capitalism, so called because it is practised in English-speaking countries. It is based on the economics of the Chicago School of economics and the ideas of Adam Smith.
3 Savings to be made through staff 'rationalisations' – i.e. job losses – have always been an important justification for a takeover. Fred Goodwin of RBS was known as 'Fred the Shred' for the cuts he made. Ironically, in 2013 RBS had computer problems when thousands of customers lost payments in the weeks before Christmas. In 2012, a major IT failure locked many RBS, NatWest and Ulster Bank customers out of their accounts for several days. The IT problems for which the company notorious for were blamed by chief executive Ross McEwan on several decades of under investment in new IT.
4 The then Prime Minister, Gordon Brown, keen at the time to have some good news to boost his personal standing, was said to have played a key role in bringing the two institutions together in order to save HBOS. In reality, however, Lloyds had been interested in merging with HBOS for some time.
5 Kay Review (2012: 121): 'Several leading former HBOS Executives suggested to the commission that the company's impairments were the result of the financial crisis and the seizure of wholesale funding markets, which affected its customers. The chairman (Lord Stevenson) and both former CEOs (Crosby and Hornby) all three put the emphasis on the unprecedented closure of the wholesale markets.'
6 Northern Rock Building Society was formed in 1965 as a result of the merger of two north-east building societies: the Northern Counties Permanent Building Society (established in 1850) and the Rock Building Society (established in 1865). During the thirty years that followed, it expanded by acquiring fifty-three smaller building societies, most notably the North of England Building Society in 1994. Along with many other UK building societies in the 1990s, Northern Rock chose to demutualise and float on the stock exchange.

7 The scandal also called into question the accounting practices and activities of many corporations in the USA and was a factor in the creation of the Sarbanes–Oxley Act of 2002. The company's collapse was a major factor in the subsequent dissolution of the Arthur Andersen accounting company. Enron filed for bankruptcy protection during late 2001.

Chapter 8

1 This research was carried out over a two-week period in July 2012 and covered only the main broadsheet newspapers.
2 It might be argued that these categories are too broad and arbitrary in that 'economic news', for example, also includes economic commentaries which are not strictly news stories.
3 Market cap is different from turnover, which is the total sales that a company makes. Most economists would agree that the market cap is an artificial reflection of a company's value, as it can change due to factors that the company cannot change, such as 'market sentiment'. Turnover, however, is for the most part real and tangible and should be a reflection of what the company is doing.
4 The FTSE 100 Index, also called FTSE 100, FTSE or, informally, 'the Footsie', is a share index of the 100 companies listed on the London Stock Exchange with the highest market capitalisation. It is one of the most widely used stock indices and is seen as a gauge of business prosperity for businesses regulated by UK company law. The index is maintained by the FTSE Group, a subsidiary of the London Stock Exchange Group. The index began on 3 January 1984 at the base level of 1000. After falling during the financial crisis of 2007–10 to below 3500 in March 2009, the index recovered to a peak of 6091.33 on 8 February 2011, fell under the 5000 mark on the morning of 23 September 2011, but reached 6,840.27 (its highest since September 2000) on 22 May 2013. On 19 March 2015 it topped 7000 (https://uk.finance.yahoo.com/q/hp?s=^FTSE).
5 The so-called 'Cardiff Study' (see below) does contain an analysis of business news but it is news that occurs in the domestic news pages and could therefore contain news on, for example, personal finance products. The HCfCCR study looked at only the business pages and supplements.
6 The study by the Cardiff team (Professor Justin Lewis, Dr Andrew Williams, Professor Bob Franklin, Dr James Thomas and Nick Modsell) also produced two journal papers in Journalism Studies and Journalism Practice.
7 The broadcast media were: BBC and ITV evening news bulletins, Radio 4's World at One and the Today programme.
8 The Cardiff Study originally treated 'wire' stories (see note 9) the same as PR-sourced stories. However, after protests from PA this was altered. 'The most commonly used journalistic source for domestic stories was the PA wire service (47% of press stories in our sample replicated at least some copy

from PA), followed by Mercury 17% with 11% of stories replicating stories from other media.' Fiona Walsh, the Guardian's online business editor, believes there is no problem with using agency copy: 'We use it as a source and where appropriate it will be re-written.'
9 Wire services provide news reports to media outlets; they may also be called news services. They prepare hard-news articles, features and other material to be used by media outlets, with little or no editing needed. Some wire services also provide photos, infographics and broadcast reports. The services charge for access to their material.
10 Ian King is now the Business Editor of Sky News.

Chapter 9

1 For her analysis of how business and financial news is constructed in UK newspapers Doyle carried out a series of ten semi-structured and four unstructured interviews with financial journalists who were working or had worked with the *Financial Times*, *The Sunday Times*, the *Telegraph*, *Investors Chronicle* and CNN in March and April 2005.
2 A conceptual metaphor is an understanding of one idea in terms of another; for example, understanding quantity in terms of directionality (e.g. 'prices are rising').
3 Significantly, as Koller says (2004: 76), an opposite of a war metaphor would be one featuring romance, and these are quite hard to find in business and financial media discourse: 'Their relative strength or weakness in quantitative terms (of a romance metaphor) therefore mirrors the demographic structure of the publication's overwhelmingly male readership, indicating the magazines' and newspapers' orientation towards their audience.'
4 These media appearances are important for the companies the commentators work for – they are good publicity for them and demonstrate their expertise.
5 This did not include the *Daily Express*, which was not available on the Lexis news database at the time.

Chapter 10

1 The Stock Exchange is not connected to the government, even though it carries out regulations enacted by the government. The Stock Exchange is a public company and its shares are listed on the Exchange just like those of any other public company.
2 Kay, in his Review, provides many examples of UK companies which have grown through having a long-term growth strategy, contrasting their success with examples such as RBS which attempted to grow through acquisition rather than concentrating on organic growth.

3 Mergermarket is a mergers and acquisitions (M&A) intelligence service. It provides intelligence to the investment banking, legal and private equity markets.
4 There were very few women working in the City at senior levels, their functions being confined to support roles such as typists and secretaries.

Chapter 11

1 Butskellism refers to the political consensus of the 1950s when the Labour and Conservative parties followed relatively similar policies when in power and opposition. The term combines the names of the Conservative Chancellor of the Exchequer, R.A. Butler, and his opposite number in the Labour Party, Shadow Chancellor Hugh Gaitskell.

Bibliography

Ahamed, L. (2009) *Lords of Finance: The bankers who broke the world*, William Heinemann, London.
Aldrick, P. (2007) 'This is Barclays' show', *Daily Telegraph*, 23 April.
Anderson, G. M. and Tollison, R. D. (1982) 'Adam Smith's analysis of joint-stock companies', *Journal of Political Economy* 90 (6), 1237–1256.
Anon, http://www.economist.com/help/about-us [accessed 6 February 2013].
Anon, (1943) *The Economist, 1843–1943*, The Economist Newspaper, London, p. 15.
Bagehot, W. (1867) *The English Constitution*, Champan Hall, London.
Bagehot, W. (1873) *Lombard Street*, Henry King & Co, London.
Balen, M. (2009) *A Very English Deceit: The secret history of the South Sea Bubble and the world's first great financial scandal*, Fourth Estate, London.
Bakan, J. (2004) *The Corporation*, Constable, London.
Bargiela-Chiappini, F., Nickerson, C. and Planken, B. (2007) *Business Discourse*, Palgrave Macmillan, London.
BBC2 (2006) *Tory! Tory! Tory!* (documentary), Episode 1: 'Outsiders' (March).
Beharrell, P., Philo, G. and Hewitt, J. (1977) 'Strategic Policies', in Peter Beharrell and Greg Philo (eds) *Trade Unions and the Media*, Macmillan, London.
Berelson, B. (1952) *Content Analysis in Communications Research*, Illinois Free Press, Glencoe, IL.
Black, Jeremy (1992) 'The Eighteenth Century British Press', in Dennis Griffiths (ed.) *The Encyclopaedia of the British Press, 1422–1992*, Macmillan, London.
Blackden, R. and Thelwell, E. (2007) 'The biggest hitters in British banking', *Daily Telegraph*, 23 April.
Blackhurst, C. (2000) 'How the City was spun', *Management Today*, January/February.
Blyth, M. (2013) *Austerity: The history of a dangerous idea*, Oxford University Press, Oxford.
Bowers, S. (2005) 'Three face jail over Mirror share fraud', *Guardian*, 8 December.
Boyce, D. G. (2011) 'Harmsworth, Alfred Charles William, Viscount Northcliffe (1865–1922)', *Oxford Dictionary of National Biography*, Oxford University

Press, Oxford, www.oxforddnb.com/view/article/33717 [accessed 4 August 2014].

Brittan, S. (1995) *Capitalism with a Human Face*, Edward Elgar, Aldershot.

Brown, L. (1992) 'The British press 1800–1860', in Dennis Griffiths (ed.) *The Encyclopaedia of the British Press, 1422–1992*, Macmillan, London.

Brummer, A. (2004) 'Why Fred must keep growing', *Daily Mail*, 20 February.

Burnham, E.F.L. (1995) *Peterborough Court: The story of the Daily Telegraph*, Cassell, London.

Butterick, K. (2012a) Interview with the author.

Butterick, K. (2012b) Interview with the author.

Butterick, K. (2012c) Interview with the author.

Butterick, K. (2012d) Interview with the author.

Butterick, K. (2012e) Interview with the author.

Cain, P. and Newton, S. (2011) 'Crisis and recovery: historical perspectives on the Coalition's economic policies', *History and Policy*, www.historyandpolicy.org/policy-papers/papers/crisis-and-recovery-historical-perspectives-on-the-coalitions-economic-poli [accessed 10 June 2014].

Calomiris, C. W. (2009) 'The subprime turmoil: what's old, what's new, and what's next', *Journal of Structured Finance* 15 (1), 6–52.

Cave, A. (2008) 'HBOS man leads banking pack', *Corporate Communications*, online exclusive, September, www.corpcommsmagazine.co.uk/news/236-online-exclusive-hbos-man-leads-banking-pack [accessed 21 May 2014].

Cave, T. and Rowell, A. (2014) *A Quiet Word: Lobbying, crony capitalism and broken politics in Britain*, Random House, London.

Chapman, C. (2011) *Selling the Family Silver: Has the privatisation worked?*, Random House, London.

Chenoweth, N. (2001) *Rupert Murdoch, the Untold Story of the World's Greatest Media Wizard*, Crown Business Press, New York.

Citigate Dewe Rogerson (2011) 'Investor relations survey: extraordinary times', Citigate Dewe Rogerson, London

Clarke, T. and Monkhouse, E. (1994) *Rethinking the Company*, Financial Times, Pitman, London.

Cole, P. and Harcup, T. (2010) *Newspaper Journalism*, SAGE, London.

Conboy, M. (2004) *Journalism in Britain, a Historical Introduction*, SAGE, London.

Cooper, G. (2010) *The Origin of Financial Crises*, Harriman House, Petersfield.

Corporate Synergy (2006) *Financial Public Relations*, Corporate Synergy Research, London.

Coyle, J. (2004) 'Flattery will get you everywhere', *Observer*, 18 April.

Crouch, C. (2012) *The Strange Non-Death of Neoliberalism*, Polity Press, Cambridge.

Daily Mail (1896) [London, England] 'Chat on "Change"', 4 May, p. 2, *Daily Mail Historical Archive*, Web [accessed 14 November 2014].

Daily Mail (1896) [London, England] 'Advice to Investors', 4 May, p. 2, *Daily Mail Historical Archive*, Web [accessed 14 November 2014].

Daily Mail (1897) [London, England] 'A £3,000 Settlement', 11 May, p. 3, *Daily Mail Historical Archive*, Web [accessed 14 November 2014].

Daily Mail (1898) [London, England] 'Hooley Disclaimers', 11 August, p. 3, *Daily Mail Historical Archive*, Web [accessed 14 November 2014].

Daily Mail (1923) [London, England] 'Mr. Charles Duguid', 15 December, p. 15, *Daily Mail Historical Archive*, Web [accessed 14 November 2014].

Daily Mail (1929) [London, England] 'The Hatry collapse and its sequel', 21 September, p. 10, *Daily Mail Historical Archive*, Web [accessed 14 November 2014].

Daily Mail (1937) [London, England] 'Quack Remedies', 17 December, p. 10, *Daily Mail Historical Archive*, Web [accessed 13 November 2014].

Daily Mail (1966) [London, England] 'This is where we come in', 28 September, p. 17, *Daily Mail Historical Archive*, Web [accessed 14 November 2014].

Dale, R. (2004) *The First Crash: Lessons from the South Sea Bubble*, Princeton University Press, Princeton, NJ.

Davenport, N. (1964) *The Split Society*, Victor Gollancz, London.

Davies, M. (2014) 'Militancy or manipulation', *Babel, The Language Magazine* (February), 19–24, University of Huddersfield.

Davies, N. (2009) *Flat Earth News*, Vintage, London.

Davis, A. (2000) 'Public relations, business news and the reproduction of corporate elite power', *Journalism* 1: 282–304.

Davis, A. (2002) *Public Relations Democracy: Politics and the mass media in Britain*, Manchester University Press, Manchester.

Davis, A. (2006) 'The role of the mass media in investor relations', *Journal of Communication Management* 10 (1), 7–17, Emerald Publishing.

Davison, S. and Harrison, K. (2015) *The Neoliberal Crisis*, Lawrence & Wishart, London.

Dawson, F. G. (1990) *The First Latin American Debt Crisis: The City of London and the 1822–25 loan bubble*, Yale University Press, New Haven, CT.

Downie, J. A. (1979) *Robert Harley and the Press*, Cambridge University Press, Cambridge.

Doyle, G. (2006) 'Financial news journalism: a post-Enron analysis of approaches towards economic and financial news production in the UK', *Journalism* 4, 433–451.

Duguid, C. (1902) *How to Read the Money Article*, E. Wilson, London.

Edwards, R. D. (1993), *The Pursuit of Reason, 'The Economist', 1843–1993*, Harvard Business School, Boston, MA.

Edwards, R. D. (1993) 'A Scotsman inside everyman, James Wilson', *The Economist*, 11 September.
Elfenbein, J. (1960) *Business Journalism*, 2nd edition, Harper and Brothers, New York, USA.
Fairclough, N. (1989) *Language and Power*, Longman, New York.
Fairclough, N. (1993) 'Critical discourse analysis and the marketization of public discourse: the universities', *Discourse and Society* 4 (2), 133–168.
Fairclough, N. (1995) *Media Discourse*, Edward Arnold, London.
Fairclough, N. (2000) *Language and* Power, 2nd edition, Longman, New York.
Fairclough, N. (2002) 'The dialectics of discourse', *Textus* 14 (2), 3–10. Retrieved from www.ling.lancs.ac.uk/staff/norman/2001a.doc [accessed 17 April 2012].
Farndale, N. (2011) 'The Telegraph at 50', www.telegraph.co.uk/news/sunday-telegraph-at-50/8300953/The-Sunday-Telegraph-at-50.html [accessed 23 May 2014].
Fay, S. (1997) *The Collapse of Barings*, W.W. Norton & Co., London.
Fay, S. (2011) 'Big City, bright lights', *British Journalism Review* 22, 1 March, pp. 48–53.
Farber, D. (2013) *Everybody Ought to be Rich: The life and times of John J. Raskob*, Oxford University Press, Oxford.
Feather, J. (1985) *The Provincial Book Trade in Eighteenth Century England*, Cambridge University Press, Cambridge.
Ferguson, C. (2012) *Inside Job*, Oneworld, Oxford.
Financial Crisis Inquiry Report (2011) *Final Report of the National Commission on the Causes of the Financial and Economic Crisis in the United States*, www.gpo.gov/fdsys/pkg/GPO-FCIC/pdf/GPO-FCIC.pdf.
Fiske, J. (1994) *Media Matters: Everyday culture and political change*, University of Minnesota Press, Minneapolis, MN.
Fontana, B. (1985) *Rethinking the Politics of the Commercial Society:* The Edinburgh Review, *1802–1832*, Cambridge University Press, Cambridge.
Fowler, R. (1996) *Language in the News: Discourse and ideology in the press*, Routledge, London.
Fraser, M. (2009) 'Five reasons for crash blindness', *British Journalism Review* 20 (4).
Freedman, S. (2009) *Binge Trading: The real inside story of cash, cocaine and corruption in the City*, Penguin, London.
Friedman, M. (1970) 'The social responsibility of business is to increase its profits' *New York Times Magazine*, 13 September.
Galbraith, J. K. (1980) quoted by William Keegan in 'It's just like the 1980s', *Observer*, November, 2010.
Galbraith, J. K. (1993) *A Short History of Financial Euphoria*, Penguin, London.

Galbraith, J.K. (2009) *The Great Crash of 1929*, Penguin, London.
Galtung, J. and Ruge, M. (1965) 'The structure of foreign news: the presentation of the Congo, Cuba and Cyprus crises in four Norwegian newspapers', *Journal of International Peace Research* 2 (2), 64–91.
Gambles, A. (1999) *Protection and Politics: Conservative economic discourse, 1815–1852*, Royal Historical Society, London.
Gavin, N. T. (ed.) (2000) *The Economy, Media and Public Knowledge*, Leicester University Press, Leicester.
German, C. (2000) 'Kenneth Fleet, journalist who brought financial news to the city', *Guardian*, 6 October.
Ginns, B. (2012) Interview with the author.
Glasgow University Media Group (1976) *Bad News*, London, Routledge.
Glasgow University Media Group (1980) *More Bad News*, London, Routledge.
Glasgow University Media Group (1982) *Really Bad News*, London, Routledge.
Glasgow University Media Group (1983) *Getting the Message*, London, Routledge.
Greenhill, S. (2008) '"It's awful why did nobody see it coming?" The Queen gives her verdict on the global credit crunch', *Daily Mail*, 6 November.
Gregory-Smith, I., Thompson, I. and Wright, P.W. (2014) 'CEO pay and voting dissent before and after the crisis', *Economic Journal* 124 (574), 22–39.
Groth, O. (1928–1930) 'Die Zeitung: Ein System der Zeitungskunde', in *Journalistick*, 4 vols, Bensheimer, Mannheim, 1: 22–90.
Habermas, J. (1973) *Theory and Practice*, Beacon, Boston, MA.
Hall, S. (1973) *Encoding and Decoding in the Television Discourse*, Centre for Contemporary Cultural Studies, Birmingham.
Hall, S. (1981) 'Cultural studies and the centre: some problematics and problems', in Stuart Hall, Dorothy Hobson, Andrew Lowe and Paul Willis (eds) *Culture, Media, Language*, Hutchinson, London, pp. 15–47.
Hall, S., Crichter, C., Jefferson, T., Clarke, J. and Roberts, B. (1978) *Policing the Crisis: Mugging, the State and Law and Order*, London, Macmillan.
Hamilton, G. (2004) 'Delane, John Thadeus (1817–1879)', *Oxford Dictionary of National Biography*, ed. H. C. G. Matthew and Brian Harrison, Oxford University Press, Oxford, www.oxforddnb.com/view/article/7440 [accessed 2 November 2013].
Harcup, T. (2006) *Journalism Principles and Practice*, SAGE, London.
Harcup, T. and O'Neill, D. (2001) 'What is news? Galtung and Ruge revisited', *Journalism Studies* 2 (2), 261–280.
Hayagreeva, R. and Sivakumar, K. (1999) 'Institutional sources of boundary-spanning structures: The establishment of investor relations departments in the Fortune 500 industrials', *Organisational Science* 10 (1), 27–42.
Hayek, F. A. (1944) *The Road to Serfdom*, Routledge Press, London.

HBOS (2001) *Annual Report 2001*, HBOS, Edinburgh.
Hellier, (2003) 'Revealed: The City's most influential financial PRs', City AM, 8 March, www.cityam.com/article/revealed-city-s-most-influential-financial-prs#sthash.FfFTmEUd.dpuf.
Henry, F. and Tator, C. (2002) *Discourses of Domination*, University of Toronto Press, Toronto, ONT.
High Pay Centre (2013) 'FTSE 100 CEO pay briefing 2013: Have new rules on top pay had any impact?' High Pay Centre, London.
Hilton, B. (2001) *A Mad Bad and Dangerous People? England 1783–1846*, Clarendon Press, Oxford.
Hirsch, F. and Gordon, D. (1975) *Newspaper Money: Fleet Street and the search for the affluent reader*, Hutchinson, London.
Hollingsworth, M. (1986) *The Press and Political Dissent: A question of censorship*, Pluto Press, London,.
Hoppitt, J. (2000) *A Land of Liberty? England 1689–1727*, Oxford University Press, Oxford.
House of Commons Treasury Committee (2009) Banking Crisis, Volume 1, Oral evidence, HC144-1 [Incorporating HC1167 i–iv, Session 2007–08], House of Commons, London, The Stationery Office, www.publications.parliament.uk/pa/cm200809/cmselect/cmtreasy/144/144i.pdf [accessed 17 April 2014].
Howe, A. (1997) *Free Trade and Liberal England 1846–1946*, Clarendon Press, Oxford.
Hutton, W. (1995) *The State We're In*, Jonathan Cape, London.
Jackson, B. and Sandos, R. (2012) *Making Thatcher's Britain*, Cambridge University Press, Cambridge.
Jameson, D. A. (2009) 'Economic crises and financial disasters, the role of business communication', *Journal of Business Communication* 46 (4), 499–509.
Jeffries, L. (2010) *Critical Stylistics*, Palgrave Macmillan, London.
Jeremy, D.J. (1998) *A Business History of Britain: 1900–1990s*, Oxford University Press, Oxford.
Jones, A. (2013) 'Life as an industrial correspondent', *The Work Foundation*, 20 October, www.theworkfoundation.com/blog/228/Life-as-an-Industrial-correspondent.
Jones, D., Petley, J., Power, M. and Wood, L. (1985) *Media Hits the Pits: The media and the coal dispute*, Campaign for Press and Broadcasting Freedom, London.
Jones, N. (1986) *Strikes and the Media: Communication and conflict*, Basil Blackwell, Oxford.
Jones, N. (2002) *The Control Freaks*, Politicos Publishing, London.
Jones, N. (2011) *The Lost Tribe: Whatever Happened to Fleet Street's Industrial Correspondents?*, Nicholas Jones, London.

Kavanagh, D. A. (1987) *Thatcherism and British Politics: The end of consensus?*, Oxford University Press, Oxford.
Kay Review (2012) *Kay Review of Equity Markets and Long Term Decision Making*, Department of Business Innovation and Skills, London (July).
Keegan, W. (2010) 'Its just like the 1980s – except the riots have already begun', *Observer*, 14 November.
Keegan, W. and Pennant-Rae, R. (1979) *Who Runs the Economy? Control and influence in British economic policy*, Temple Smith, London.
Kelly-Holmes, H. and Mautner, G. (eds) (2010) *Language and the Market*, Palgrave Macmillan, London.
Keynes, J.M. (1930) *The Great Slump 1930, The Nation & Atheneaum issues of December 20 and December 27, 1930*, British Periodicals Ltd., London.
Keynes, J. M. (1936) *The General Theory of Employment, Interest and Money*, Palgrave Macmillan, London.
Kindleberger, C. P. and Aliber, R. Z. (2005) *Manias, Panics and Crashes, A history of financial crises*, Palgrave Macmillan, London.
King, I. (2011) Interview with author.
Kjaer, P. and Slaatta, T. (eds) (2007) *Mediating Business: The expansion of business journalism*, Copenhagen Business School Press, Copenhagen.
Kleinman, M. (2008) 'HBOS directors bought stock at bargain prices', *Daily Telegraph*, 23 March.
Koller, V. (2004) *Metaphor and Gender in Business Media Discourse: A clinical cognitive study*, Palgrave Macmillan, Basingstoke.
Kynaston, D. (1994) *The City of London, Volume 1: A world of its own 1815–1890*, Pimlico, London.
Kynaston, D. (1998) *The Financial Times: A centenary history*, Viking, London.
Lawson, N. (1992) *Views from Number 11. Memoirs of a Tory radical*, London, Bantam.
Lewis, J., Williams, A., Franklin, B., Thomas, J. and Modsell, N. (2008) *The Quality and Independence of British Journalism: Tracking the changes over 20 years*, Cardiff School of Journalism, Media and Cultural Studies, Cardiff University.
Lewis, M. (2011) *The Big Short*, Penguin, London.
Mahate, A. A. (1994) 'Contagion effects of three late nineteenth century British Bank failures', *Business and Economic History* 23 (1), 102–115.
Mair, J. and Keeble, R. L. (2009) 'Playing footsie with the FTSE? The great crash of 2008 and the crisis of journalism', *Ethical Space: The International Journal of Communication Ethics* 6 (3–4), 79–92.
Maltby, J. (1998) 'UK joint stock companies legislation 1844–1900: accounting publicity and "mercantile caution"', *Accounting History* 3 (1), 9–32.
Marston, C. (1996) 'The organisation of investor relations function by large UK

quoted companies', *Omega, International Journal of Management Science* 24, (4), 477–488.

Marston, C. and Straker, M. (2001) 'Investor relations: A European survey', *Corporate Communications* 6 (2), 62–93.

Martin, I. (2013) *Making it Happen. Fred Goodwin and the men who blew up the British economy*, Simon & Schuster, London.

Marx, K. and Engels, F. (1965) *The German Ideology*, London, Lawrence and Wishart.

McCabe, D. and Sydney-Smith, M. (2013) *Enders Analysis: Regional and local press 2013 sector update*, Enders Alanlysis Ltd, London.

McCord, N. (1968) *The Anti-Corn Law League 1838–1846*, Allen & Unwin, London.

McCusker, J. J. (1991) 'The demise of distance: the business press and the origins of the information revolution in the early modern Atlantic world', *The American Historical Review* 110 (2), 1–28.

McCusker, J. J. and Gravensteijn, C. (1991) 'The beginnings of commercial and financial journalism: the commodity price currents exchange rate currents, and money currents of early modern Europe', *Nederlandisch Economisch-Historisch Archief* 3 (11), 21–31, Amsterdam.

McKay, C. (1852) *Memories of Extraordinary Popular Delusions*, Vol. 1, Strand, London.

McLellan, D. (1986) *Ideology*, University of Minnesota Press, Minneapolis.

McQuail, D. (2000) *McQuail's Mass Communication Theory*, Sage, London.

Micklethwait, J. and Wooldridge, A. (2005) *The Company*, Phoenix, London.

Millman, G. J. (2006) 'No longer just Gray: business journalism takes off', *Financial Executive*, October.

Millward, R. (2010) 'The family silver, business efficiency and the City, 1970–1987', *Business History* 52 (1), 169–185.

Morgan, E. V. and Thomas, W. A. (1962) *The Stock Exchange: Its history and functions*, Elek Books, London.

Morris, A. J. A. (2004) 'Bottomley, Horatio William (1860–1933)', *Oxford Dictionary of National Biography*, Oxford University Press, www.oxforddnb.com/view/article/31981 [accessed 20 September 2013].

Murphy, A. (2009) *The Origins of the English Financial Markets*, Cambridge University Press, Cambridge.

National Audit Office (2014) 'The Privatisation of Royal Mail', Report by the Comptroller and Auditor General, Department for Business, Innovation and Skills, HC 1182, Session 2013–14, www.nao.org.uk/wp-content/uploads/2014/04/The-privatisation-of-royal-mail.pdf [accessed 17 March 2014].

Nel, F. (2010) '"Laid off", what do UK journalists do next?', University of Central Lancashire, In collaboration with Journalism.co.uk.

Oakley, D. (2014) 'Kay Review chimes with the spirit of the times', *Financial Times*, 23 July.
O'Brien, D. P. (1970) *J. R. McCulloch, a Study in Classical Economics*, George Allen & Unwin, London.
Odlyzko, A. (2010) 'Collective hallucinations and inefficient markets: the British railway mania of the 1840s', School of Mathematics and Digital Technology Center University of Minnesota, www.dtc.umn.edu/~odlyzko/doc/hallucinations.
O'Neill, D. (2007) 'From hunky heroes to dangerous dinosaurs', *Journalism Studies* 8 (5), 813–830.
ONS (Office of National Statistics) (2013) *Ownership of UK Quoted Shares 2012*, www.ons.gov.uk/ons/dcp171778_327674.pdf.
Parliamentary Commission on Banking Standards (2013) 'An Accident Waiting to Happen: The failure of HBOS', *HL Paper 144 HC Paper 705* by the authority of the House of Commons, London, The Stationery Office.
Parsons, W. (1989) *The Power of the Financial Press*, Edward Elgar, London.
Paul, H. (2011) *The South Sea Bubble: An economic history of its origins and consequences*, Routledge, London.
Picard, G. R., Selva, M. and Bironzo, D. (2014) *Media Coverage of Banking and Financial News*, Reuters Institute for the Study of Journalism, University of Oxford.
Pickering, P. A. and Tyrrel, A. (2000) *The People's Bread: A history of the Anti-Corn Law League*, Leicester University Press, Leicester.
Poovey, M. (2002) 'Writing about finance in Victorian England: Disclosure and secrecy in the culture of investment', *Victorian Studies* 45, 17–21.
Porter, D. (2004) 'Marks, Harry Hananel (1855–1916)', *Oxford Dictionary of National Biography*, Oxford University Press, Oxford, www.oxforddnb.com/view/article/47898 [accessed 19 September 2013].
Porter, D. (1986) '"Trusted guide of the investing public": Harry Marks and the *Financial News*, 1884–1916', *Business History* 28, 1–17.
Porter, D. (1998) 'City editors and the modern investing public: establishing the integrity of the new financial journalism in late nineteenth-century London', *Media History* 4 (1), 49–60.
Porter, D. (2000a) *Play it Safe or Think Big? The Daily Mirror, its readers and their money, 1960–2000*, LSE Business History Unit, London.
Porter, D. (2004b) 'Alsager, Thomas Massa (1779–1846)', *Oxford Dictionary of National Biography*, Oxford University Press, Oxford, www.oxforddnb.com/view/article/41071 [accessed 19 September 2013].
Prebble, J. (2000) *The Scottish Dream of Empire*, Birlinnn, Edinburgh.
Preda, A. (2009) *Framing Finance: The boundaries of markets and modern capitalism*, University of Chicago Press, Chicago, IL.

Preston, P. (2011) 'The gates have closed for good on the industrial correspondent', *Guardian*, 27 March.
Pugh, P. (1998) *The Strength to Change: Transforming a business for the 21st century*, Penguin Books, London.
Richardson, J. E. (2007) *Analysing Newspapers: An approach from critical discourse analysis*, Palgrave Macmillan, Basingstoke.
Richardson, R. (1993) 'Hayek on trade unions: propagandist or social philosopher', *CEPDP* 178 Department of Industrial Relations and Centre for Economic Performance, London School of Economics.
Ringshaw, G. (2004) 'The heart said yes, the head said no', *Daily Telegraph*, 19 September.
Robb, G. (2002) *White Collar Crime in Modern Britain: Financial fraud and business morality 1845–1929*, Cambridge University Press, Cambridge.
Robinson, J. (2008) 'Why didn't the City journalists see the financial crisis coming?', *Observer*, 13 October.
Rosevare, H. (1991) *The Financial Revolution 1660–1760*, Longman, London.
Roush, C. (2006) *Profits and Losses: Business journalism and its role in society*, Marion Street Press, Oak Park, IL.
Sanders, D. (1991) 'Government popularity and the next general election', *Political Quarterly* 62 (2), 235–261.
Sanders, D. (1996) 'Economic performance management, competence and the outcome of the next general election', *Political Studies* 44 (2), 203–231.
Sanders, D. (1999) 'Conservative incompetence, labour responsibility and the feelgood factor: why the economy failed to save the Conservatives in 1997', *Electoral Studies* 18 (2), 251–270.
Sanders, D., Marsh, D. and Ward, H. (1993) 'The electoral impact of press coverage of the British economy 1979–1987', *British Journal of Political Science* 23 (2), 175–210.
Schiffrin, A. (2011) *Bad News: How America's business press missed the story of the century*, The New Press, New York.
Scott, W. R. (1951) *The Constitution and Finance of English, Scottish and Irish Joint Stock Companies to 1790*, 3 volumes, Peter Smith, New York.
Smith, A. (1776) *Wealth of Nations*, www2.hn.psu.edu/faculty/jmanis/adam-smith/wealth-nations.pdf [accessed 19 April 2013].
Starkman, D. (2009) 'How could 9,000 business reporters blow it?', *Mother Jones*, January/February.
Stedman Jones, D. (2012) *Masters of the Universe: Hayek, Friedman and the birth of neoliberal politics*, Princeton University Press, Woodstock.
Stock Exchange (2010) *A Guide to Listing on the Stock Exchange*, White Page, London.
Storey, G. (1951) *Reuters Century, 1851–1951*, Max Parrish, London.

Stout, L. (2012) *The Shareholder Value Myth: How putting shareholders first harms investors, corporation and the public*, publisher, San Francisco, CA.

Sutherland R. (2010) 'Financial journalists must learn what ordinary people think are big deals', *Observer*, 10 January.

Tambini, D. (2010) 'What are Financial Journalists For?', *Journalism Studies* 11 (2), 158–174.

Taylor, J. (2012) 'Watchdogs or apologists? Financial journalism and company fraud in early Victorian Britain', *Historical Research* 85 (230) November, 632–650.

Temple, M. (2008) *The British Press*, Open University Press, London.

Tetlock, P.C. (2007) 'Giving content to investor sentiment: the role of media in the stock market', *The Journal of Finance*, 72 (3), 1139–68.

Tett, G. (2010) *Fool's Gold*, Abacus, London.

Thatcher, M. (1993) *Downing Street Years*, Harper Collins, London.

Treanor, J. (2009) 'Stop demonising bankers, warns BBA chief', *Guardian*, 25 September.

Tumber, H. (1999) *News: A reader*, Oxford University Press, Oxford.

van Dijk, T. A. (1988) *News as Discourse*, Erlbaum, Hillside, NJ.

Van Oss, S. F. (1898) 'The limited company craze', *Nineteenth Century*, 43, 48–63.

Walsh, C. (2005) 'Tips and sells saga winds up as fallen slickers await their fate', *Observer*, 11 December.

Walsh, F. (2011) Interview with the author, May 2011.

Wheen, F. (2000) *Karl Marx*, Fourth Estate, London.

Wilson, J. (1839) *Influences of the Corn laws: As affecting all classes of the community, and particularly the landed interests*, Longman, Orme, Brown, Green, and Longmans, London.

Wilson, J.F. (1995) *British Business History, 1720–1994*, Manchester University Press, Manchester.

Wodak, R. and Ludwig, C. (eds) (1999) *Challenges in a Changing World: Issues in critical discourse analysis*, Vienna: Passagenverlag.

Wren-Lewis, S. (2015) 'The Austerity Con', *London Review of Books* 37 (4), 9–11, 19 February.

Websites

www.economist.com/help/about-us.
www.fticonsulting.co.uk.

Index

2008 financial crisis 83, 90, 92, 98, 111, 180
50p tax campaign 177

ACAS 133
Addey, John 144
Adam Smith Institute 161
advertising: financial products 76; new share issues 45, 53; newspapers – dual product 111; railway shares 26
AIG 93
Aldrick, Philip 89
Alsager, Thomas Masa 19, 20, 23, 38, 79
Applegarth Press 18
Amazon 180
analysts: stock market 88, 131
announcement process 139, 140
Answers to Correspondents, 34
anti-business 180
Antwerp Stock Exchange 3
Argentina 55
Ashley, Mike 104; Sports Direct 104; Newcastle United 104
austerity 170, 171; Blyth, 171
Australia 55

Bagehot, Walter 20, 21, 23; Stuckey & Co 23; *English Constitution (1867)* 24; *Lombard Street (1873)* 23, 24
Baines, Edward 26
Bank of England 10, 16, 29, 55, 69, 72, 103
banking correspondent 97

Barber, Lionel 84
Barclays Bank 89
Barings 54, 55, 60
Barnes, Thomas 19, 20
Barr, John 47
Barrons 62
Basham, Brian 151, 154
Beharrel, Peter 134
Bell, Sir Tim 143
Bentham, Jeremy 156
Bhoyrhul, Amil 80, 81
Bicycling News 34
Big Bang 77, 144, 145, 147
Binns, Peter 148; Buchanan Communications 148
Blair, Tony 85, 168
Blank, Sir Victor 155
Blunt, Sir John 11, 13
Bolger, Dan 83
Bolivia 16
Bottomley, Horatio 52
Bracken, Brendan 73
Bradford & Bingley Building Society 92
British Airways (BA); allegations of dirty tricks 152; takeover battle with Virgin Airways
British Bankers Association 97, 98
British Gas 149
British Petroleum 148
British Rail 142
British Steel 138
British Telecom 148, 149
Brittan, Samuel xi, 163, 164, 165, 175
Brontë, Charlotte 26, 30; Emily 26

INDEX 201

Brummer, Alex 86, 91, 117
Brunswick Public Relations 145, 150
Bubble Act 13, 17, 31
bucket shops 52
Buenos Aires Water Supply & Drainage Company 54
business discourse 120
Business news pages, 101, 108
Business Week 62
Butt, R. 165
'Butskellism' 160
Butterfield, George 43

CBI 107, 180
Callaghan, James 164, 165, 166
capitalism: Anglo-Saxon 88, 126; 'casino capitalism' 65
Cardiff University 108
Carpetright plc 141
Castaing John 5, 6
Centre for Policy Studies 161
Chat on Change 36, 41
Chief executive, high pay 129–130; importance 122
Chile 16, 53
Churnalism 113
Citigate 150
Citigate Dewe Rogerson 94, 148
city article 19, 36; column, comment 88
city editor 37
Clarke, Philip 141
Clement, William Innell 19
Coalition government 103, 128, 168, 170; Conservative and Liberal Democrats 170
Cobden, Richard 22, 156
collateralised debt obligations (CDOs) 83, 86
companies, public, x 103; fraudulent 7, 12; joint-stock x, 1, 7, 14, 143; large cap 103; small cap 103
company news stories 139
company promoters 7, 30, 38, 61, 62

Conservative government 79, 167
Corn Laws 21–23, 68; Anti-Corn Law Association 21; Anti-Corn Law League 21
'corporate elite' 125
Corporate Synergy 143
Course of the Exchange 5, 6
Coyle, John 144, 145; Broad Street Associates 151
credit rating agencies 83
Crosby, James 92, 94, 95, 124
Cummings, Peter 93

Daily Courant 8, 10
Daily Express 73, 74, 135
Daily Herald 68, 69
Daily Mail 32, 34–6, 40, 50, 62, 64, 69, 74–6, 78, 86, 88, 98–9, 115, 135, 151, 157, 174; *Money Mail* 86, 88; *Mail Online* 115
Daily Mining News 43
Daily Mirror 49, 74, 75, 76, 80, 81, 133; City Slickers 49, 80, 174; Maguire, Kevin 133
Daily Sketch 74
Daily Telegraph 13, 32, 33, 74, 76, 77, 78, 79, 89, 94, 102, 108, 167, 133, 135, 151, 152, 153 165; *Sunday Telegraph* 77, 78, 86, 94, 152, 166
Davenport, Nicholas 68
Davis, Aeron x, 108, 124, 125, 128, 133, 150
Davies, Nick 113
Davies, Matt 135, 136
Dawson, Jo 14
Delane, William 21
Derek, Dale 74, 174
Dewe Rogerson 148
Doyle, Gillian x, 100, 118, 121, 122, 124, 132
Drapers Record 54
Duguid, Charles 32, 34, 37, 39, 40, 50, 58, 62, 75, 78, 174
Duke of Cambridge 33

East India Company 14
economic news 101
Economist Intelligence Unit
    (EIU) 175
Economist, The 20, 21–4, 27–31, 63,
    69, 158, 160, 174
Edict of Nantes 7
Edinburgh Review 21, 156
Eisenger, Jess 122
Ellis, Mike 14
Emmott, Bill 174
English, H. 15
Enron 100; Ken Lay 122
Ethical Space ix
ethics 174
equity markets 84
Evening News 35
Evening Post 10
Exchange Alley 5

Financial & Mining News 43, 45, 46
financial bubbles 86, 172
financial crisis 2008 vii, 83–100, 111,
    127, 130, 169, 171, 174, 175, 176,
    178, 179
Financial Dynamics 141, 154
financial journalists 110, 114;
    background, 117
financial media 172, 173
Financial News 43, 47–9, 51–3, 55,
    56, 58, 59, 61, 62, 64, 69, 73, 78,
    81, 157
Financial Post 56
Financial PR 79, 106, 107, 110, 137,
    140, 142, 143, 144, 147, 148, 152,
    153, 154
Financial Services Authority
    (FSA) 95, 152
Financial Times xi, 43, 50–6, 58–9,
    61–5, 73, 74, 84, 86, 91, 100, 107,
    115, 124, 155, 157 165, 166, 167,
    169, 173, 175
Financial Truth 56
Forte, Rocco 150
Fortnightly Review 156

Fortune 62
Fleet, Kenneth 78, 79, 174
Freedman, Seth 81, 82
Friday night drop 152
Friedman, Milton 128, 159, 162, 165,
    167
FTI Consulting 123, 154
FTSE 104
FTSE 100 Index 104, 129,
    180; British Land, G4S, JD
    Sports, M&S, SERCO, Tesco,
    Vodaphone 104, 180
FTSE 250 and 350 105
Fuggers 3
Fuller, Jane 91–2
fund managers 140

Galbraith, J.K. 65, 167, 172
Galtung, John 120
Gambles 1999 21
Germany 60, 66, 69
Ginns, Bernard 110, 117
Goodwin, Fred 87, 90, 123
Google 180
Gowers, A. 100
Granada, takeover of Forte 128
Grant, Albert 38, 61, 65, 81
Granville, Lord 24
Great Exhibition 1851 60
'Greek debt crisis' 103, 108
Grenfell, W.R. 49
Griffiths, Katherine 97, 109
Gross Domestic Product 55
Guardian 102, 106, 112, 113, 115,
    132, 153, 174, 175
Guinness 54

Hall, Stuart 169
Hansard Publishing 52
Hanson plc 132, 142, 151
Harcup, Tony 120, 121
Harmsworth, Alfred 34, 35, 41
Harney Peak Tin Company 49
Harper's Magazine 156
Hartwell, Lord 78

INDEX 203

Haskins, Chris 169
Hatry, Clarence 64
Hayek, Friedrich 159, 160, 161, 167; influence on President Regan and Margaret Thatcher 158
HBOS 13, 14, 54, 85, 88, 92, 93, 95, 96, 100, 155; Halifax Building Society 55, 147, 148; Bank of Scotland 93
High Pay Centre 130
Hipwell, James 80, 81
Honduras 16
Hooley, Ernest Terah 38, 40, 50
Hornby, Andy 14
House of Commons Treasury Select Committee ix, 84, 92, 98, 117
Huddersfield Centre for Communication and Consultation Research (HCfCCR) xi, 101, 103, 108, 109, 113, 118, 131, 152
Hudson Bay Company 1
Huguenots 7
Hume, David 156, 165
Hunt Thornton 33
Hutton, Will 86

ICI plc 142, 143
ideology 120, 124, 125; in financial and business news 126
Illustrated London News 34
Independent 98, 102, 108
industrial revolution 60
information asymmetry 2, 174, 180
Informa Goup 5
Initial Public Offerings (IPOs) 140, 146, 147, 148; 'floating a company' 142;'going public' 142, 147; Institute of Economic Affairs 161, 165, 166
Investors UK 178
Investor Relations 148
Investor Relations Society 149

Jackaman, Tim 145; Square Mile Communications 145

Jaskob, John 65; *Ladies Home Journal* 65
Jay, Douglas 69, 163
Jay, Peter xi, 70, 163, 164, 166
JJB plc, shares 80
John Addey Associates 144, 151
John Bull 52
Joint-stock Companies Act 31
Jonathan's Coffee House 4, 6; Jonathan Miles 5
Jones, Nicholas 134, 154, 173

'kaffir' boom 49
Kay, John Professor 2; Kay Review 2, 6, 87, 129, 137, 138, 139, 140, 146, 178, 179
Keegan, William 86, 88, 164
Keynes, J. M. 60, 66, 67, 68, 158; *Economic Consequences of Peace (1919)* 66; *General Theory of Employment, Interest & Money (1936)* 68; Keynesianism 72, 73, 158, 161, 162–164, 167
Kindelberger & Aliber 173
King, Ian 118
Knight, Angela 97
Koening steam press 18
Koller, Veronica 126
KPMG 88

Labour correspondents 134
Labour Finance & Industry Group 169
Labour Party 160, 166; government, 1945 72, 73; New Labour 85, 154, 168
Laissez-faire 17, 21, 25, 31, 68, 157, 158, 159, 171
Laski, Harold 73
Lawson, Nigel 78
Leeds Mercury 26
Lambert, Richard 107
Law Times 29
Lehman Brothers 169
Leopold, Graham 51

Levy, Joseph, Edward 33; Levy-Lawson; Moses 33
Lewis et al. 108, 112, 113
Liberal Party 33
LIBOR 90
Lidderdale, William 55
Lloyd, Edward 4, 5
Lloyd George, David 59
Lloyds Banking Group: Lloyds/ TSB, 92, 97, 155
Lloyds List 5, 6
local newspapers 116
London & Globe Finance Corporate 56
London & Leeds Bank 47, 48
London Coffee Houses 4; (Wills, Grecian, Toms, St. James, Cocoa Tree, Nandos)
London County Council 48
London Financial Guide 50
London School of Economics 157
London Stock Exchange 6, 37, 49, 51, 56, 58, 62, 63, 79, 102, 104, 109, 114, 125, 132, 138, 138, 141

McFall, John 98
McKay, Charles (1852) 11–14, *Memories of Extraordinary Popular Delusions of the Madness of Crowds* 172
MacRae, Curtice & Co. 52
MacRae, Douglas Gordon 52, 56
McMurdo, Edward 43
main market index 103
Major, John 168
Makinson Cowell 150
Mandelson, Peter 154
manias 173
Marine National Bank 46
Market Abuse Directive 90
Marks, David 43
Marks, Harry 20, 43, 45–7, 49–50, 56–7, 81, 174
Marshall, Alfred 67, 158
Matthew, Colin 14

Maxwell, Robert 78
mergers, acquisitions, takeovers 134
Metropolitan Board of Works (MBW) 48
Mexico 16, 45
Mill, J. S. 156, 165
Mississippi Scheme 172
monetarism 167
Mont Pelerin Society 160
Morgan, Piers 81
Morning Chronicle 18, 19
Morning Herald 18
Morning Post 18, 33
Morris cars 162
Muscovy Company 2

National Audit Office 177
nationalisation 73
Nation & Atheneaum 66
New Deal 69
New Journalism 32, 33, 34, 41
New Statesman 66, 68
New York World 43
National Review 23
neoliberal 79, 167, 168; neoliberalism 158, 160, 161, 171
news values 120; and ideology, 124
Nineteenth Century 38
Nobel Prize 167
North, Colonel, J.T.; Pactolus 53
Northern Pacific Railway 45
Northern Rock 92, 98, 155
Norman, Montague 69

Observer 20, 86, 167
Occupy protest movement 169
Office of National Statistics (ONS) 178
oil dependency 161
O'Neill, Deirdre 120, 121
online newspapers 111; digital platforms 114; subscribers 115
O'Riordan, Shane 96
Overend Gurney 23

INDEX

Pall Mall Gazette 40, 48
Parker, Paul 142
Parliamentary Commission on Banking Standards 92; *An Accident Waiting to Happen* 92, 93
Parsons, Wayne x, 6, 23, 42, 62, 65, 66, 68, 69, 70, 156, 157, 162, 164, 165
Payne, Will 65
Pennant-Rae, R. 164
Pension funds 178
Personal finance journalism 75, 77, 101
Peston, Robert 86, 87, 98, 99, 133, 155, 174
Picketty, Thomas 130
Postboy 10
Postman 10
Porter, Dilwyn, x, 29, 39, 40, 41, 43, 44, 47, 50, 57, 62, 75, 76, 80
Poyais 15; George McGregor 16
Press Association 109, 112, 133
press releases 145, 150
PRIME 106
profits warning 141
Property market 85
Puckle's machine gun 12

Quarterly Journal of Economics 158

Randall, Jeff 86
railway companies
Railway mania 24; Darwin, Charles 26; Gladstone, William 26; Liverpool & Manchester Railway 24; Mill, John Stuart 26; Palmerston, Lord 26; Peel, Robert 26; Thackery, William 26; Tooke, Thomas 25;
rating agencies 83
Rees-Mogg, William 163, 165
Regulatory News Services (RNS) 109
Reuters Institute vii, 90
Revelstoke, Lord 54, 60

Ringshaw, Grant 94, 95, 125
Rolls Royce 132
Rothchilds 20
Royal Bank of Scotland/RBS 54, 85, 87, 91, 123; takeover of ABN AMRO 87, 89
Royal Economic Society 157
Royal Mail 148, 177
Ruge, Mari 120
Russell, Lord John 22

'Safe conduits' 38, 79, 95, 176, 177
Salisbury, Lord 35
Sampson, Marmaduke 38, 79
Santender: bid for Abbey National 94
Seattle Times 122
Second World War 71, 72, 159
sector correspondents 91, 93, 94; banking correspondents 97
Seldon, Arthur 166
Sergeant, Patrick 79
Share ownership changes 177, 178
Share price movement, 138
shareholder spring 130
shareholder value theory 127, 131
share ramping 80, 82, 174
Slater, Jim 78
Sleigh, Colonel Arthur 33
Standard & Poor 500 129
Standard Chartered Bank 22
Stead, W.T. 48
Stevenson, Lord 92
Storthard, Peter 77
Smiles, Samuel 157; *Self-Help* 157
Smith, Adam 15, 157, 165; *Wealth of Nations* 15
South Africa 49
South America 9, 15, 54
South Sea Bubble 6, 8, 16, 86, 137
South Sea Company 9–17
Stamp Act 1712 8
Stanhope, Viscount 14
Starbucks 180–1
Statist, The 57, 158

stockbrokers 143, 144; stock-
jobbers 10, 144

Talton, Jon 122
takeovers: hostile, contested 149;
AMEC and Kvaerner 152
takeover panel and code 152
Tesco plc 141
Tett, Gillian 83, 84
Thatcher, Margaret 79, 134, 146, 166, 167; Thatcherism 78
Times, The 18–19, 27, 28, 31, 33, 37–9, 41, 74, 102, 108, 115, 118, 151, 155, 157, 163, 164, 165, 166, 167; *Daily Universal Register* 18; *Sunday Times* 33, 77, 97, 115, 153
trade unions 133; BA cabin crew strike 133; enemy within 134; militant 135; public interest 134; public sector workers strike 135; RMT 135
Trafford Park Industrial Estate 38
Trustee Savings Bank 148
Tit-Bits 34
'Tulipomania' 172

UK 85, 161, 163
USA 60, 65, 66, 69, 85, 90, 161, 163

Van der Molen 3
Vanity Fair 57
Venezuala 16
Vodaphone 133

Wall Street Crash 60, 63, 65
Wall Street Journal ix
Walpole, Robert 11, 14
Walsh, Fiona 112, 115, 116
Walter, John I 18; Walter, John II 29
Weekly Journal 10
Welch, Jack 122
Westminster Gazette 40
Westminster Review 156
Whelan, Dave 80
Whiston's Merchants Weekly Rembrancers 6
Wilson, James 20–21; *Influences of Corn Laws Affecting All Classes of the Community (1839)* 22
Wren-Lewis, S. 170
Wright, Whitaker 56
World Bank 72, 101

Yorkshire Post 110, 116, 117
zero hour contracts 105

www.ingramcontent.com/pod-product-compliance
Lightning Source LLC
Chambersburg PA
CBHW032035290426
44110CB00012B/808